DISCARD

The
Sponsor's
Toolkit

J

The
Sponsor's
Toolkit

Anne-Marie Grey & Kim Skildum-Reid

Sydney New York St.Louis San Francisco Auckland Bogotá
Caracas Lisbon London Madrid MexicoCity Milan Montreal
New Delhi SanJuan Singapore Tokyo Toronto

McGraw·Hill Australia

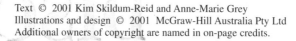

*A Division of The **McGraw·Hill** Companies*

National Library of Australia Cataloguing-in-Publication data:

Skildum-Reid, Kim.
The sponsor's toolkit.

Bibliography.
Includes index.
ISBN 0 074 710656

1. Corporate sponsorship—Australia. 2. Special events—Marketing. 3. Marketing—Australia. I. Grey, Anne-Marie. II. Title.

658.820994

Published in Australia by
McGraw-Hill Australia Pty Ltd
4 Barcoo Street, Roseville NSW 2069, Australia
Acquisitions Editor: Javier Dopico
Production Editor: Sybil Kesteven
Designer (cover and interior): Lara Scott
Illustrator: Alan Laver, Shelly Communications
Typeset in 9/15 pt Daily News Regular by Post Pre-press Group
Printed on 80 gsm woodfree by Prowell Productions Ltd, Hong Kong.

Forewords

Kim and Anne-Marie have put something in your hands of great value. If you're reading it, you're lucky. Not just because it's a really smart book but because you are, I believe, in the best business there is.

If you're new to the business of sponsorship, the tools in this kit will help you build a foundation of knowledge. If you're an experienced professional, reviewing them and making sure your team is using them is just smart marketing.

In the next page or two, I'd like to provide you with a very brief look at the environment in which you'll put these tools to work. Is it all encompassing? Hardly. Is it representative of all geographies? For the most part, yes. Is it insightful? Well, I'll let you be the judge of that.

It's safe to say that the marketing environment we're currently in is more dynamic than at any point in history. The rate of change, the type and amount of change at times defies belief. In many cases, today's truism is tomorrow's sorry miscalculation.

That said, it behooves us to try to stop our gyrating world for a moment, step back and observe. It further behooves us to identify trends that are shaping our world and make some conclusions that will lead us to better decisions.

A couple of those trends and observations follow. To be sure, there are many others.

If It Moves, Logo It!

Over-commercialisation is at once a trend and a threat—worldwide. As a matter of fact, I believe it is the single largest threat to the sponsorship industry now and, unfortunately, for the foreseeable future.

We have now sponsor names and/or identification inside arenas, on uniforms, seat backs, urinals and the field of play itself. If we can't paint it on the field, we insert it electronically. Australian Rules footballs are logoed. Discussions regarding logos on jockeys in the Kentucky Derby are being held. Are horses next? The American practice of sponsor names on buildings is beginning to creep around the world.

And, all of this, to what end? Awareness increases and image enhancement? Most brands I see engaged in these practices really need neither. But in any event, in too many cases to consumers it's all just a blur. Take a look at any NHL ice hockey arena.

We have seen the enemy and it is us! If we, as sponsors, agencies, rights holders, arena owners—all buyers and sellers—don't restrict ourselves we'll wake up one day and find that those we're trying to reach are numb and more importantly, we've greatly devalued the very asset we so desperately sought an association with in the first place.

The Emergence of the Brand Experience

What is it? It's a sponsor owned and controlled environment. And it is one antidote for over-commercialisation. It's an immersion in the brand—a communication of its soul.

The ability to create brand experiences is a huge advantage for tangible product marketers. The opportunity to see, feel, touch and use a product in this created environment leads to a true consumer connection to the brand. It's the opposite of a contrived, transparent, surface association.

For General Motors, as you might guess, the brand experience centres on driving.

Measurement as Imperative

A focus group of one tells me that no more than one in five sponsors today is engaged in the consistent, comprehensive measurement of the results of its efforts. The good news is that a decade ago, that number was closer to one in twenty.

I won't bore you with why you must do it. You know that. But I will tell you that unless you set aside funding, significant funding, to do it you will not do it. It's only in the last 10–12 years that sponsors have truly embraced dedicated *leveraging* budgets. I would submit to you measurement budgets today are where leveraging budgets were 10–12 years ago.

But there's a broader, more important reason to measure—and that concerns our industry's growth. Only through on-going, disciplined, systematic measurement will sponsorship prove its true effectiveness and gain the share of marketing spend it deserves.

I'm proud to say that at GM, we've (finally) turned the measurement corner.

In closing, I would ask that you use these thoughts and the tools in this kit to build a strong sponsorship foundation for your brand. Use them to build your business and in turn our industry. As we enter the 21st century, it is the most exciting, creative and impactful that the marketing world has to offer.

All Good Luck,

Bob Heussner
President
GM EventWorks

Understanding the who, what, where, when, why and how of sponsorship for an organisation are the keys to building strong and mutually beneficial partnerships.

Sponsorship is a vital part of the marketing mix and if not chosen and managed correctly can have a negative impact on a company's image and brand values. A sponsorship needs to fit with where a company is going and what it wants to achieve.

All of McDonald's sponsorships—in sport, the arts, environmental programs and youth activities—not only reflect the company's brand values but also suit the organisation's vast geographic and demographic situation. With more than 700 restaurants across Australia, operating in metropolitan, suburban and regional areas, it is important that the sponsorships we choose have these communities and our broad customer base in mind. As well, each sponsorship or alliance is a long-term commitment between McDonald's and the program and participants it supports.

Sponsorship is a partnership and both the organisation's stakeholders and those of the sponsored party should feel good about the partnership, for it to work effectively. This is something that is key in our business. McDonald's employs more than 55 000 people so it is important to us that our entire organisation knows about—and feels good about—our alliances.

The Sponsor's Toolkit is a fantastic workbook for any company, to evaluate or revitalise its current sponsorship needs. From planning what you want to achieve from a sponsorship, to effectively managing the sponsorship to suit both the needs of your organisation and that of the sponsored party, this book is vital to that process. It is a step-by-step approach to evaluating a sponsorship and making a sponsorship work and should therefore take pride of place on every sponsor's bookshelf.

John Blyth
Vice President—Director of Public Affairs
McDonald's Australia

Contents

About the authors

Anne-Marie and Kim met in 1996, when both served on the board of the Australasian Sponsorship Marketing Association. In addition to their own pursuits, they have been working together since then, developing and presenting a series of workshops for both sponsors and sponsorship seekers around the world. Their first book, *The Sponsorship Seeker's Toolkit*, was published in May 1999 to rave reviews and continued strong sales. It is considered by many to be the definitive guide for sponsorship seekers.

Kim Skildum-Reid

Kim Skildum-Reid is widely recognised as one of the top corporate sponsorship consultants in the Asia-Pacific area, with 17 years experience across the US, Europe, Asia, and Australia/New Zealand.

Over the better part of a decade, she worked for numerous Fortune 500 companies in the US on their sponsorships of blue chip properties as diverse as the Superbowl, US Open Golf, and the International Chili Society Cook-Offs, as well as dozens of major professional sporting organisations and national concert tours.

Kim moved to Australia in September 1992, and in January 1994 she started her own consultancy, Skildum-Reid Consulting, specialising in corporate-side sponsorship strategy. Her clients are some of the top sponsors in Australasia, and have included Lion Nathan Australia, Toyota, Qantas, ANZ Bank, Australia Post, Cable & Wireless Optus, City of Sydney, Dunlop Tyres, Ansett Australia, Volvo, NEC, Lion Breweries, ABN AMRO, Peters Ice Cream, James Hardie Industries, Canberra Milk, AAPT, Queensland Main Roads, Vic Roads, Orix Australia, George Weston Foods, and Daewoo.

In June 2001, Kim entered into a strategic alliance with Clemenger Communications, part of the global BBDO advertising agency group, to provide sponsorship expertise and training to their agencies and clients across Australasia, in addition to her own busy consultancy.

In August 1997, Kim retired after four years as President of the Australasian Sponsorship Marketing Association, Inc., an organisation of which she was a founder.

During her presidency, Kim led the growth of the organisation from 30 to one of the strongest and most active sponsorship associations in the world.

Kim is recognised around the world as a dynamic and insightful speaker. She also writes, with many dozens of articles to her credit, and provides expert commentary on sponsorship to organisations such as CNN, CNBC Asia, ABC, and the Canadian Broadcast Corporation, among others. In 1999, she retired from the prestigious position of sponsorship columnist for *Professional Marketing* magazine, Australia's largest circulation marketing publication.

Anne-Marie Grey

Anne-Marie Grey is Vice-President of Marketing and Strategic Alliances for the United States Fund for UNICEF. Anne-Marie oversees the US Fund's marketing activities including Corporate Partnerships and Alliances, Trick or Treat for UNICEF, Products and Licensing, and Cause-Related Marketing.

Prior to joining the US Fund, Anne-Marie held the position of Director, Creative Enterprises and Marketing at Share Our Strength, one of the country's leading anti-hunger and anti-poverty organisations, working with Evian, American Express, Tyson Foods, Williams-Sonoma and Coors.

Before joining Share Our Strength, Anne-Marie established Grey O'Keefe and Associates, an Australian-based consulting firm specialising in developing strategic alliances between cultural, sporting, non-profit organisations and the private sector. Anne-Marie has led campaign teams for cultural and non-profit organisations including the National Museum of Australia, The Australian National Gallery, the Australian Sports Commission, and the Australian Healthcare Association.

Anne-Marie studied at Colby College, the Australian National University, and the Graduate School of Management at the University of New South Wales.

Introduction

Sponsorship is romantic. It sounds silly when we say it like that, because it's not romantic at all, but to many companies, sponsorship is treated in exactly that way. It is romanticised. Somehow, because sponsorship often has to do with freakishly talented athletes or artists or humanitarians, and it often has to do with fun events, that means it's okay to be less than diligent about the business of investing these marketing funds.

But that is what sponsorship is—an investment. Sponsorship is an investment made in a commercial partnership through which you should be achieving quantifiable marketing returns. And, while we will grant that a few of the very best sponsorships do have some art or magic working for them, most of the best performing sponsorships around the world don't. Doing sponsorship well—using this most powerful of marketing media to its greatest effect—boils down to good business practice. If you have the right approach, systems, tools and teamwork, you will do it well. It really is that simple.

Part of knowing how to do sponsorship well is knowing how it got here. Sponsorship has changed more in the past three to four years than it has in the entire history of modern sponsorship, but there are shadows of all those other incarnations that we deal with every day, both inside and outside of our organisations.

During the 1970s, sponsorship was about awareness and exposure. Investments (when not based upon the whims of some senior executive) were made based on how many 'impressions' that sponsorship could deliver. One person seeing a logo one time is one impression. It wasn't uncommon for an event taking place in a city of one million people to deliver 50 million or more impressions over the course of the promotional period. Was that delivering on marketing objectives? That's a good question, because very few companies ever bothered to quantify their investments. There was a gut feeling that sponsorship had marketing power, but were they tapping into it simply by putting their logos in front of people? In most cases, no.

The 1980s saw sponsorship receiving greater notice, with many companies increasing their investments in this area, as well as using a greater degree of acumen in

> If you have the right approach, systems, tools, and teamwork, you will do sponsorship well.

In the 1980s,
Michael Jordan
changed
sponsorship
forever.

The underlying
power of
sponsorship is in
creating emotional
connections with
your market.

their selection. This shift was driven in large part by the number of top athletes doing endorsements, and the number of companies who were staking their entire brands on these relationships, with Nike—and everyone else sponsoring Michael Jordan—very clearly leading the way.

Companies started to realise that, in order for sponsorships to be effective, they had to be worked. The 1-to-1 rule was born, calling on sponsors to support their sponsorships with a minimum of one additional dollar for every dollar spent on the sponsorship fee. They began creating promotions around them, usually just simple drawings. These activities, while not particularly interesting, started selling a lot of product, which was a big improvement on the previous decade.

The focus was squarely on sales and the results of those sales promotions. Investments were quantified in terms of dollar return, with much of the long-term brand-building value of sponsorships either overlooked or assigned a number arbitrarily, with the result being that the perceived return on investment shifted vastly based on who was doing the math.

The early to mid-1990s ushered in a far more expansive view of how sponsorship can affect and improve brand marketing. Investments became objective-driven, and the creativity used in developing leverage programs (e.g. sponsorship-driven promotions, publicity or other activity) grew by leaps and bounds. So grew the clutter across the sponsorship arena. It was becoming more and more difficult to make an impact, even with well-planned and executed programs. The 1-to-1 rule became the 2-to-1 rule. The Olympics in Barcelona and Atlanta brought ambush marketing, the controversial practice of a company implying that it is a sponsor of an event when it isn't, into the lexicon of marketers everywhere. Quantification, like selection, became about objectives, as marketers realised that the potential power of sponsorship to shift people's attitudes wasn't quantifiable in money. The gap between good sponsors and bad widened as increasing numbers of companies began to identify and use the power of the medium.

In the late 1990s and early 2000s, companies started going beyond using sponsorship as a functional tool—albeit an excellent one—to identifying and using the underlying emotional power of a sponsorship to connect with their markets. The new approach centres around reflecting and enhancing not only your market's interests (e.g. golf), but the specific emotional drawcards associated with them. This approach, if integrated across marketing media, results in a strong degree of consumer identification, not just to the product, but to the brand and its premise. It's not just consumer buy-in, it's consumer join-in.

'If you charge for tangible things, you're in the goods business. If you charge for activities you perform, you're in the service business. If you charge for the time customers spend with you or the spiritual connection your brand offers, you're in the experience business. And, providing experiences can transform the value of what you produce.'
Lesa Ukman, Founder and President, IEG, Inc.

The most interesting part about these big shifts in sponsorship is that consumers are clearly driving that change. They are expecting companies to provide brands that not only meet their functional needs—quality, price, etc.—but that say something about who they are as individuals or who they want to be.

Consumers are also now expecting to be rewarded for their loyalty. It started in earnest with frequent flyer programs. This was followed by credit cards offering preferred concert seating to cardholders and hundreds of frequent buyer schemes. All of these activities, and so many others, worked to create relationships with consumers where once there were only transactions. Now, adding value has moved beyond simply giving people freebies with their purchases. It has shifted from focusing on largely irrelevant perks toward enriching and enhancing people's lives—using sponsorship to get your audiences closer to and more involved with something that they care about.

Looking forward, it is impossible to say exactly where sponsorship will be in ten years time. But we are certain that things won't be going backward, and the big changes we have seen in the past few years will continue to evolve, probably driven in large part by advances in technology. Those companies that embrace the full potential of sponsorship now will clearly have the edge, as they will be able to adapt their strategies to the fast-changing world.

A few of the key concepts that will see the best sponsors running even further ahead of the pack into the future are also the keys to doing sponsorship well now:

➤ Sponsorship is not about connecting your brand with the event. It is about connecting your brand with your target market.

➤ While visibility used to be the ultimate goal, now everything you do—from selection to maximisation to quantification—is about objectives.

➤ The best sponsors *never* measure column inches, they measure changes in their markets' perceptions and behaviours.

➤ If you are not segmenting your markets psychographically, you will not do sponsorship well.

'What have you done for me lately?' is a sentiment that runs deep.

➤ Sponsorship should not be 'supported' by other media. It is a catalyst that can make any or every other part of the marketing mix achieve better results.

➤ If you do not have broad buy-in and participation from across your company, you are missing opportunities and probably wasting money.

Throughout this book, we will be working through all of these facets of this amazingly versatile media. In the meantime, don't despair if you think your company is years, or even decades, behind the times. This is not at all uncommon and is certainly not impossible to fix. There are dozens of things that you can do right now that will move your portfolio into the modern age, while creating far more value from the investments you currently have.

Acknowledgments

We would like to acknowledge a number of people for their assistance, support, and expertise during the development and production of *The Sponsor's Toolkit*.

First and most importantly, we would like to extend our thanks to all of our clients and everyone who has attended our workshops around the world for being so open about your wins and your challenges. You inspire us with your commitment to doing sponsorship well, you have so many great ideas, and you definitely keep us on our toes. Keep up the great work!

Thanks to our contributors, Lionel Hogg for your great contract pro forma, Anne Bicknell and Donald McBain, media gurus extraordinaire, Peter Raper of Sports Marketing and Management for your special expertise and insights, Ty Speer, Simon Baggs and Jim Moser for your all-round help, and John Blyth and Bob Heussner for your terrific forewords. We also want to thank all of our colleagues and clients who have allowed us to share their experiences with our readers, including Terry Hearity, Tim Salt and Rowan Johnstone.

Thanks to the whole crew at McGraw-Hill Australia, especially Tony Wong, Firgal Adams, Javier Dopico, Bob McLeod, and Sybil Kesteven for supporting our vision and making us look so good.

Kim would like to thank . . .

I want to thank my family and friends for supporting my hectic career and especially for putting up with me as I obsessed over every detail of this book; the Drummoyne Women's Rugby Team and the Union gang, for all the fun and friendship; and Caren Ann Petrulo, for being an inspiration from the very beginning. Thanks to Anne-Marie for the gossip, the collaboration, and keeping me sane in this crazy business we're in. Over to you, darl! And an extra big thanks with a hug and kiss for Andy for being so wonderful and especially for keeping the house renovations on track while this book was coming together. What a champion.

Anne-Marie would like to thank . . .

I want to thank my family: Kieran, Declan, and Katie; Sarah Temple, who ensures I keep doing gorgeous things; Diane Whitty, for providing me with unparalleled opportunities to grow, bigger challenges, and ensuring I take risks; Lisa Fielding, for providing a wonderful sounding board and keeping things moving along; Susan Power, for her delightful and witty repartee; and Clare Micuda, for keeping me on track, on deadline, and on time. My most grateful thanks are for Kim, who pushes me to do things I never thought I could do and enjoys the margaritas with me along the way.

Finally, we need to thank Edward once again. If it wasn't for you, we might not be authors at all.

How to use this book

The Sponsor's Toolkit is just that, a toolkit. It is a book to be used, not just read. It is a process that both you and your peers can use to get significantly more value from your current investments, while taking steps to make your overall portfolio better reflect your needs as you move forward.

We believe that you will find the entire book a beneficial resource, whether you need a tune-up or a complete overhaul. But we also understand that you might have one or more pressing issues that need addressing straight away, before you have time to complete the whole book.

Given that, you've got a couple of options for using *The Sponsor's Toolkit*:

1. Read it front to back, doing the exercises and working through the tools as you go.
2. Determine your specific needs in terms of skill building, tools and techniques, and review the sections that pertain to your immediate needs first. In this section, we have included a Sponsorship Self-Test as well as a number of typical scenarios that will help you to determine the best sections for you.

Whichever way you choose to use *The Sponsor's Toolkit*, here are few tips that will help you get more out of it:

➤ check out the resources we have outlined in Appendix 2 on page 185. Start increasing your knowledge level right away

➤ use the exercises collaboratively whenever possible. Throughout this book, we advocate a team approach as the key to getting the most out of your sponsorship program. These exercises can also be great ice-breakers to get your team started

➤ keep your peers in the loop. There are always a lot of stakeholders in a strong sponsorship program—from brand management to sales to research to loyalty marketing and more. Keeping them informed is essential. Getting them involved is even better

➤ have fun with the process. Your job as a sponsor is to connect with people through their passions—what they care about, how they have fun. If you don't

> For best results, get your peers involved in the process.

bring a similar sense of passion and creativity to the process, you won't be fully effective as a sponsor.

Some people pick and choose the tools and exercises they use, implementing a few before changing over to this process completely. While this is not absolutely ideal, it is normal. Based on our experience, the changes that come about from using just a few tools, such as the Proposal Guidelines on page 66, are enough to convince organisations to go all the way.

We have written *The Sponsor's Toolkit* so that it will be useful to both experienced and new sponsorship marketers. If you are just beginning in this business, we strongly suggest coming back to it as you gain confidence and your skills improve. You will find that many suggestions, tips, and tools that may not have seemed relevant when you were just starting out will have gained far more usefulness for you.

Special notes

Throughout this book, we often use the generic term 'event' to describe a sponsorship opportunity, whether it is an event, team, venue, individual, cause, organisation, or program. Also, although we use the word 'consumer' quite a lot, the strategies outlined can be applied equally well to your trade, employees, stockholders, and to business customers. Finally, if there is a term that you don't understand, be sure to check out the Glossary in Appendix 1 starting on page 178.

Sponsorship self-test

This test is a tool you can use to determine your sponsorship strengths and weaknesses. Check true or false for each of the statements below. Scoring and assessment information is found at the end of the test.

If you don't understand a term, check the Glossary.

Section A

	T	F	
1.	☐	☐	Sponsorship is not a priority for our company, although we do invest substantial funds in it.
2.	☐	☐	Responsibility for individual sponsorships rests with the brand manager or group.
3.	☐	☐	We do not have enough human resources to manage effectively our sponsorship portfolio.
4.	☐	☐	We have a group of people from several departments that meets regularly to discuss sponsorship.

5.	❐	❐	We define our target markets primarily by demographics (e.g. 18–24-year-old males).
6.	❐	❐	We define our target markets primarily by psychographics (e.g. sophisticated, status-oriented up-and-comers).
7.	❐	❐	We do not generally do research around individual sponsorships.
8.	❐	❐	We regularly invest in upgrading the sponsorship skills of internal stakeholders from a range of departments.
9.	❐	❐	We don't have a complete list of all of the sponsorships in our portfolio because brands/states/regions/sales often invest in sponsorships without telling anyone else.
10.	❐	❐	We have a Sponsorship Policy and it has been signed off by senior management.

Section B

	T	F	
11.	❐	❐	Sponsorship selection is ad hoc and follows no set criteria.
12.	❐	❐	We select sponsorships that will achieve multiple marketing objectives.
13.	❐	❐	We are bargain-oriented and regularly enter into sponsorships that we wouldn't ordinarily invest in, just because they are cheap.
14.	❐	❐	We select sponsorships that are strong target market matches and generally require a sponsorship seeker to provide research before we will invest in a sponsorship.
15.	❐	❐	We value exposure or awareness as a main goal of sponsorship.
16.	❐	❐	We make it easy for potential sponsees to understand our needs.
17.	❐	❐	We regularly sponsor events that represent the personal interests of senior executives.
18.	❐	❐	We negotiate benefits based upon the needs of our brands and target market(s).
19.	❐	❐	We negotiate to win.
20.	❐	❐	When entering a sponsorship, we always have a contract or letter of agreement in force.

Section C

| | T | F | |
| 21. | ❐ | ❐ | We do not leverage our sponsorships as well as we could. |

22.	❏	❏	We always integrate our investments across multiple marketing media.
23.	❏	❏	We communicate poorly with current sponsees, sometimes communicating only at renewal time.
24.	❏	❏	We work with sponsees to achieve mutual objectives.
25.	❏	❏	We do not have adequate funding for leveraging sponsorships.
26.	❏	❏	We are adept at renegotiating if our needs change.
27.	❏	❏	We either don't quantify investments or quantify them in terms of dollar returns.
28.	❏	❏	We quantify investments based upon objectives.
29.	❏	❏	We often blame the sponsee when a sponsorship doesn't work.
30.	❏	❏	We regularly invest time and money in upgrading the skills of our sponsees.

Section D

	T	F	
31.	❏	❏	We have been ambushed by a competitor more than once.
32.	❏	❏	We have never been ambushed by a competitor.
33.	❏	❏	We ambush our competitors whenever we get the chance.
34.	❏	❏	We ambush rarely, and only if it supports overall marketing strategy.
35.	❏	❏	Ambush marketing is unethical and that very fact should stop companies from doing it.
36.	❏	❏	We assess all of our major sponsorships to determine where our competition might have an opportunity to ambush us.

Scoring

Give yourself one point for each odd-numbered 'true' and one point for each even-numbered 'false'. Score each section separately.

Section A

This section has to do with preparation, which is the single most important thing to get right if your sponsorship program is to be successful.

If you scored . . .   Then

More than 6   Your internal approach to sponsorship is in disorder and is probably a major contributing factor to your not getting the most from your sponsorship investments. Luckily, it is never too late to turn this part of your program around. You need to read, do the exercises, and start implementing the strategies contained in Part 1—Preparation as a matter of urgency. If you do, you will start to see results in the short term and these results will increase as your company gets comfortable with a more effective approach.

3 to 6 points   You are doing some things right, but definitely need to refine and refresh your approach to sponsorship internally. Part 1—Preparation will provide you with some new tools and ideas that will get you back on track quickly.

Less than 3   Congratulations. Your internal systems, tools, and approach are quite strong. If you are not achieving the results you want from sponsorship, chances are the problems are occurring somewhere else in the process. You could pick up some pointers and new tools by going through Part 1—Preparation.

Section B

This section has to do with selection and negotiation. If you don't invest in the right sponsorships with the right benefits, no amount of time, effort, or money is going to make them work.

If you scored . . .   Then

More than 6   Your approach to selection and negotiation is not working. Your sponsorship portfolio is likely to be littered with sponsorships that will never perform for you because they weren't great matches from the start. Although we can't make those sponsorships go away any faster, changing your selection process will make an immediate improvement in both the quality of sponsorships in which you invest and the type of relationship you have with these new sponsees. Part 2—Selection and negotiation is going to be of particular interest to you, with information and tools to make this a far more effective and easier process. There is also a chapter on Salvaging a bad situation, starting on page 146, that might help you to gain more appropriate benefits during a less-than-ideal contract.

3 to 6 points   You are in the middle ground, here. In all likelihood, your general approach to selecting sponsorship is sound, but you may be lacking the systems and tools to objectify and streamline the process. Part

2—Selection and negotiation will be very valuable to you, providing loads of this type of information.

Less than 3   Your selection and negotiation process is in good shape. Part 2—Selection and negotiation may have some tips and tools that will help you to fine-tune what you are currently doing.

Section C

This section has to do with management and maximisation—getting the most out of your sponsorship investments while minimising the drain on human and financial resources.

If you scored . . .   Then

More than 6   Your approach seems to be the opposite of 'take the money and run'. You literally write the cheque and run. Maximisation is what provides you with the value from a sponsorship investment, and you are not making the most of that opportunity. The good news is that, not only is maximisation one of the fastest things you can fix, it is also one of the easiest and most fun. There is plenty to help you in Part 3—Maximisation and management.

3 to 6 points   While you are doing a number of things right, you still aren't getting the most out of your investments. You might need to get more peers involved in the process, or perhaps creativity is the key to making your sponsorships work harder. Part 3—Maximisation and management will help to pinpoint where you can improve.

Less than 3   You are doing plenty right, and should be wringing value out of your sponsorship program. If it is still looking a bit lacklustre, you may just need to freshen things up. There are some exercises in Part 3—Maximisation and management that will help you to update your leverage activities so they have even more impact.

Section D

Ambush marketing is often misunderstood. Whether you choose to partake in ambushing or not, you need to understand what it is and how it works, otherwise you are a sitting duck.

If you scored . . .   Then

3 or more   Part 4—Ambush marketing is a must-read for you. You are either getting ambushed, ambushing too often, or both, and the only thing that accomplishes is wasting money.

1 or 2 points   You're doing reasonably well, but ambushers can be a pretty clever group, so it pays to stay on your toes. An ambush checklist and exercise can be found in Part 4—Ambush marketing.

Typical scenarios

If you are having a specific or immediate sponsorship challenge, you can pick and choose specific sections and chapters that will help you. Below, we have outlined some typical sponsorship scenarios, as well as the recommended reading.

No leverage funds

This is a very typical challenge, usually revolving around the belief that it takes more money to maximise a sponsorship than it does to pay the fee. Thankfully, this is not the case if you approach maximisation with creativity, teamwork, and resourcefulness. We would strongly recommend reading Part 3—Maximisation and management before you go begging for more money from the marketing budget, because you probably don't need it.

Sponsorships not delivering on objectives

You're already on the right track, because at least you are thinking in terms of objectives. Getting sponsorships to perform, however, is a different kettle of fish. Because there could be a number of reasons for this lack of performance, you will need to refer to a few areas. We would suggest you read both Part 2—Selection and negotiation, to ensure you are selecting and negotiating sponsorship most effectively, and Part 3—Maximisation and management, to ensure your sponsorships are well leveraged.

Need to reduce or substantially change sponsorship portfolio

Whether you need to reduce your sponsorship budget or you are just trying to do fewer things and do them better, this can be tricky. We suggest you have a look at Chapter 13—Portfolio management, as well as Chapter 11—Salvaging a bad situation.

About to do a big negotiation or renegotiation

Big sponsorships last a long time, so you want to get the negotiation right. We recommend that you read Chapters 1 and 2, which have to do with understanding what you need from sponsorship, then move on to Chapters 7 and 8, which are about negotiation and contracts.

Hiring a new sponsorship manager or rethinking how sponsorship management is structured

The sad truth is that restructuring sponsorship management is easier to get wrong than right, and the same goes for hiring a sponsorship manager. You can find information on management structures that work (and a few that don't), and a Sponsorship Manager Job Description template in Chapter 1 on page 19.

Facing internal issues about sponsorship

Internally, sponsorships have a tendency to be either very political or completely ignored—there usually isn't much middle ground. If you are having difficulty getting everyone working together, we would strongly recommend reading Part 1—Preparation and particularly Creating a sponsorship team in Chapter 1 on page 13.

Overview of sections

The book is broken into five general sections. Below is an overview of what you will find in each of them.

Part 1—Preparation

In this section, you will define what you want to achieve from sponsorship and create a comprehensive plan to achieve it. You will learn invaluable tricks for gaining internal buy-in. You will also work through budget issues and learn that more money doesn't necessarily make a better sponsorship program.

Part 2—Selection and negotiation

If you've got the preparation right, selecting the right sponsorship partners and negotiating strong, win–win relationships become relatively straightforward. In this section, you will learn about evaluating proposals against your needs (and getting the right proposals in the first place). You will learn how to say 'no' so that it doesn't backfire and, should you get to that next stage, how to navigate even the trickiest negotiations. This section contains many tools, templates and forms that will make this whole process run smoothly.

Part 3—Maximisation and management

Sponsorships don't run themselves. Many overworked sponsorship managers wish they would, but they don't. There are dozens of tricks, techniques and tools in this section that can be used to make sponsorships run more effectively, as well as more easily. We address maximisation as well as management, ensuring that all of your sponsorships—both current and new—are performing as well as they possibly can.

Part 4—Ambush marketing

Love it or hate it, ambush marketing is here to stay, and this section covers it thoroughly. In this section, you will find insights as to why it works, why it doesn't, how to prevent being ambushed, and how to select and ambush an event. Even if you would never dream of carrying out an ambush—and a lot of companies wouldn't—it is imperative that you understand how it works. It is only by knowing how to do one that you will be able to spot your weaknesses and stop an ambush happening to you.

Part 5—Appendixes

Sponsorship is an ever-changing medium. If you want to keep up, you will need to continually develop your resources and skills. To that end, we have included a comprehensive listing of resources, including associations, conferences, publications, and Internet sites from all over the world, as well as books that we recommend.

Also in the Appendix is an outstanding Sponsorship Agreement Pro Forma template, provided by one of Australia's foremost experts on sponsorship law. Finally, we have included a section on options for structuring sponsorship management and a sponsorship manager job description.

Part 1

preparation

Chapter 1

Internal planning

Does this sound familiar? A sponsorship is entered into based on gut feel, objectives are created to fit the event, little if any effort is put into maximising the program, and then the sponsee is blamed for its failure. Many companies trick themselves into thinking that their sponsorships don't work because the sponsee has somehow failed, but the fact is that most fail because of inadequate preparation on the part of the sponsor.

Sponsorship is a complex and sophisticated pursuit. Doing it right can achieve extraordinary results, while there are few faster ways to waste money than doing it wrong. There is a myth which says that sponsors who consistently get great results from their sponsorship investments are either very smart, very lucky, swimming in cash, or all three. In reality, the biggest difference between the bad, the good, and the great is in their preparation.

Internal planning will ensure that:

➤ you know what you want to achieve from sponsorship

➤ you know who your target markets are

➤ both of the above are tied into your overall marketing strategy

➤ your peers are supportive of and involved in the change

➤ you select a management structure that gives you the best result

➤ you have a policy and strategy that provide both a stringent framework and flexibility.

If you read only one section of the book, make it this one. It will have a greater impact on what you get out of your sponsorship program than any other.

If you only read one section of this book, make it this one.

The approach

As with all internal planning, we need to start with your mindset. We can provide you with all the great tools in the world, but if your direction is unclear, all those tools will serve to do is get you to the wrong place more quickly.

Unfortunately, there are far more out-of-touch sponsors than any other kind.

Fortunately, if your company falls into this category, it is a relatively straightforward process to adjust your approach and get far more out of your sponsorship program. In addition, if you change your approach now, with most sponsors not being as effective as they could be, you will have less competition for people's attention and your sponsorships will have more impact.

Even if you are a good sponsor and get consistently strong returns, refining your approach can reap you big gains. It is only a very short step from being good to being great, but most companies don't bother. It is worth it.

The power of sponsorship

There are two factors that make sponsorship the single most powerful of all marketing media, and if you want to maximise the effectiveness of your sponsorship portfolio, it will be imperative to keep both of these firmly in mind:

1. Sponsorship is the most emotional and personally relevant of all marketing media. It is about what people care about, and because of this, it is the most powerful tool we have to foster our relationships with consumers and add value to those relationships in a meaningful way.
2. Sponsorship is the most integrateable of all marketing media. If a sponsorship is well chosen, there is no limit to the number of marketing activities that can use the sponsorship to better achieve objectives.

If you are not taking advantage of these two areas, you may as well not be doing sponsorship, because you are missing out the most powerful aspects of this very potent medium.

Harnessing that power

Sponsorship used to be about connecting the sponsor and the sponsee as indelibly as possible, using lots of signs and logos and contests, with the assumption that an audience will somehow just 'get it'. Most people, however, don't.

Some day, on the way out of a game or event, ask yourself how many sponsors you can recall. Then ask yourself if any of the ones you can remember actually managed to change the way you think about their brands or whether they will make you run right out to buy their products. You're in marketing, we're in marketing—we pay more attention to this type of message that your average Joe on the street. And yet, chances are we won't remember many sponsors and they won't affect us in any meaningful way. Most of your marketplaces won't pay as much attention as we would, and the effect on them will be even less.

In the last few years, the way switched-on companies approach sponsorship has

> If your sponsorship is not emotionally relevant and fully integrated, you should not be investing in this medium.

Sponsorship isn't about what's sexy, it's about connecting with your audience.

changed dramatically as many sponsors have realised that their job isn't to connect with a sponsee, it is to connect with their target markets. The sponsee is simply a conduit— a set of mechanisms through which that connection can take place.

This recent realisation that it is the brand's relationship with the audience, not the sponsee, that is important, has given sponsors access to a wider variety of potential investments and maximisation opportunities. It's not about what's sexy anymore, it's about what fosters the most effective connection with your audience.

Even with the best of sponsees, the responsibility for making this connection with a target market rests with you, the sponsor. There are a number of key components that are imperative for you to get right if you are going to make the most of a sponsorship investment.

Throughout the book, we will be discussing all of these components in detail, along with many other aspects of sponsorship, but here from the outset we do want you to get a feel for the approach from the outset.

Objectives

First and foremost, you need to know what you are trying to accomplish, who your target markets are, and how you will quantify your success. If you don't know what you are trying to achieve with absolute certainty, you will not be effective in selecting, negotiating, maximising, or quantifying your sponsorship investments.

Integration

Easily the most frequent, and usually the first, comment that people tell us in relation to maximisation is that they don't have enough funds for effective leveraging. Many people talk about the '1-to-1 rule' or the '2-to-1 rule'. But, even if we could wave a wand and give you a big stack of extra money for leveraging, we wouldn't, because doing that misses the point of sponsorship leverage, which is:

Marketing activities should not be created for sponsorship. Sponsorships should be creating more impact within existing marketing activities.

Using sponsorship as a catalyst will not only increase the effectiveness of other marketing media, but will provide funding from other areas of your company if the opportunities or benefits provided by a sponsorship replace, enhance, or make more cost-effective their already budgeted activities.

Teamwork

A very important step in getting your sponsorship program off the ground is to accept that there are a lot of stakeholders, both inside and outside your company, who could benefit from sponsorship. A well-chosen sponsorship could make these stakeholders' jobs easier, more effective, and less costly.

Creating a Sponsorship Team is one of the best ways to create value around your investments by using the unparalleled power of sponsorship to make your other marketing activities more effective. If you gain the team's buy-in, you will very quickly see sponsorship becoming a core marketing function, rather than a peripheral activity with little activation and little support.

Finally, if you have experts involved, you job will be infinitely easier. You won't be doing tasks that could be done more easily and effectively by people who specialise in those areas, such as database marketing, publicity or trade relations.

Relationships

You have competitors—probably a lot of them—and your target market is free to pick any one of them at any time. Engendering loyalty has become a big priority for many companies, a bigger priority in many cases than finding new customers. Because sponsorship uses an event or activity that interests your target market, the opportunities for fostering loyalty are vast.

Sponsorship has now gone way beyond simply sponsoring an event because you know (or are guessing) that your target market has an interest in it. It is now about identifying and acknowledging the specific emotional and functional reasons that your market is interested in that event—what draws people to it—and ways in which their experience can be improved and enhanced. Your job, as a sponsor, then becomes about adding value to that experience, creating real impact.

An example of this difference could be a bank targeting young families for first time home loans. They could:

➤ sponsor a community event and set up a booth where people can get information,

or

➤ sponsor a community event, provide free child-minding and kids' activities at its booth, and provide free parking close to the event for families with children under five. The bank may or may not require that a family pick up a parking voucher at one of its branches or through automatic tellers, but either way, the impact of the sponsorship is much greater.

Relevance

Sponsorship is an excellent way to enhance the relevance of your product to your target market and their lives. It can be used as a vehicle for educating the marketplace about your brand or to shift or underpin product positioning. This is often accomplished by aligning one or more key attributes of your brand with attributes of the event that are important to your target market, then using those attributes across a range of marketing activities.

Creativity

There is so much clutter in sponsorship today that breaking through it is a major issue. Ensuring that creativity in both selection and execution is the rule, rather than the exception, is very important if you want your sponsorship program to capture the imagination of your target market and deliver the best possible results. With it, your Sponsorship Team will go a long way towards achieving those results.

Changing the way your organisation thinks

As you have probably determined, this approach isn't nearly as easy as putting up a few signs, but it is effective. By concentrating on results against your marketing objectives and on building relationships and relevance with your target markets, those results will be sustained far longer than most sponsorships 15, 10, or even five years ago ever could.

The good news is that changing or fine tuning your own approach to sponsorship is relatively simple. The better news is that changing your whole organisation's approach to sponsorship isn't much more difficult. It's mostly just a matter of education. People see sense, and this approach is sensible. Part of the reason that sponsorship isn't more fully embraced by companies is that so much of the way it's done in those companies doesn't make sense. That's history talking. This is your chance to make new history.

This book is full of exercises and tools that will be very useful to you as you educate the stakeholders. They are fun, they are easy, and they will help that light bulb go on over people's heads.

Case study: Lion Nathan Australia

As one of the two largest brewers in Australia, Lion Nathan Australia is invested in a wide range of sponsorships, big and small, and has a major commitment to making these investments deliver for them. To that end, they recently reviewed their sponsorship activities and approach. Although they have implemented a number of strategies to make their investments more productive, the single most important thing that they did was to change the fundamental way their company thinks about sponsorship.

From brand management to regional sales to loyalty marketing to media, Lion Nathan has several dozen genuine sponsorship stakeholders. Shifting the mindsets of one or two people wasn't going to make a noticeable impact, so they embarked upon a multi-tiered program of collaboration and education, including:

- interviewing all of the key stakeholders to ensure their needs were taken into account when developing their new strategy
- providing sponsorship workshops for stakeholders, so that their understanding of sponsorship and their skills are up-to-date
- creating a highly consultative process for selecting, maximising, and quantifying sponsorship
- instituting a system of information sharing, so that all stakeholders learn from both the big wins and the challenges.

By taking these steps, Lion Nathan has created a company culture that has left behind old school thinking and embraces the power of sponsorship. And while most of these stakeholders will never be experts at sponsorship, they are now asking the right questions, participating in the process, and using sponsorship to create more value in their marketing activities.

Understanding what you want to achieve

All too often, a company will invest in a sponsorship, then create objectives for it. This never works. Think about it: what is your job as a marketer? Is it to align your brand with football? The arts? A cause? No. Your job as a marketer is to do your part in achieving the marketing objectives set for the brand. The fact that you use sponsorship to do it doesn't change your job. You just have a more interesting tool with which to accomplish those goals.

The first step to doing sponsorship well is to understand exactly what you want to achieve from sponsorship. This isn't rocket science. Sponsorship is just another marketing activity—albeit a powerful one—and just as with all other marketing activities, it needs to support overall marketing objectives. Get your hands on the most up-to-date marketing plan for your brand. Those objectives are your sponsorship objectives.

No one sponsorship will achieve every marketing objective, but a well-selected sponsorship can perform against a number of them.

Your job is to achieve objectives for the brand, not to align with the sponsee.

NOT	INSTEAD
X Align the brand with football	✓ Increase market share by 5 points within target market of sports-oriented males under 30
	✓ Increase share of people in target market who identify brand as 'tough' and 'masculine' by 25%
	✓ Anchor major autumn sales promotion
	✓ Provide relevant content for Web site
	✓ Increase Web site visits of over 30 seconds duration by 30% over the key autumn/winter period
	✓ Develop a database with no fewer than 24 000 customers and qualified prospects within next financial year for new loyalty program

Your menu of objectives should number 10–15.

An important step to becoming objective-oriented is to make a list of objectives that can be achieved through sponsorship. We've listed a few below. Some of these may work for you, others won't, but it will be a good starting place to develop your own menu of objectives. You should endeavour to have around 10–15 objectives on your list. This will give you enough flexibility to be able to consider a wide range of potential partnerships, while ensuring that each sponsorship has a far-reaching impact. This is the beauty of sponsorship. It is as comprehensive as it is flexible.

Sample menu of objectives

➤ Communicating a marketing message to a target market

➤ Increasing sales to a target market

➤ Building a database of qualified prospects

➤ Adding value to current and potential consumers

➤ Increasing consumer understanding of your product/brand

➤ Shifting consumer or trade attitudes towards your brand

➤ Enhancing brand positioning

➤ Creating a focal point for promotions (consumer, trade, retail, media, sales, on-line, loyalty)

➤ Providing content for a Web site

➤ Gaining benefits for use in a loyalty program

➤ Product display or demonstration

➤ Promoting trial via sampling and/or couponing

➤ Forcing trial through on-site sales exclusivity

➤ Gaining on-site sales (exclusive or non-exclusive)

➤ Product endorsement by individual or organisation

➤ Adding value to retail/trade relationships

➤ Trade hospitality

➤ New product launch

➤ Launching an existing product/brand to a new market

➤ Brand re-launch

➤ Increasing awareness within target market (new products only)

➤ Creating a focal point for trade promotions

➤ Creating a focal point for above-the-line advertising (or supporting an existing theme)

➤ Increasing employee morale

➤ Employee retention

➤ Increasing employee knowledge level

➤ Networking with other sponsors, government decision-makers, and other key participants

When listing your objectives, be sure you make them specific to your company and brand. You also want to be sure you don't include any objectives that can't be objectively quantified through one or more mechanisms. See Quantification on page 149 for more information.

Seven bad reasons to sponsor

Many sponsorship selection and negotiation processes are driven by factors that are not particularly strategic and, in some cases, even undermine the positioning of the brand.

In some cases, one or more of these factors might affect your decision, but in no case should any of these 'objectives' be the primary reason for an investment. Sponsorship must be a strategic fit, meeting multiple strategic objectives, or it won't work.

1 The awareness trap

If you have found yourself focused on 'awareness' or 'exposure' in relation to sponsorship, you are definitely in need of a re-think. The weakest part of sponsorship is its ability to make you visible. If all you want to be is visible, there are easier, cheaper, more effective ways to do it. More importantly, though, if you are focusing on awareness, you are missing out on the strongest part of sponsorship—its ability to build and enhance relationships between your brand and your markets.

If you can't quantify it, it's not an objective.

Generating
'awareness' shows
only that you exist,
nothing more.

This is an easy trap to fall into. These terms are used freely by both sponsors and sponsorship seekers, and it's hard to believe, at least at some level, that putting your logo in front of enough people won't do *something* for your brand. The fact is that the only thing that generating awareness does is prove that you exist. It says nothing about your product, your message, or your brand. And, if you think that the values of the event are rubbing off on your product just because you've got your logo on it, think again. Consumers have become a very savvy bunch. They don't connect signage or logos with an event any more than they connect a commercial for refrigerators to NYPD Blue.

Your goal, with sponsorship, should always be to connect with your target markets. This can be done in a number of ways, including adding value and experiential marketing. Experiential marketing is the creation of ways that your target market can, through your sponsorship, actually experience or participate in the event in a deeper, more special, or more personal way. If you are accomplishing these things with your sponsorship program, then any signage or other visibility you may get becomes a strong reinforcement of your activities. On its own, however, exposure is very low impact.

Of course, there is an exception that proves the rule. If you have a new product or you are launching an existing product to a new marketplace, then generating awareness is an appropriate approach to sponsorship. But do understand that, if you do your job right, your market will know the product exists within a short period of time. Within 12 months, it will be time for a new approach.

2 The myth of good corporate citizenship

Sit down and take a deep breath because what we're about to tell you is going to shatter a myth that is a feature of a great many corporate sponsorship programs: there is no such thing as good corporate citizenship.

The term 'good
corporate
citizenship' tends
to obscure the
true objectives.

'Good corporate citizenship' is a euphemism that in and of itself means nothing. 'Giving back to the community' is the same. They mean one thing to one company and something entirely different to another, and as long as sponsorship professionals hang onto those terms, the real objectives will be obscured.

If you are spending marketing funds to become a good corporate citizen, there must be some underlying result that you are aiming to achieve. It is extremely unlikely that a company will spend funds that are expected to generate some type of marketing return on *truly* altruistic activities. That doesn't mean for a minute that you can't do great things *and* achieve a marketing return, you simply have to put your finger on exactly what objectives you are trying to achieve.

The next time you find yourself wanting to use the terms 'good corporate citizenship' or 'giving back to the community', try to be more definite. If it helps, you may want to ask yourself two questions:

➤ What does generating 'good corporate citizenship' mean for our brand?

➤ If we succeed in achieving 'good corporate citizenship', how will this affect our consumers or trade? How will it affect their perceptions or behaviours?

Chances are, you will come up with at least one or two genuine, quantifiable objectives. You might want to increase trust in your company. You may want to increase your target market's propensity to buy your product. You may want to underpin your 'localness' in your company's home town or solidify your positioning. Whatever answers you get, these are your true objectives. You don't necessarily have to change what you sponsor, you just need to focus it.

3 Blocking the competition

It happens all the time. A company will sponsor an event—even if it's not a strategic fit—simply to block a competitor from getting it. This accounts for an enormous amount of sponsorship involvement, and has littered many sponsorship portfolios with investments that don't work for them.

If a sponsorship is a strategic fit, delivers on multiple objectives, and the exclusivity offered keeps your competition out of it, go ahead. If not, at best, you will end up with a dud sponsorship. At worst, you will end up with a dud sponsorship at an inflated price after the sponsee instigates a bidding war. In our experience, it's not worth it.

4 Chairman's choice

Although 'chairman's choice' has a nice ring to it, any executive with influence over budgeting could be guilty of this very outmoded practice of diverting sponsorship funds to organisations or events that are of personal interest. The classic example is an executive authorising the sponsorship of his or her favourite football team, but art galleries, charities and any number of other types of organisations have benefited from this practice. Unfortunately, the sponsor very rarely benefits.

One of the most blatant examples that we know of is the state road safety organisation whose job it is to educate people about safe driving. Its core target market is men 18–24, yet the board—a considerably older bunch—decided to invest in a sponsorship of the opera. Not only that, but this particular opera spent a significant portion of time touring outside the state. Did the organisation achieve any marketing objectives? Did the organisation reach its target market at all? Highly unlikely.

'Chairman's choice' is a dying breed.

Personal interests should not play any part in sponsorship in this day and age—we don't care how big the title. If a sponsorship cannot stand up to stringent, objective assessment, it doesn't belong in the portfolio, because that money could be used to make better investments and because the downside can be so great. With corporations now answerable to boards, shareholders, employees, and, increasingly, consumers, a closer eye is cast upon them to ensure that expenditures are made strategically. Wasting money is, in these stakeholders' minds, akin to lower profits, fewer benefits, and higher prices.

5 Buying sales

Gaining exclusive vending rights or preferred supplier status as part of a strategic sponsorship is great. We're all for it. Unfortunately, overpaying for vending rights or preferred supplier status is often justified by strictly imagined marketing benefits (signage-based exposure is common), when the only real benefit is the sales.

On the other hand, sometimes a sponsorship will not be able to achieve multiple objectives, but it is *still* a good investment for gaining sales (i.e. the cost of the investment is lower than the profit margin). In this case, the prudent thing to do is to negotiate for the lowest level of sponsorship possible that still includes exclusive sales rights, then don't maximise it. Spending leverage funds on a non-strategic sponsorship is a waste of money and is often counterproductive to the positioning of the brand.

6 Sentimentality

We all feel for worthy causes, no question about it. But, this is not a reason in itself for investing marketing funds in them. Sponsorships of causes and other non-profits can be extremely powerful marketing tools. If the investment is a good strategic fit, then sponsor the organisation, maximise it—providing additional marketing punch to the sponsee, as well—and gain a marketing return. If the investment is not a good fit, and you still want to make a donation, then do it from your philanthropic budget.

A great book on this subject is *Brand Spirit* by Hamish Pringle and Marjorie Thompson. Information on this book can be found in the Recommended reading section of Appendix 2.

Another way that sentimentality can adversely affect a sponsorship program is if you continue sponsoring something simply because you've been sponsoring it for a long time. If it still has potential to work for you, freshen it up and continue. If not, you need to make a difficult choice. Advice on how to leave a long-term sponsorship with the least amount of downside to both parties can be found in the Exit strategies section on page 158.

7 Appeasing your critics

If you are thinking of using a sponsorship to significantly change your approach to an issue over which you have been criticised, such as globalisation, the environment, or health, then it can work really well. Non-profits often have a grassroots understanding of the effects of and possible solutions to social issues that your organisation is facing, and can be very helpful in facilitating a more responsible or enlightened approach.

If, on the other hand, you are considering using sponsorship simply to counteract bad PR, with no intention of using the sponsee's expertise or resources to make some meaningful change, don't do it. Consumers and the media will see right through you, and the result is that you will not only be criticised but also be named a hypocrite.

> If you sponsor a cause, you have to be prepared to walk the walk, not just talk the talk.

Creating a Sponsorship Team

As you began to think about the range of objectives you want to achieve through sponsorship, you no doubt noticed that many of these objectives involve departments or areas outside of sponsorship. This is normal and, in fact, is the healthiest and most cost-effective way to do sponsorship.

Sponsorship, when done well, should be a catalyst for your company to do any or all marketing activities better. You shouldn't be running a mail-in contest through the sponsorship department when your database marketing, research, and sales promotion departments are not only better placed to get the job done well, but could replace one of their existing (and not so effective) activities with a more interesting sponsorship-driven promotion. It's self-defeating to have multiple activities out in the marketplace. You end up competing against yourself. It's better to spend the dollar once and spend it well.

> Spend a dollar once and spend it well.

This approach, of course, requires teamwork. Developing a vibrant, diverse, and committed Sponsorship Team is absolutely imperative to getting the most out of your sponsorship investments.

There is a whole section on how to use your Sponsorship Team to maximise sponsorships, found in Part 3—Maximisation and management. We believe, however, that the importance of having and using a team approach to sponsorship is so important that you really need to start thinking about it now.

What can a Sponsorship Team do?

Although maximisation is an obvious way to use a Sponsorship Team, don't stop there. Use the creativity, expertise and resources of that team to make your sponsorships work better in many ways.

A team won't work if you're not prepared to share the credit.

Your team can:

- bring a fuller understanding of what they are trying to achieve and the opportunities around their areas
- help to decide whether or not to invest in a sponsorship, as well as ensuring that their needs are met when negotiating benefits
- maximise a sponsorship cost-effectively by using it as a catalyst for making their current activities work better
- provide in-kind benefits, and possibly funding, that will help to pay for sponsorships
- implement sponsorships through their departments or areas
- point out potential trouble spots, and help to devise ways around them
- provide contacts that will be helpful to the implementation of the program (e.g. subcontractors, merchandise manufacturers)
- quantify sponsorships against objectives.

Again, there is a whole chapter in Part 3—Marketing and management that fully explores how you can use your team to maximise, manage, and quantify sponsorship investments more effectively.

How do I start a team?

There are four steps in creating and managing your Sponsorship Team. The four steps are:

1. Identify the sponsorship stakeholders.
2. Educate them about your company's approach to sponsorship—you don't need to make them experts, but they should at least understand the basic concepts outlined in The approach on page 2.
3. Get them involved in the process of selecting, maximising and quantifying sponsorship as part of your Sponsorship Team.
4. Share the credit.

This last point is really important. We had a client whose Sponsorship Team was so effective that he was afraid they would do him out of a job, so he disbanded them. It's unfortunate when the organisation is ready for a change and the sponsorship manager isn't.

The makeup of the Sponsorship Team will obviously be different from one company to another, but here are some suggestions as to who might be involved:

- Brand Manager
- Sales Manager
- Trade Relations Manager
- Ad Agency

- Internet Marketing Manager (or whatever your company calls this enigmatic role!)
- Research Manager
- CRM/Loyalty Marketing
- PR
- Community Relations
- Regional Marketing
- Sponsorship Director/Manager
- Marketing Director
- Senior Executives
- Employee Representatives
- Corporate Relations (or whoever communicates with shareholders).

It is imperative that you set the minimum number of meetings per year in which each team member is expected to participate at the outset. Nine or ten of the monthly meetings should be sufficient, perhaps fewer for a senior executive. This will ensure that the people who get involved realise that it is a commitment, not just something for the résumé.

In addition, you need to ensure that all team members have the authority to make things happen within their departments or areas. It is no good to you if all the seats are full, but no one can make a decision.

Finally, it is in your best interest, and the best interest of your company, if you try to select team members that are forward thinking, creative, and not risk-adverse. We're not saying that sponsorship is risky, but some people do see it that way, so not being afraid to try something new or different is a good attribute.

Involving key outside organisations in these meetings can also be very useful. It is a great idea to involve one or more retailers, if applicable, because they will often tend to come on board for a retail promotion more readily if they have a hand in designing it. The involvement of associated companies, such as parent companies or organisations with common ownership, could also be valuable. If they target a similar marketplace with a complementary product, as is often the case, this provides a strong platform for cross-promotions.

If you will be discussing the maximisation of a specific sponsorship, it is often very beneficial to include a couple of representatives of the sponsee in the meeting. Involving sponsees in the creative process will do two things: they will gain a fuller understanding of both your objectives and challenges, and they will have the opportunity to use their expertise about the event to provide cost-effective ideas that may not have been come out otherwise.

Try to find team members with a 'Why not?' attitude.

Choosing the best management structure

Every company has its own way of managing sponsorship. Trouble is, most of these management structures create more problems than they solve.

We have two suggestions for management structures that work. This is followed by an overview of a couple of common management structures that are unlikely to give you the best result, and why.

Structures that do work

Semi-centralised

This is our favoured approach in most situations, providing a high degree of ownership and consultation by key stakeholders while ensuring an expert approach.

The semi-centralised structure centres on the brand group. As the custodians of brand health and the area held responsible for results, it makes sense that this group is the cornerstone for selecting, managing and maximising sponsorships. The other major area held directly responsible for results are regional marketing/sales teams. Because they have a lot at stake, they also need to be a key part of the sponsorship process.

The sponsorship manager has overall responsibility for the sponsorship portfolio and, in many ways, acts like a consultant, providing high-level expertise through the process. The sponsorship manager should not be implementing sponsorships, but rather providing the advice, resources and impetus so that the brand team and other stakeholders can make it happen and reap the rewards.

The sponsorship manager's responsibilities include:

➤ overall responsibility for management (but not implementation) of the sponsorship portfolio

➤ assisting brand groups with the integration of sponsorship across marketing activities and the development of strategies

➤ assisting brand groups with assessment and selection of opportunities

➤ making recommendations for new investments by brand groups (including reviewing proposals for one brand that might be better for a different brand)

➤ facilitating the Sponsorship Team

➤ creating sponsorship maximisation, implementation, and quantification plans in concert with brand teams

➤ running, or assisting with, sponsorship negotiations and renegotiations

➤ running, or assisting with, negotiation of promotions, including promotional media

Every company has their ideal way to manage sponsorship.

➤ assisting with the sell-in of opportunities across departments/states/retail outlets

➤ strategically assisting with specific sponsorship opportunities or challenges, as needed

➤ managing sponsorship education program (publications, workshops, conferences), including providing sponsorship workshops to key stakeholders and sponsees, as needed

➤ facilitating sponsorship research by sponsees and brand groups

➤ acting as a clearing house for sponsorship information, proposal and contract filing, sponsorship contacts, educational resources, etc.

➤ being the frontline face of sponsorship.

The positives of this approach include:

➤ ensures sponsorship is linked to overall strategies

➤ centres 'ownership' with the group responsible for overall brand health

➤ fosters strong involvement across stakeholders

➤ ensures that sponsorship expertise is not wasted on low-level implementation and that other stakeholder expertise (e.g. PR, direct marketing) is used to its best effect

➤ minimises activation costs.

Negatives include:

➤ must invest in experienced sponsorship talent

➤ requires education of an array of stakeholders.

Brand centred

If there isn't the budget or senior management support for in-house sponsorship expertise, this approach is the next best option.

The roles are similar to the above, but without a sponsorship manager, the overall responsibility for the direction of the sponsorship portfolio rests with the Sponsorship Team. Key decisions about specific sponsorships remain with the brand team.

The major positive to this approach is that it is managed from the seat of brand marketing strategy. Negatives include:

➤ lack of specialised sponsorship expertise

➤ requires a lot of driving to ensure sponsorship doesn't fall by the wayside, as can happen (brand teams tend to have a lot on their plates)

➤ without a sponsorship manager to drive the Sponsorship Team, this approach tends not to be very consultative.

> Semi-centralised sponsorship management usually provides the best result.

Structures that don't work

Just as there are structures that work well, there are also structures that don't.

Fully centralised

This is the typical scenario, often anchored with one or more sponsorship managers. In this situation, sponsorship activities tend to take place outside of the umbrella of overall marketing strategies—almost as a satellite—rather than being an effective and intrinsic part of the marketing plan.

Hallmarks include:

➤ tends to be disconnected from the overall marketing plan, with objectives being created for sponsorship, rather than sponsorship being selected and maximised to meet larger brand objectives

➤ lack of ownership by other departments, brand management, and senior management

➤ many opportunities to add interest to existing marketing activities will fall by the wayside

➤ sponsorship support will be far more expensive if it is being maximised with sponsorship dollars rather than being used as a catalyst for increasing the effectiveness of other marketing activities.

State/regionally driven

While there is clearly a positive around having your local office involved in local sponsorships, there are a number of major drawbacks:

➤ lack of strategic focus—regional offices are not always well-connected to overall marketing plans or brand plans

➤ lack of expertise

➤ sponsorships are often selected, negotiated, and managed by people who primarily do another job, and this is reflected in the sponsorships. For example, if sponsorships are managed by the local trade marketing manager, they will tend to be focused on hospitality and trade incentives, rather than a wider array of objectives

➤ many opportunities for optimisation are lost.

In fact, the marketing departments of many companies that take this approach have absolutely no idea what sponsorships the company has, and if sponsorship is to function as the marketing power tool it is, this can't be a good thing.

Sponsorship manager job description template

 Job1.doc

This position fits into the semi-centralised sponsorship management model that we recommended. That is, the overall responsibility for selecting, maximising, managing, and quantifying a sponsorship sits with each brand group, with overall management of the portfolio sitting with the sponsorship manager.

This position will function largely like an internal consultant, providing expert support and assistance, as well as ensuring that key functions for making sponsorship work do not fall by the wayside (as can happen).

What follows is a job description and requirements for a sponsorship manager. Also included are some questions you should ask, the answers to which will provide a lot of insight to an applicant's approach and abilities.

Providing strategic assistance

- Taking overall responsibility for management of the sponsorship portfolio
- Assisting brand groups with the integration of sponsorship across marketing activities and the development of strategies
- Assisting brand groups with assessment and selection of opportunities
- Making recommendations for new investments by brand groups (including reviewing proposals for one brand group that might be better for a different brand)
- Creating sponsorship maximisation, implementation, and quantification plans in concert with brand teams
- Running, or assisting with, sponsorship negotiations and renegotiations
- Running, or assisting with, negotiation of promotions, including promotional media
- Assisting with sell-in of opportunities across departments/states/retail outlets
- Strategically assisting with specific sponsorship opportunities or challenges, as needed
- Managing sponsorship education program (publications, workshops, conferences), including providing sponsorship workshops to new key stakeholders and sponsees, as needed
- Facilitating sponsorship research by sponsees and brand groups
- Acting as a clearing house for sponsorship information, proposal and contract filing, sponsorship contacts, educational resources, etc.
- Being the frontline face of sponsorship for [*company*]

Keeping the balls rolling

➤ Facilitating Sponsorship Team meetings, brainstorms

➤ Managing (not doing) the implementation process

➤ Managing (not doing) the quantification process

➤ Ensuring that all sponsorships are evaluated, addressed and updated every six months, at minimum

➤ Ensuring that Proposal Guidelines for all brands are kept up to date and distributed to all stakeholders

➤ Ensuring most recent Proposal Guidelines are made available to potential sponsees through all appropriate channels, including over the Internet

➤ Ensuring all other tools, guidelines, etc. are kept up to date

Required experience

Please note, a marketing degree or MBA is not a strong indicator of whether or not a person will be suitable as a sponsorship manager. Experience and personality/approach will give you a far better indication. We recommend the following:

➤ minimum of three years experience managing multiple sponsorships from the sponsor side

➤ experience managing projects involving multiple internal stakeholders (brand groups, loyalty marketing, research, sales, etc.)

➤ experience managing projects involving outside stakeholders (ad agencies, retail/trade, strategic partners).

Required attributes

➤ Very strong abilities in both analytical (left brain) and creative (right brain) areas

➤ The weight of authority to lead sponsorship within [company]

➤ Diplomacy and creativity to manage multi-disciplinary teams

Key questions to ask

➤ Why do sponsors invest in sponsorship? The answer will show whether s/he is objective-oriented

➤ What can sponsorship achieve that other forms of marketing can't? The answer will show whether s/he understands the power of sponsorship (emotional connections and integratability)

➤ What can a good sponsorship bring to the sponsee? The answer will show whether s/he is partnership-oriented or transaction-oriented

➤ In the 21st century, who are the stakeholders in sponsorship? Whether s/he includes consumers, employees, and shareholders will indicate a grasp of the wider ramifications of sponsorship

Sponsorship policy

A Sponsorship Policy is a document that lays out, in general terms, your company's commitment to sponsorship, internal responsibilities and reporting, and how sponsorships are to be conducted. It is not your game plan—that's your strategy—the policy is the rules by which you play the game.

Before seeking or entering into a sponsorship agreement, it is important that your organisation has a Sponsorship Policy in place.

Why you need one

There are four reasons that your organisation should have a Sponsorship Policy:

1. Any company, particularly public companies, spending substantial marketing funds should define the key components, objectives, and administration guidelines of the program.
2. A policy will ensure that a uniform approach is taken to sponsorship throughout your organisation, including protecting your marketing budget from 'chairman's choice'.
3. A policy outlines accountability and responsibility within your organisation and your expectations of sponsees.
4. A policy can assist you greatly through the process of a sponsorship audit.

Components of a Sponsorship Policy

A Sponsorship Policy does not need to be a tome, but it should contain the following information.

Background

The background outlines your company's history with sponsorship, as well as your overall approach and the objectives you are aiming to achieve. This is a good place to include your menu of objectives.

Definitions

You need to define what does and does not constitute sponsorship, particularly if you are engaged in both sponsorship and philanthropy.

A strategy is your game plan. A policy is the rules of the game.

EXAMPLE

Sponsorship is an investment in sports, the arts, a cause, educational organisation, community or government event or program, individual or broadcast. Sponsorship investments have a reasonable expectation of achieving at least five marketing objectives and are generally made from a marketing or brand budget.

Philanthropy is a gift made with no expectation of commercial return and is not generally funded from marketing or brand budgets. Philanthropy has a separate policy that is held in the corporate affairs department.

Also, if sponsorship-type activity is carried out by multiple departments, you might want to make that distinction. For instance, your corporate affairs department might 'sponsor' a government conference for reasons that have nothing to do with marketing.

Situational analysis

The situational analysis identifies all current issues that may impact on your sponsorship program. These can include, but are not limited to:

➤ competitor activities

➤ the economy

➤ company changes, initiatives, or issues.

Accountability

This section is very simply about who is responsible for what, including:

➤ selection and approval of sponsorships (often different people will have authority for different levels of sponsorship)

➤ management of the overall sponsorship process, including the Sponsorship Team

➤ management of sponsee relationships

➤ quantification

➤ stakeholder education

➤ representation of sponsorship issues to the board or executive committee.

Guidelines

The most important thing that the guidelines section will include is an overview of the process by which sponsorship will be selected, negotiated, and managed, as well as the systems and tools that will be used in that process. As you develop and refine your processes and tools, be sure to document all of the steps in this section of your policy.

This is the area where you will outline any exclusions you might have. Try not to put too many constraints on the types of sponsorships that you will consider, because there are new things happening in sponsorship all the time. Something that may once have been inappropriate for your company might become appropriate in a new incarnation.

EXAMPLE

We will consider sponsorships in all categories, but as a brewer, it is inappropriate for us to sponsor any event or program where the primary audience is under legal drinking age.

Quantification and evaluation should also be included in the guidelines section. Our recommendation is that you evaluate the performance of the sponsorship separately from the performance of the sponsee. This is because it is possible to have strong sponsorship results while having a difficult relationship with the sponsee. It is also possible to have a strong relationship with the sponsee while the sponsorship itself may not have performed as anticipated.

EXAMPLE

The results of each sponsorship will be evaluated against the objectives set for that sponsorship at the outset. These results will be quantified by the Sponsorship Team member with the most expertise and resources in that field (e.g. the number and quality of new entrants to the database will be reported by the customer loyalty department).

We will evaluate our relationship with the sponsee separately. This evaluation will be based on:

➤ *whether or not all benefits were delivered as promised*

➤ *the timeliness and relevance of reports*

➤ *the degree to which the sponsee added value to our investment*

➤ *whether or not we were kept in the loop by the sponsee*

➤ *the overall ease of the working relationship.*

Review and evaluation

A policy is a living document. It needs to be continually reviewed, evaluated, and updated. Be sure to include a timeframe and process for keeping it up to date. Every six months is generally adequate.

Policy checklist

If you have addressed all of the questions listed below in your Sponsorship Policy, you can be assured that you have a sound foundation on which to build your sponsorship program.

Background

➤ Why is your organisation engaging in sponsorship?

➤ What are your objectives? (Include your menu of objectives here.)

➤ What is your general approach (e.g. partnership-oriented, objective-driven)?

➤ Have your objectives or overall approach changed significantly in the past few years? If so, how has this affected your sponsorship program?

Definitions

➤ How do you define sponsorship?

➤ How does this differ from philanthropy and/or grants?

Situational analysis

➤ Are there any internal issues that could affect your sponsorship program (e.g. restructure, takeover, resistance to change)?

➤ Are there any competitor developments that could affect your program?

➤ Are there any economic or industrial issues that could impact your program?

➤ Are there any other issues that will impact on your sponsorship program?

➤ What sponsorship issues do staff and management need to be aware of?

➤ How are your stockholders likely to react to the sponsorship program?

➤ How are your retailers/distributors and end-users likely to react to the sponsorship program?

Accountability and responsibility

➤ Who is responsible for evaluating sponsorship opportunities?

➤ Who is responsible for negotiating sponsorships?

➤ Who can approve sponsorships and to what dollar level?

➤ Who is responsible for managing sponsorship programs and ensuring all investments are maximised?

➤ Who is responsible for ensuring employee and stockholder interests are served?

➤ Who is responsible for quantifying and reporting sponsorship results?

➤ Who makes up your Sponsorship Team?

➤ Who represents sponsorship issues to the board or executive committee?

Guidelines

➤ What are your organisation's guidelines for investing in sponsorship properties?

➤ What is the process for selecting sponsorships?

➤ What types of properties are deemed inappropriate and why?

➤ How will you ensure sponsorship programs are integrated with other marketing programs?

➤ What procedures/approaches will you use to maximise your investments?

➤ What contra resources are available for use during sponsorship negotiations to minimise cash expenditure?

➤ How will you quantify sponsorship opportunities?

➤ How will sponsee performance be evaluated?

➤ How will you keep stakeholders informed about sponsorship activities? (Stakeholders could include staff, management, subcontractors and agencies, stockholders, distributors, retailers, and end-users.)

➤ How will you ensure that sponsorship expertise is kept up to date?

Policy review and evaluation

➤ How often will this policy be reviewed?

➤ Who will be involved in the review?

➤ Who is responsible for any changes required?

Chapter 2

Sponsorship strategy

A Sponsorship Strategy is a document that provides, over time, an outline of exactly how your objectives will be achieved through sponsorship. It will outline the systems and tools you will use to carry out the strategy. It usually will also assess each sponsorship in your current portfolio against these strategies.

The usual timeframe for a Sponsorship Strategy is 2–4 years, although it should be noted that a strategy is a living document and should be revisited regularly as your needs and situation change.

In this chapter, we will go through a number of critical areas that you need to understand and assess before you will be prepared to develop your own strategy. These areas will form key sections of your strategy document. We then provide a framework for your strategy, showing you how to structure the document so it makes sense both to you and to the other stakeholders in your company.

Understanding your target markets

In the past few years, marketers of all types have started to understand that their job is not to 'talk at' their audience, it is to create relationships. More than any other form of marketing, sponsorship has the raw materials to develop and foster relationships with consumers and trade. The key is to understand your target markets—not just who they are, but what they want and what motivates them. If you understand your target markets, your role as a sponsor will become very clear. Your markets will tell you how to sell to them.

The goal is to use sponsorship to move your audience further down the relationship continuum from understanding your brand to using it to becoming a loyal user, with the ultimate goal that the consumer becomes an advocate of your brand.

> Your goal is not to get people to buy your brand, it is to get them to *join* your brand.

Ignorance ⟩ Understanding ⟩ Acceptance ⟩ Repertoire ⟩ Loyalty ⟩ Advocacy ⟩

➤ Ignorance—Have heard of your brand, but don't understand it

➤ Understanding—Understand your brand's premise, but haven't determined its specific relevance to them

➤ Acceptance—Accept your brand, but don't regularly use it—think it's 'okay'

➤ Repertoire—Brand is part of the repertoire of brands in the category (e.g. soft drink, airline) that the consumer uses regularly

➤ Loyalty—Only use your brand

➤ Advocacy—Only use your brand and advocates it to others.

Figure 2.1
Relationship
continuum

Profiling and segmentation

Do this little exercise: take five minutes and write down ten words or short phrases that you would use to describe yourself. Imagine you are going to hand this piece of paper to a total stranger and that, solely based upon what you've written, your goal is for that person to understand fully who you are. You may write some big, important things about yourself. You may have some little things that provide great insight. Do it now before you move on.

It used to be that markets were segmented mainly by demographics—hard information such as income, gender, age, how many kids, and what kind of car you drive. Now, savvy companies are throwing demographics out the window in favour of psychographic segmentation. Psychographics are like psychological demographics. They are about how people define themselves, what motivates them, and what they care about. An example of the difference between the demographic and psychographic profiles of the same person can be found below.

Demographic

➤ Male

➤ 35 years old

➤ Married

➤ Professional

➤ Household income $100 000+

➤ Urban

➤ Drives 4WD

➤ Owns a computer

➤ Travels for business and pleasure

➤ Primary grocery buyer

Psychographic

➤ Adventure-sport enthusiast

➤ Work hard, play hard

➤ Social

➤ Environmentally responsible

➤ Egalitarian

➤ Experience-oriented/try anything once

➤ Fun

➤ Pierced navel

➤ Rugby player

➤ Loves to cook

> Demographics are about *what* you are, psychographics are about *who* you are.

Which one of these lists gives you more understanding of this person? It's the same person, but the psychographic profile will have drawn for you a much different and much more accurate description of who he is.

Now, look at the ten ways you've described yourself. Chances are you didn't include much, if any, demographic information. Just as with the example shown above, you have most likely listed not only ten definitions of yourself, but ten ways in which a brand could foster a relationship with you by adding value to the things that are important to you and aligning with your values in a meaningful way. But how many companies select sponsorships based on demographics, rather than psychographics? Too many.

For all market segments, your job as a switched-on sponsor becomes to provide experiences and opportunities to your target markets that allow them to be more a part of something they care about. It is about adding value. Knowing the answers to a few key questions will be very important to knowing how to add this value. We have included these types of questions in our sample survey that follows, but generally, you will need to know your markets and their views on brands and events.

Around your brand/product category (e.g. car manufacturer)

➤ What are the key psychographic attributes of each market segment?

➤ Why do these people buy (or not buy) your brand, or other brands?

➤ How and under what circumstances do they use your or your competitor's brands?

➤ What is their favourite brand of any product and why? (Whether their answer is functional or emotional will say a lot about how you should market to them.)

➤ What attributes do they believe your brand has?

Around events

➤ Why does your target market attend games or an event? What is the emotional motivation?

➤ Why do these people watch it on TV? Where? What is the motivation (e.g. an excuse to go to the pub with mates, or relaxing on a Sunday afternoon on the couch)?

➤ How can the emotional part of their experience be enhanced?

➤ How can the functional part of their experience be enhanced?

➤ Are there any barriers or challenges to them participating in or enjoying their experience?

➤ Are there any parts of the experience that could be improved?

If you build and drive your sponsorship program based upon the answers to these questions, the result will be that you will connect with your marketplace, not just expose your brand to them. That connection will create long term shifts in people's perceptions and understanding of your brand, as well as their behaviour (e.g. loyalty, advocacy, frequency of purchase).

'Broadcasting' vs 'narrowcasting'

Broadcasting is the practice of communicating to a mass market with little, if any, targeting. The up-side is that it reaches an enormous amount of people. The downside is that by trying to be all things to all people, broadcast marketing doesn't tend to do any of them very well. Plus, you are likely marketing to many people who aren't genuine prospects for your product or service.

Narrowcasting is just the opposite. It means that you are communicating with a specific, or narrow, market and that you are aligning with them very closely and to the exclusion of other marketplaces. The downside is that the number of people reached is far smaller. This is fully made up for by the increase in effectiveness of the marketing activity and the fact that you are targeting people who are most likely to be receptive to it.

If you are trying to align with and develop a relationship with a target market, clearly narrowcasting is going to work better for you. This does not mean that you should go out and dump all of your big, broad-based sponsorships (although, if you are spending a lot of money and your target market makes up only 10% of the audience, you might want to think about it). It simply means that the activities that you develop around the sponsorship—promotions, PR, etc.—need to be targeted specifically at your market. It is not at all uncommon for a company to use a large sponsorship in a number of totally different ways to reach two or three or more divergent target markets.

> Narrowcasting doesn't mean you should dump all of your big sponsorships, you just need to focus your activities.

There are also market segments that demand to be approached as groups unto themselves. They won't accept being lumped in with the mass market, to such an extent that they will be turned off by any message that identifies them that way. Examples of this are the status-oriented consumer, who wants to be acknowledged as being a cut above, and the very individualistic consumer, such as extreme sports enthusiasts.

Case studies: Making the connection

TOM'S OF MAINE, manufacturer of natural personal care products, focuses squarely on working with community and environmental organisations that are supported by their core consumer base, engendering loyalty by aligning their brand very closely with the values of their target market. They measure not only the benefits that the sponsorship brings to their brand, but the results that these non-profits reap from promotions done by Tom's, such as increasing membership or raising awareness of their cause.

MASTERCARD INTERNATIONAL doesn't focus on whether people are aware of their major sponsorships of sports such as ice hockey, baseball, and motorsport. Instead, they maximise sponsorships based on their 'Priceless' marketing strategy, providing sponsorship-driven priceless moments for cardholders. They then measure the effectiveness of sponsorships based on consumer buy-in to the concept of 'Priceless'. See more at www.mastercard.com.

ALTHOUGH they are a great family activity, baseball games can take a long time, and kids can get bored. Minute Maid juices made their sponsorship of the Houston Astros baseball team even more of a fun family affair by building a huge baseball-oriented play area for children at the stadium.

PEOPLE attend parades for the atmosphere, and Santa.com made the crowd an even bigger part of the atmosphere at the Santa.com Holiday Parade. They filled the streets with camera-wielding elves that snapped hundreds of digital photos of attendees, which were then shown on parade floats for everyone to see—instant holiday stardom!

Research

You can't understand your markets if you don't do research. That is the bottom line.

There are two different kinds of research, both of which can offer strong insights into your markets:

1. Quantitative—This type of research is based on individual surveys (phone, Internet, in person) or questionnaires. It uses a series of questions and tick-boxes to collect and analyse both demographic and psychographic aspects of your target markets.

2. Qualitative—This type of research is most commonly done with focus groups— small groups of people with one or more similar characteristics—but can also be

done individually, through interviews. Although the interactions follow a general plan, the structure is much more free-flowing than with quantitative research, and a wide variety of opinions, suggestions and areas for improvement can be canvassed openly.

So, which one should you do? If you have specific things that you want to know, as well as the right mechanisms to reach the marketplace effectively, quantitative research will work best for you. If, on the other hand, you are more interested in understanding a whole range of preferences and motivations, then qualitative research will probably work better. This is particularly the case if you do focus group research, because different personalities in the room will tend to play off one another, providing you with considerable insights.

Who should be researched?

The short answer is everybody. This includes:

➤ current and potential consumers (your target markets)

➤ attendees, members, and people interested in your sponsees

➤ trade (retailers, brokers, agents, etc.).

Research gathering

Because you are probably already carrying out target market research, you should be able to work with your researcher to ensure that both psychographic questions and questions relevant to sponsorship are included.

It is likely that many of your sponsees also do research. If this is the case, work with them to include questions that will assist you in understanding people's perceptions of your brand, their buying habits, and to identify areas where you can add value to their experience with the event.

Read the attached research questionnaire templates for some ideas on questions you might want to ask.

Market research on a shoestring

If your sponsee doesn't do research, or for some reason you can't piggyback on what it does do, don't despair just yet. Although it is certainly possible to spend a great deal of money on gathering quantitative research, it isn't absolutely necessary.

When the budget was tight and we had a strong idea of what we needed to find out, we have had a great deal of luck with the following approach. It is not statistically perfect by any means, but it is inexpensive and can provide some direction about how

You can't understand your markets if you don't do research.

to strengthen sponsorship activities and an impression of how your sponsorships are impacting your marketplace:

1. Contact a marketing or business instructor at your local university, TAFE, business college or Vo-Tech. Ask them to select a couple (or group) of students that want to do some work experience.

2. Work with those students to develop a questionnaire and plan of attack to get the information you need. Give them a good brief—ensure that they understand both your marketing objectives and who you are trying to reach. You will probably want to start with a questionnaire that is around 90% right already. Two questionnaire templates are attached to get you started.

3. Arrange for the students to get access to the sponsee's audience (you should have already cleared this with the sponsee). They could gather information by phone, mail, or in-person surveys, which tends to be fastest.

4. Once the students have analysed the data, ask for a presentation, as well as a copy of the raw figures on disk. The students usually do a very good job of analysing the data, but even if they do miss on a couple of areas, you will have all the raw data so you can analyse it yourself.

Keep in mind that these students are not your own personal lackeys. You need to give them opportunities not only to gather data, but to plan the survey and analyse it. If you do that, this type of research shouldn't cost more than a few hundred dollars and will provide the students with a *valuable* learning experience, while you gain valuable insight.

You can use the same approach to get specific, sponsorship-oriented research about your target markets by collecting surveys in places where you know a large proportion of your target market will be, such as at a shopping mall, downtown at lunchtime, at the beach.

Audience profile questionnaire

 Research1.doc

1. Is this your first visit to a professional women's basketball game?
    - ❐ Yes
    - ❐ No

2. How many games have you attended this season?
    - ❐ This is my first

❐ 2–4

❐ 5–10

❐ More than 10

3. Where did you hear about tonight's game? Check all that apply.

❐ I have season tickets

❐ Friend or relative

❐ Radio ad

❐ TV ad

❐ Newspaper ad

❐ Internet

❐ Another sporting event

❐ From a television or radio program or print article (please specify)

❐ Other (please specify)

4. What did you think of the stadium? Check all that apply.

❐ Good visibility

❐ Comfortable

❐ Easy to get to

❐ Good food/drinks

❐ Found parking difficult/expensive

❐ Found public transportation difficult

❐ Food/drinks too expensive

❐ Food/drinks poor quality

5. What are the top three reasons you decided to attend this game?

❐ Atmosphere at the game

❐ Quality of play

❐ I like to support women's sport

❐ Rivalry between the teams

❐ Good day/night out

❐ Good value for families

❐ I follow a particular player (please specify)

❐ I just wanted to check it out

❏   Easier/cheaper to get tickets than for men's games

❏   I came as a favour to someone else

❏   Other (please specify)

6.   Did the game live up to your expectations?

❏   Yes

❏   Mostly

❏   No

7.   If you could change one thing about your experience, what would it be?

8.   Including yourself, how many people are in your group today?

❏   1

❏   2

❏   3–4

❏   5–9

❏   10 or more

9.   Who are you here with?

❏   Another family adult

❏   Non-family adult

❏   Child/children

❏   School group

❏   Other organised group

10.   What is your zip code?

Questions 11–14 for Non-Tri-State residents only

11.   How long are you staying in the Tri-State area?

12.   Are you staying in paid accommodation?

❏   Yes

❏   No

13. What other activities have you done/do you plan to do during your stay? Check all that apply.

- ☐ Attend another sporting event
  - ☐ Basketball
  - ☐ Football
  - ☐ Baseball
  - ☐ Ice hockey
  - ☐ Other
- ☐ Attend a non-sporting event
- ☐ Visit a museum or gallery
- ☐ See a concert, play, or show
- ☐ Sightseeing
- ☐ Shopping
- ☐ Other (please specify)

14. Now, thinking of things you do for pleasure. When was the last time, if ever, did you yourself do the following for pleasure?

	IN PAST WEEK	1–4 WEEKS AGO	1–6 MTHS AGO	MORE THAN 6 MTHS AGO	NEVER OR DO NOT KNOW
Go to the movies	1	2	3	4	5
Attend a professional sporting event	1	2	3	4	5
Play sport or do an exercise program	1	2	3	4	5
Eat out at a restaurant	1	2	3	4	5
Go to a concert or play	1	2	3	4	5
Garden or work around the yard	1	2	3	4	5
Visit a museum, art gallery or exhibition	1	2	3	4	5
Go to the beach	1	2	3	4	5

15. For each of the following statements, please tell me if you agree or disagree that it describes you personally:

	AGREE	DISAGREE	DO NOT KNOW
I am very fashion conscious	1	2	3
I want to achieve a lot	1	2	3
I love sports of any kind	1	2	3
I am really a homebody	1	2	3
I will try anything once	1	2	3
I hate getting dressed up	1	2	3
I try to be environmentally responsible	1	2	3
I like to garden and potter around the house on weekends	1	2	3
I would rather watch TV on Saturday than go out	1	2	3
I thrive on the company of other people	1	2	3
I do not like sport, either watching or taking part	1	2	3
I would rather take part in something than watch it	1	2	3

16. Are you employed in paid work? What is your occupation?

    ❐ Yes

    ❐ No

    ❐ Occupation: ....

17. How old are you?

    ❐ Under 18 years

    ❐ 18–24 years

    ❐ 25–34 years

    ❐ 35–49 years

    ❐ 50+ years

18. What is the highest level of school you have completed?

    ❐ High school

    ❐ Trade/technical or business college

    ❐ University degree (undergraduate)

    ❐ Advanced university degree

19. Which of these categories does your total annual household income fall into?

☐ Under $25 000

☐ $25 001 – $40 000

☐ $40 001 – $60 000

☐ $60 001 – $80 000

☐ $80 001 – $100 000

☐ Over $100 000

20. How likely are you to attend a women's professional basketball game again in the next 12 months?

☐ Very likely

☐ Somewhat likely

☐ Not very likely

☐ Not at all likely

☐ Do not know

Thank you for your help.

21. Record gender of respondent:

☐ Female

☐ Male

Date of interview: ....

I certify that this interview was conducted in accordance with briefing instructions and the Code of Professional Behavior, and that the information gathered is true and accurate.

Signed by interviewer: ....

Sponsorship impact questionnaire

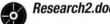

Research2.doc

1. Who are the major sponsors of the 10th Annual Contemporary Art Awards?

2. I would be more likely to buy a product made by a company that sponsors the arts.

❐ Agree

❐ Agree somewhat

❐ Neutral

❐ Disagree somewhat

❐ Disagree strongly

3. When I see products made by companies who sponsor and support the Contemporary Art Awards, I am more likely to purchase their products.

❐ Agree

❐ Agree somewhat

❐ Neutral

❐ Disagree somewhat

❐ Disagree strongly

4. When I see products made by companies that do not support the arts, I am less likely to purchase their products.

❐ Agree

❐ Agree somewhat

❐ Neutral

❐ Disagree somewhat

❐ Disagree strongly

5. Can you name any other sponsors of the arts?

6. When did you first try California Blender's Choice Sparkling Wines?

❐ Tonight

❐ In the last month

❐ In the last three months

❐ More than six months ago

❐ In the last year

❐ I have never tried California Blender's Choice Sparkling Wines

7. Would you purchase California Blender's Choice Sparkling Wines in the future?

❐ Yes

❐ Likely

❐ Perhaps

❐   Unlikely

❐   No

8.   When is the last time you purchased wine?

     ❐   In the last two weeks

     ❐   In the last month

     ❐   In the last three months

     ❐   More than six months ago

     ❐   In the last year

     ❐   I have never purchased sparkling wine

9.   If you have purchased wine, which brand or style did you last purchase?

     ❐   French Champagne

     ❐   Other imported sparkling wine

     ❐   California Blender's Choice

     ❐   Gallo of Sonoma

     ❐   Fetzer

     ❐   Robert Mondavi

     ❐   Berringer

     ❐   Other American Wines

     ❐   Chilean Wine

     ❐   Australian Wine

     ❐   Other import (Please specify.)

10. If you have purchased wine more than once in the last six months, which brands or styles did you purchase? (Choose all that apply.)

     ❐   French Champagne

     ❐   Other imported sparkling wine

     ❐   California Blender's Choice

     ❐   Gallo of Sonoma

     ❐   Fetzer

     ❐   Robert Mondavi

     ❐   Berringer

     ❐   Other American Wines

     ❐   Chilean Wine

     ❐   Australian Wine

❐   Other import (Please specify.)

11. What are the main reasons you purchase a particular wine for the first time? (Choose all that apply.)

❐   Recommendation from friend/family

❐   Expert recommendation (e.g. wine critic, wine steward)

❐   I had heard of it, but I'm not sure where

❐   Read the description on the label

❐   I had the opportunity to try it and liked it

❐   Brand supports the arts

❐   Trusted the brand

❐   I liked the bottle/label

❐   Price

❐   Other: ....

12. Are you a member of a wine club?

❐   Yes

❐   No

❐   I was a member, but am not one at this time

13. How would you rate the Contemporary Art Awards exhibition?

❐   Excellent

❐   Above Average

❐   Fair

❐   Poor

Be sure to include basic database generating questions.

Determining brand needs

In addition to understanding your target markets and knowing your overall objectives, you will need a full understanding of what your brand needs before you are ready to develop your strategy. This analysis covers your brand's positioning, its life stage, new initiatives, your competitive situation, and other factors that could affect brand health.

Brand positioning

Brand positioning is about the personality of your brand. It encompasses the attributes of your brand, as well as the core brand values. Usually, there will be a larger number of attributes, reflecting a wide variety of aspects, and only one or two of the much deeper values that are the true essence of the brand.

Some companies reflect brand positioning graphically. Some of these are very complex, and some are quite simple. An example of a simple graphic that could reflect a fast food chain is found in Figure 2.2.

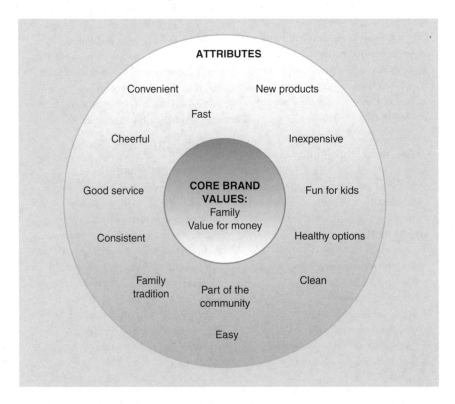

> Brand positioning is about the personality of your brand.

Figure 2.2 Possible attributes and values of a fast-food chain

However you identify the attributes and values of your brand, you need to keep them firmly in mind when selecting sponsorships. Matching one or more key attributes with a sponsee creates a more natural fit, and one that will seem far more seamless to the all-important target markets.

Case study: American Express and the Museum of Contemporary Art

The Museum of Contemporary Art is one of Australia's pre-eminent cultural organisations. It was seeking an interesting way of displaying part of its extensive permanent collection and developed the concept 'Plastic Fantastic' around a planned exhibition of the use of plastic from the 1960s through to the current day.

At the same time, American Express was preparing to introduce a new Blue Card, aimed primarily at a young, up and coming audience.

This 1997 sponsorship is an outstanding example of a sponsor and sponsee who are matched in all three ways.

Target market matching

American Express was trying to reach younger, sophisticated professionals living in the Sydney metropolitan area—not the core marketplace for their other cards. This matched extremely well with the Museum's audience:

- 45% were 25–34 years old
- 50% were earning over $50,000 annually
- 63% were single
- 53% were professional
- 74% resided in inner suburbs
- 60% socialised in cafes and bars.

This is a good example of a sponsee delivering a new target market to a sponsor.

Attribute matching

The Blue Card was being launched with the taglines 'young, funky and individual' and 'life's there, go out and grab it'. These attributes are virtually a perfect match with the well-known attributes of the Museum of Contemporary Art.

Matching a charge card or 'plastic' and an exhibition of plastic items is also strong.

The match was further extended with the commission of a large, blue plastic sculpture, the 'Blue Boy', which was displayed prominently outside the Museum in its prime city location throughout the exhibition.

Objective matching

One of American Express' key objectives was to create added value for its cardholders. Two of the Museum of Contemporary Art's objectives were to sample the exhibition to opinion leaders in their target demographic market and to sell more merchandise in their store.

The two organisations worked together to achieve these objectives by offering American Express members special discounts in the Museum store, as well as by creating cardholder days at the Museum, when members got free entry.

Brand lifecycle

In order to work for your company, both the sponsorship and the negotiated benefits should match the product's lifecycle stage (see Figure 2.3).

In brand infancy, your company's primary goal should be developing awareness and understanding of the brand and its core premise. In adolescence, your goal should be creating relevance—*why* should a person care about your brand?—as well as educating consumers on brand attributes and positioning. In brand maturity, it is all about creating and nurturing relationships with consumers.

Just as key objectives change across a lifecycle, what sponsorship can provide to a brand also shifts as the brand moves through the lifecycle.

Figure 2.3 A brand's lifecycle
follows a simple bell curve

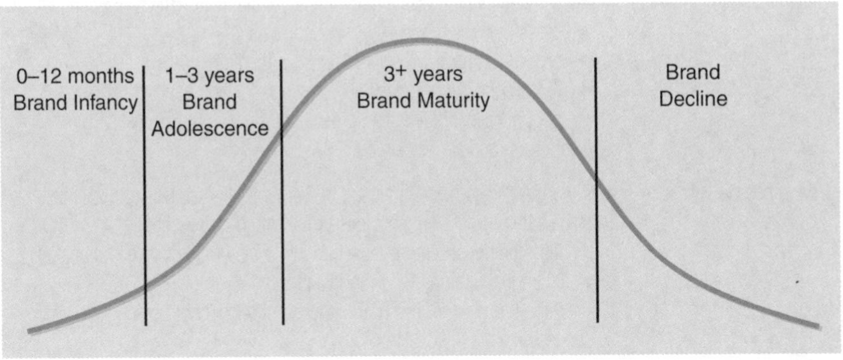

| 0–12 months Brand Infancy | 1–3 years Brand Adolescence | 3+ years Brand Maturity | Brand Decline |

LIFECYCLE STAGE	APPROPRIATE SPONSORSHIPS/BENEFITS
Brand infancy	Short-term (6–12 months) exposure-based sponsorships that provide: • exposure of brand • exposure of positioning statement • sampling/trial • trade promotions to introduce brand to trade and incite product support • relationship-building opportunities with opinion-leaders (early adopters) • research to understand consumer values, awareness of the brand, and understanding of brand positioning.
Brand adolescence	Longer term, relevance-building sponsorships (three years plus option to renew) that provide: • opportunities to create relevance with key customer groups • opportunities to involve consumers in sponsorships and/or supporting promotions (consumer/trade) • opportunities to involve trade in sponsorships and/or supporting promotions • retail promotion • communication of marketing messages—brand benefits, positioning statements • research to gauge product understanding, positioning, and perceived alignment to customer values.
Brand maturity	Longer term, relationship-building sponsorships (three years plus option to renew) that provide: • added value benefits/experiences for key consumers

- excitement and interest around a brand that might be perceived as static or stale
- reinforcement of brand values, attributes
- a variety of promotional techniques (media, retail, direct marketing, etc.)
- cross-pollination with other sponsorships
- cross-promotion with other sponsors/media partners
- research to gauge consumer interests, creating new sponsorship opportunities or ideas for sponsorship-driven promotions.

See also 'Brand adolescence'.

Brand decline	If the brand is to be re-launched to the same marketplace, the sponsorship strategy would be the same as for 'Brand adolescence'.
	If the brand is to be re-launched into a new marketplace, the strategy would be the same as for 'Brand infancy'.
	If the brand is not being re-launched, it should not be supported with sponsorship.

In addition to understanding your current needs, you also need to look to the future.

New initiatives

In addition to understanding your current needs, you also need to look to the future. Because most sponsorship contracts run for multiple years, taking planned or potential new initiatives into consideration is very important. Ask yourself the following questions:

➤ Are you going to be launching any new products for this brand?

➤ Are you launching this brand into any new markets (target market and/or geographic)?

➤ Is this brand going to be relaunched with a new look or positioning?

➤ Is your retail (or other sales mechanism) situation changing?

➤ Will you be embarking upon any other new initiatives, such as starting a loyalty program or setting up a destination Web site?

Competitor analysis

While you should always play your own game, you cannot ignore your competitors. Be sure you think about the following questions:

➤ What are their key sponsorships? Do any of them conflict with yours?

➤ Are they increasing or cutting back their sponsorship portfolio?

➤ Are they moving towards or away from your brand's positioning?

➤ Do they seem to get a lot of value from their sponsorships? Are they 'good sponsors'?

➤ Do they have any sponsorships that are naturally a better fit with your brand? Do you have any that are a more natural fit with your competitors?

➤ Have you ever been ambushed by a competitor? Are they still engaging in this type of activity?

➤ Have you ever ambushed a competitor? Are you experiencing any backlash from them, the public, or the media?

➤ How are your competitors perceived by sponsees? Good, bad, or indifferently?

Other factors

This area is really a catch-all of factors that could affect your brand, your overall marketing results, or your sponsorship program. For the most part, these factors will be out of your hands, but you still need to take them into account.

Economic

➤ How is the economy behaving? Is consumer confidence high, low, or on the move?

➤ How will the economy affect sales of or perceptions of your brand?

➤ How will the economy affect how people spend their leisure time/money?

Industrial

➤ Is your industry undergoing any changes? Do/will people perceive it differently?

➤ Does your industry have any consumer problems (e.g. airline strikes, pollution, etc.)?

Political

➤ Are there any new policies or laws that will affect your company/brand?

➤ Are there any new policies or laws that will affect how sponsorship works (e.g. changing how sponsorship is viewed by the Tax Department, or the banning of tobacco sponsorship)?

| Budget

We have already determined that sponsorship is the most emotional of all marketing media, and that emotion is not confined to your consumers and trade. Nowhere are these internal passions more problematic than in the case of budgeting.

It is very typical for one region or department to think (incorrectly) that sponsorship is simply a big waste of time, so they do not want one dollar of their budget going towards it, even if the reality is that they are benefiting greatly from the investment. On the other hand, some regions or departments may be overly attached to some sponsorships, and will fight tooth and nail against dropping a sponsorship that is clearly off strategy. Other departments know that sponsorship is achieving a great deal for them, but they don't want to pay for it. No wonder sponsorship budgeting can be such a nightmare!

Before you will be able to sort out your budgeting woes, you will need to get broad buy-in for your Sponsorship Strategy. This can be achieved quite easily, but will require a few simple steps:

> when developing your strategy, ensure you get input from all key stakeholders as to what they want to achieve
> educate those stakeholders about the benefits to each of their areas
> ensure they understand the strategy and the procedures that are in place to select and maximise the best sponsorships
> be sure they are represented on the Sponsorship Team when deciding what sponsorships to invest in *and how to pay for them*
> keep everyone in the loop.

Although you may have one or two holdouts, most budget situations will fade away as soon as the stakeholders believe that their needs are being met and that sponsorship is being approached in a way that reflects good business practice.

Rules vs getting real

'How much should we budget, over and above the cost of sponsorship fees, for maximising our sponsorships?' This is one of the most common questions we hear, the answer to which has changed an enormous amount in the past 26 years.

1975—'Maximisation? What's maximisation?'

Back when sponsorship started taking off, maximisation wasn't even a consideration. Results were measured in logo impressions, with signage, PR, and TV coverage being all important.

1985—The '1-to-1' rule

For every one dollar spent on a sponsorship fee, another one dollar should be spent to activate it. This was a step in the right direction, but kept sponsorship outside of overall marketing plans and budgets. Sponsorship was supported by other media, rather than truly integrated with them.

1995—The '2-to-1' rule

With increasing clutter in the marketplace, sponsorship budgets grew, with most of it going towards activation. Results were better, but it still wasn't being truly integrated.

'Maximisation', 'activation', and 'leverage' are the same thing. They all refer to the activities carried out by a sponsor around their sponsorship investments.

2001—The Get Real Rule (okay, so we made that up!)

This rule was born of necessity. We had several clients in a row who were spending many millions on sponsorship, but had only 10% or so to leverage their investments. Our first impression was that it would never work, but then we realised that sponsorship should work as a catalyst. No more is it about creating marketing activities to support sponsorship, it is about using the power of sponsorship to support marketing activities. Sponsorship support budgets have become about providing seed funding to jump-start new initiatives that will benefit and eventually be funded by other departments.

Our approach now is that the better a sponsorship program is working, the lower the additional support funds that are put behind it. Having 10% is no longer a disaster, it's the ideal.

How much of your marketing budget should you spend on sponsorship?

Sponsorship has grown enormously as a proportion of overall marketing spending. Back when sponsorship was done based upon gut feel or chairman's choice, it only made up a small percentage of most companies' marketing budgets. Now, a typical sponsorship portfolio could make up anywhere from 5–20% of an overall budget. For some categories, such as beer and soft drinks, it tends to make up an even larger percentage.

The proportion that you spend is really what works for you. Using your current spending as a benchmark, think about the following:

Do you increase?

If your current marketing portfolio is not really connecting with your markets, and that portfolio is light on sponsorship, you may want to consider increasing your spend. Of course, if you follow the Get Real Rule, you could well find yourself increasing your spending on sponsorship fees, while reducing your dependence on additional support funding. Your sponsorship budget could go down, even as you increase your portfolio.

Do you reduce?

If, on the other hand, you are sponsoring everything that moves and you don't have the human, creative, or financial resources to maximise them all, you may want to consider reducing your portfolio and concentrating on doing fewer things better. Many sponsors from around the world are taking this approach and reaping excellent rewards.

Do you stay level?

Most companies that are just starting to get their sponsorships right are best served by keeping the sponsorship budget level until they are familiar and comfortable with what sponsorship can achieve. If you make savings on sponsorship support by following the Get Real Rule, invest it in stakeholder training and top up opportunistic funding (see below) rather than increasing your sponsorship commitments straightaway.

Who spends what

While many companies do not disclose the percentage of their marketing budget that goes towards sponsorship, a few do. As you can see below, the amount companies commit to sponsorship varies greatly from one company or category to another.

- Born Footwear – 85%
- Jamba Juice Co. – 30%
- Nautica – 15%

- Charles Schwab & Co – 10-15%
- Auto manufacturing – average 8%
- Wireless communications (e.g. mobile phones) – average 8%
- Gateway (computers) – 7%
- Foxwoods Casino – 2%

All of these figures are for US companies. Source: *IEG Sponsorship Report*. Full contact details are found in the Appendix.

Opportunistic funds

Every company should have some opportunistic funds set aside in case a great sponsorship opportunity comes along that isn't in the budget. Approximately 5–10% of the total sponsorship budget is usually sufficient.

If something great comes along that costs more, you might have to look to other budgets. A sponsorship that big is likely to materially benefit a number of departments; perhaps they can kick in some funds.

Who should pay for sponsorship?

Some companies pay for sponsorship activity from a specific sponsorship budget. Some rest both the decision-making process and the financial responsibility with brand groups.

The important part is not whether you pay for sponsorship with your right pocket or your left—either way works fine—it is whose responsibility it is to authorise and account for the expenditure. In most cases, this decision should be with the brand groups, because maintaining overall brand health is their responsibility, as are the costs of doing so.

What if times get hard?

In the past, when times got hard, many companies would drastically reduce their

> The responsibility for authorising and accounting for sponsorship funds should lie with the brand group.

sponsorship spending, because it was seen as an expendable luxury against such 'necessities' as above-the-line advertising. Switched-on sponsors, however, kept or increased their level of sponsorship. They realised that fostering relationships with consumer and trade markets was a key element to stabilising the brand, and that sponsorship can do that better than any other single marketing medium.

Increasing sponsorship becomes even more important if the decline is due to an overall economic downturn. If your consumer and trade markets are hurting, the added value that you can provide to their lives through sponsorship—however small—will be even more powerful.

If your company finds itself in a rocky patch, do not bail on your sponsorship program. Do it smarter. Do it better. If absolutely necessary, try to renegotiate the sponsorships to reduce the cash component. But do not treat sponsorship as an expendable luxury.

Keeping your costs under control
Become a preferred sponsorship partner

One of the best ways to keep fees for major sponsorships under control is to become a preferred sponsorship partner. That way, sponsees will tend to want to work with you rather than your competition. They will know that you will help them to achieve their objectives, not just give them money, and this counts for much with many sponsees.

Becoming a preferred partner can be achieved, over time, through a combination of activities:

➤ be clear and consistent about your objectives and needs from the start
➤ negotiate based upon achieving mutual objectives—tell them yours and find out theirs
➤ minimise the emphasis on money. Negotiate benefits for benefits, not money for benefits, providing them with access to markets and marketing vehicles that they would not be able to reach cost-effectively on their own
➤ include the sponsee in key maximisation workshops
➤ forgo any emphasis on personal relationships for an emphasis on objectives
➤ introduce new potential sponsors to them, when appropriate
➤ invest time and effort in educating your sponsees.

The attitude must be one of understanding your partners, helping them to meet their objectives, and adding real value to the relationships (e.g. by educating them). The result will be a far more productive, cost-effective, and probably cheaper investment.

> Do not treat sponsorship as an expendable luxury.

Create relationships with complementary sponsors

Even if you are a preferred sponsorship partner, there may be times that an investment will be out of reach financially. Other times, 'the big idea' for leverage will outstrip resources. In both cases, it can be very effective to partner with another company. Partnerships could include:

➤ jointly negotiating for sponsorship (new or where one company has an existing relationship). This can be a big renegotiation tool.

➤ creating co-promotions with another existing sponsor

➤ creating co-promotions with a non-sponsor

➤ making introductions to new potential sponsors when vacating a major sponsorship

➤ on-selling the benefits of large sponsorships (not ideal, as it is not pro-active).

Potential partners

Complementary products

Many software companies will partner with hardware manufacturers, creating both a strong negotiation position and an in-built platform for sponsorship-driven promotion. The mobile phone industry is similar, with handset manufacturers and wireless service providers often entering joint negotiations and running co-promotions. If your product and another are a strong natural fit, give it a try.

Related companies/brands

With common ownership among so many companies, we are seeing more instances where they are bringing each other into sponsorship deals. There are numerous examples, from the AOL Time Warner group

(AOL, Sports Illustrated, CNN, HBO, etc.) to the Pepsico group (Pepsi, Frito Lay, Tropicana), where they have used their increased negotiating and marketing power to create very strong, very effective sponsorship programs for themselves and their sponsees.

Retailers

A strong retail promotion can achieve a great deal for a brand, which is why many companies are now partnering with retailers when negotiating sponsorship. Sometimes they bring cash to the table, sometimes they simply bring their broad community reach and marketing power. Either way, if you can identify a key retailer, discuss your mutual objectives. If they are a match, you may have a great opportunity to become partners.

Putting your strategy together

Many companies have their own standard formats for writing strategy documents. Whatever format you choose for yours, it should include the following information.

Background

The background section should set the stage, and include such information as:

➤ situation analysis

➤ market influences

➤ competitor activity

➤ trade analysis

➤ economic, political, or industrial factors.

Checklists for most of these areas can be found in the Determining brand needs section starting on page 40.

Target markets

Outline all target markets for each brand, including emerging markets and any trends. Ensure you focus on psychographics, because understanding what makes a market tick will allow you to connect with them, rather than just talk at them.

Many companies will rank target markets based upon their comparative size, but this may not reflect their true importance for you. For instance, while discount vacation travellers make up a large percentage of airline seats sold, there isn't much margin in it, so many airlines focus their main marketing efforts on the higher-margin business traveller. High-tech companies often put a disproportionate amount of marketing effort into selling new products to 'tech heads', because the opinion of this small group of people will have an enormous impact on the product's success in the larger marketplace.

Some of the ways that you can prioritise your target markets are:

➤ percentage of your sales made up by each market

➤ the influence that each market has

➤ comparative profit margins

➤ potential for growth.

Information on defining your target markets can be found in the Understanding your target markets needs section starting on page 26.

Marketing objectives

These should not be your objectives for sponsorship, but rather your overall marketing

> The size of a target market might not reflect its true importance to you.

objectives. Most companies have 6–12 marketing objectives. List them all, not just the ones that have an obvious connection to sponsorship.

General strategies

Now it's time to document how sponsorship is going to achieve those objectives. Although it would seem to make sense to lay out strategies for each objective separately, in practice this doesn't really work, because most sponsorship strategies meet a number of objectives. It is usually more effective to set out a number of general strategies, with sponsorship-specific sub-strategies.

EXAMPLE

Develop database and consumer intelligence for launch of loyalty club

- *negotiate for access to sponsee databases*
- *run database-generating promotions across key sponsorship properties*
- *provide sponsorship-oriented incentives for club members to introduce new members.*

Specific strategies

You may also want to outline specific strategies for individual brands, regions, or target markets. Generally, one of these will stick out as the obvious way to address the specifics, but this will be different from one company to another.

Sponsorship audit

Using the strategies and objectives set out above, you need to assess each of your current sponsorships ruthlessly. Some sponsorships will be performing well and will need minimal adjustments to get them at their peak. Some sponsorships will have loads of potential, but will need significant work to maximise their impact. And you should prepare yourself for the fact that some of your sponsorships might not make the grade at all. This does not mean that they are not good opportunities for someone, or that they might not work for you ten years from now, just that they are not good opportunities for your brand right now.

A good tool to use as a guide for your sponsorship audit is the Proposal Evaluation Criteria document found on page 78. Just as it works to keep your sponsorship selection process stringent and objective, it is also a valuable tool for objectively assessing current relationships.

You will also want to take this opportunity to look at your portfolio as a whole. You

> Some sponsorships just aren't going to make the grade.

may be concentrating too much of your activity around one target market, one region, or one time of year. You need to note this and outline steps to address the imbalance. More information on this can be found in the Portfolio Management chapter on page 154.

New opportunities

This section outlines areas of sponsorship that you are going to explore in order to achieve your objectives. These usually come out of a combination of target market analysis, market research, strategy development, and an analysis of how your sponsorship portfolio lays out as contracts for non-performing sponsorships expire.

Systems and tools

Include an overview of the systems and tools you are using to brief, select, evaluate, manage, and maximise your sponsorships. Many of these are included in this book, and could include:

➤ Proposal Guidelines, for provision to potential sponsees
➤ Sponsorship Evaluation Criteria
➤ Sponsorship Team
➤ Negotiation Checklist
➤ Sponsorship Agreement Pro Forma
➤ Ambush Marketing Checklist.

This is also a good place to outline the on-going education and skill-building exercises that will be undertaken by your company, such as:

➤ subscriptions to publications
➤ joining associations
➤ in-house education
➤ attending seminars, conferences, and workshops
➤ fact-finding trips to your counterparts overseas.

Projected sponsorship activity

Based on the above audit, and new opportunities you are anticipating, you should be able to provide a list detailing your sponsorship activity, by year, for the duration of the Sponsorship Strategy. It will reflect activities dropping off as they reach their logical conclusion or as you drop them at the end of your contracted period, and new or periodic sponsorship activities coming on. The goal is that, by the end of the 3–4 years of this document, all sponsorships will be in line with your objectives and your portfolio will show a good balance across your key target markets.

> Don't waste your time writing a strategy if you aren't going to implement it.

Implementation plan and timeline

A strategy is no good if it isn't carried out. In this section, you should outline how each of the strategies is going to be implemented, when, and who is responsible.

Budget

The budget should be shown by financial year and broken down into three areas:

➤ sponsorship fees

➤ activation funding

➤ administration.

See the section Budget on page 45 for more information.

Case study: You can lead a horse to water . . .

Sometimes even the best strategies will have its knockers. We had a client that had a well-researched, well thought-out marketing plan. They were targeting young adults, primarily female, with a marketing message that was all about individualism. While there was a lot of scope for sponsorship and using it to add value to their target market, it wasn't to be, at least not easily. The head of marketing was stuck in the 'awareness' mindset and believed that the only thing worth sponsoring was major, male-oriented sport and that the more logo exposure they got, the better. It took considerable time and effort for the sponsorship manager and us to implement a more forward-thinking sponsorship strategy.

If you find yourself in a situation where you don't have senior executive buy-in for your new sponsorship strategy, you do have some options:

• start a Sponsorship Team. If a whole array of stakeholders is behind a change in the sponsorship strategy, it is unlikely that a senior executive will defy all of them

• enact systems and tools that objectify the sponsorship selection process (see Part 2—Selection and Negotiation on page 60 for more on this). Pretty soon, sponsorships that do not stand up to this rigorous process will start to look obvious, and fewer of them will be approved

• discuss your marketing objectives with sponsees and potential sponsees to see how you can work together to achieve them more effectively and more creatively. Even if an investment isn't the best one for your brand, you may be able to get more out of it, or, as we like to put it, make a silk purse out of a sow's ear. For more on this, see Salvaging a bad situation on page 146

• select and negotiate smaller sponsorships that are aligned with your ideal strategy, as senior management tends to pay less attention to minor investments.

Some of this is sneaky. Some is downright underhanded. But if you are being thwarted in your attempts to improve the way sponsorship is done, sometimes you have to create opportunities to demonstrate that your recommendations will work.

Research

Include overviews of any or all of the following:

➤ quantitative market research (asking sponsorship questions, if possible)

➤ qualitative market research (asking sponsorship questions, if possible)

➤ analysis of either of the above over time, showing trends

➤ market research carried out by any of your sponsees

➤ sponsorship awareness research carried out by any of your sponsees (could be included with market research).

Chapter 3

Working with a consultant

Although we have spent a big part of our careers as consultants, we truly believe that most companies have the ability to sort out their own sponsorship situations, particularly if they are provided with key skills and tools. This book should give you many of the skills and tools required to affect change on your own.

On the other hand, we also understand that asking an outsider to have an objective look at your sponsorships can be very helpful. Sometimes it can be difficult for an organisation to identify and fix problems if it has been living with them for a long time.

If you think your company is in a rut and you fall into any of the categories listed below, you *may* benefit from utilising the services of a sponsorship consultant or agency:

➤ your company is increasing its emphasis on sponsorship as a marketing medium

➤ you do not have staff dedicated to sponsorship

➤ you do not have a sponsorship strategy or internal systems in place

➤ you have a large number of sponsorships (more than 12)

➤ you have naming rights to one or more large sponsorships

➤ your sponsorship portfolio needs auditing

➤ your company is resistant to changing the approach to sponsorship.

Choosing a consultant or agency

If you are considering using a consultant or an agency, keep in mind the following:

➤ Choose a consultant that specialises in what you need—everyone has their strengths.

➤ Check their client and project list—experience counts for a lot.

➤ See that they demonstrate an understanding of your company and your industry.

➤ Ask yourself if you can work with them. Do you communicate well? Do you get on? You will be working closely, so this is important.

➤ Are they going to train your organisation so you can carry on independently? Or, are they looking for a relationship where you will be dependent on them well into the future? Either way can work, it just depends upon your needs.

➤ Use your network—good consultants are usually known within the industry.

Fees

Fees will vary widely and do not necessarily reflect the skill level of the consultant. There are three main methods of remuneration:

➤ hourly rate—this is usually the most expensive method of remuneration, as the consultant or agency has no guarantee of work over time. Some consultants charge a premium for high-level creative work

➤ project fee—this is the most prevalent method of remuneration, because it offers a finite amount of work for a finite amount of money, so it is easy to budget. At the end of the contract, there is sometimes an option to have additional work done at an hourly rate. Otherwise, a new project fee will be quoted for the new brief

➤ retainer—if there is a requirement for a wide range of consulting work, across departments, products, or a large portfolio of investments, a retainer is a good way to have guaranteed access to high level expertise on demand. The rate is usually at a substantial discount to the hourly rate, with bigger discounts for longer contracts. If you go this way, be sure to utilise all the consulting hours available to you. The downside is that it is very easy to become dependent on a consultant on retainer, making the transition to self-sufficiency more difficult.

selection and
negotiation

Chapter 4

Understanding your options

Before you can decide who or what to sponsor, you need to understand your options. Different types of sponsorships offer different types of benefits. Rather than just assuming that the category of business you are in dictates the types of sponsorships you should have, think about your sponsorship portfolio in terms of the needs of the brand and the needs of the audience. Not every investment bank should sponsor the arts. Not every beer is right for sport. Chances are, we've all been guilty of being too closed-minded about our options.

The other thing you need to be aware of is what else you could be doing with the money if you weren't investing it in sponsorship. Being able to compare the potential benefit of a sponsorship against the benefit of above-the-line advertising, for instance, will often be very useful in determining whether or not the sponsorship is right for you.

To sport or not to sport?

Although sport does attract the lion's share of sponsorship expenditure—between 60 and 85% of a typical sponsorship portfolio—that does not necessarily mean that it is the best investment for you. You need to look carefully at your target market and your objectives, and examine the entire range of options with an open mind.

The lists below outline some of the positives and potential downsides to getting involved with each major segment of sponsorship. This is by no means a definitive list, as individual organisations vary widely in their benefits and approach to sponsorship.

Sport

➤ Passionate fans
➤ High visibility
➤ 'Hero' factor

➤ Can have an enormous audience

➤ Usually have a long promotional period (teams, leagues, series)

➤ Good networking opportunities

➤ Most sporting organisations have strong supporter or member databases

➤ Most sporting opportunities have or can develop programs from elite to grassroots

➤ Sporting organisations understand that sponsorship is a commercial investment

➤ Tends to be very cluttered

➤ Can be expensive

➤ Bidding wars are becoming increasingly common

➤ Without careful management, your fortunes can rise and fall with the team or athlete's performance

Cultural organisations

➤ Tend to attract very pure demographic/psychographic markets

➤ Usually easy to take ownership, not much clutter

➤ Lots of opportunities to develop an event or activity specifically for you and your marketplace

➤ Excellent hospitality opportunities

➤ Great databases

➤ These organisations are usually full of influential VIPs (board members, patrons, etc.)

➤ Many are only just starting to understand that sponsorship and philanthropy are not one and the same—you may need to spend some time educating them

➤ Compared with sport, most cultural organisations have a fairly small reach (although there are definitely some big exceptions!)

Community events and programs

➤ Many opportunities for one-on-one interaction

➤ Geographically targeted

➤ Can be strongly psychographically targeted

➤ Very flexible—usually easy to develop programs customised for your target market and objectives

➤ Successful maximisation programs can be easily repeated with your sponsorships of other community events

➤ Sponsorship fees tend to be on the lower end

➤ Can require a higher-than-average commitment to maximisation, because their often-strapped budgets won't stretch to providing extra marketing value to you

➤ Often run by mainly volunteer organisations, although larger events are now run very professionally

Environment and causes

➤ Can be a powerful partnership that engenders deep loyalty in the target market

➤ Donations-for-purchase schemes can be a strong point of difference, if they are relevant to the consumer (e.g. a dog food company donating to the Guide Dogs, or a paper company rejuvenating native forest areas)

➤ Supporting the cause (e.g. dolphin-safe tuna, unbleached paper) is considered a strong point of difference, until all of your competitors do it

➤ Sponsors in these areas must not only talk the talk, but walk the walk, or risk controversy. If your consumers see a sponsorship as simply cosmetic, it will do more harm than good

---

Case studies: Cause sponsorships

Cause sponsorship can be a great way to achieve marketing objectives while aligning your brand very closely with your target markets. There are dozens of examples of sponsors who have done a great job for themselves, their consumers, and their sponsees. Unfortunately, it is also quite easy to get wrong. A sampling of cause relationships that have worked follows.

IN the UK, Walker's Crisps partnered with News International in the Free Books for Schools program. Over 98% of UK schools participated, with each school receiving an average of 70 books by collecting tokens from NI newspapers and packets of Walker's Crisps. In all, over 2.3 million books were distributed.

IN North America, Gloria Jean's Gourmet Coffee has developed a partnership with the Second Harvest food banks. In addition to promoting the cause to customers in all of

their 280+ stores and donating coffee to the food banks, they have developed a series of limited edition products, including their entire holiday range, donating $1.00 of the purchase price to Second Harvest. According to Second Harvest, every dollar will facilitate the distribution of 34 pounds of food to needy families.

IN Northern Ireland, the Nambarrie Tea Company worked with Action Cancer to create an award-winning cause-related marketing program. The key to their success was staff involvement. Not only were they involved in the creation of an on-pack promotion that raised over £200,000 for the charity, they also helped educate the community about Action Cancer, and calls to their help line increased dramatically. The staff wasn't prepared to end their involvement there, either, with many of them volunteering their time to the charity.

Equivalent opportunity cost

It is important to understand what you could be buying in terms of media with the same amount of money—the 'equivalent opportunity cost', as media buyers put it.

You need to know how much you would get in above-the-line media for the fee and support you are considering investing in a sponsorship, such as:

➤ how many TV commercials in peak viewing

➤ how many black-and-white pages in metropolitan daily newspapers

➤ how many colour pages in mainstream magazines

➤ how many months of metropolitan radio at 30 spots per week (30 seconds)

➤ how many supersites (huge, well-placed billboards) or 24-sheet outdoor (regular billboards).

You should get your ad agency or media buying agency to provide you with the answer to each of these questions for a set dollar amount, say, $100 000. Ensure that you are given figures based upon your bulk buying power, not casual or 'rack' rates.

Once you understand what you could be buying with your potential sponsorship investment, it often makes the decision whether or not to sponsor much more straightforward. If you and your company really believe that you would get more impact putting five 30-second commercials on '60 Minutes', then don't invest in sponsorship. On the other hand, if a sponsorship delivers on multiple objectives, is targeted correctly, and has a six-month promotional period, then the sponsorship will probably be a far more attractive option than one week of '60 Minutes'.

Owning an event

Sometimes it can seem difficult getting exactly the marketing platform you need out of a sponsorship. Although we believe that most sponsorship opportunities can be negotiated so you can achieve your objectives, an increasing number of companies are opting to own their own events. This has worked very well for many companies, and has been a complete disaster for others.

Whether you are looking to create an event from scratch or buy an existing event, there are a number of pros and cons that you need to keep in mind before you commit.

Pros

➤ You will have complete control over the event structure, production, marketing, and who else sponsors the event

➤ You can take real ownership of the event and will have almost total freedom to develop promotions that will achieve your objectives

➤ You will own the ancillary rights to the event, such as broadcast, merchandising, and other marketing opportunities. This can add up to a lot of money

➤ It is a great opportunity to involve your trade and other associated companies

➤ It is a natural for getting employees involved, so long as they are interested and you make it fun for them

➤ If the event is a success, it could be a profit centre in its own right

Cons

➤ It is a big financial commitment. Running an event is an expensive and risky business and often costs far more than the original budget, particularly if it is a start-up

➤ Kiss your weekends goodbye. Events are extremely time-intensive, even if you have an event production company working with you

➤ Securing other sponsors for the event is often difficult. Many corporate event owners need to secure a broker to handle these activities, as the skills required are outside of their expertise

➤ There are a lot of legal implications, including public liability and worker's compensation

➤ There is a fine line between owning an event and overcommercialising it to the point that it turns off your target market

➤ Having control of the event doesn't mean it will work. If the event bombs, it could be both a financial and publicity disaster

Case studies: Owning an event

GENERAL Motors favours brand ownership, as it provides a degree of control over the consumer experience that they would not have if they were merely a sponsor. General Motors' Buick Division owns one American PGA golf event, The Buick Open, and titles a number of others. They believe that, in addition to greater control, they save a lot of money by owning this major event, leaving them with more to maximise the investment.

VANS owns a number of events, including their very popular Triple Crown Series. They create the perfect opportunity to showcase their skate-inspired shoes, boarding boots, and clothing, through a series of top-quality events. These events are as diverse as snowboarding,

surfing, and supercross, with their Vans Triple Crown of Skateboarding the largest skateboard event in the world. They are able to attract not only the top competitors, but national/international television coverage, and a stable of co-sponsors who are as committed to building the sports as they are. For more information, see www.vans.com.

VOLVO has embarked upon event ownership of events, such as the Volvo Ocean Race. They prefer to own properties in large part to ensure that the event and its co-sponsors are of the right calibre for Volvo, as they believe the value of some of their past sponsorships has been undermined by other, less-than-premium sponsors.

Should you sponsor at all?

We are big believers that sponsorship can be a powerful marketing medium for almost all companies. There are a few, however, for whom sponsorship may not be a strong option for achieving objectives.

In our experience, business-to-business companies with very small target market groups (no more than a few thousand) tend to fall into this category. This is particularly the case if they can identify all of the key individuals in their entire target market and communication is carried out with them regularly. Some examples of this are investment banks, fleet leasing, and suppliers to industries with a relatively low number of companies, such as telecommunications, airlines, or car manufacturing.

Most of the time, companies in this category invest in sponsorship almost solely for the hospitality benefits. They get very little larger marketing benefit from their investments. Because of the depth of relationships already established with their customers, they don't really need the brand positioning, database building, or other benefits associated with many sponsorships.

If this is the case within your company, and you are questioning whether sponsorship is good investment for you, here are a few options:

➤ You could buy hospitality packages à la carte

➤ You could work with a sponsee organisation to develop something really special that only your customers can attend

➤ If you do need some non-hospitality benefits, but only within your narrow marketplace, you could concentrate your sponsorship activities on very targeted events, such as industry conferences or awards

---

Case study: Events without sponsorship

One of our clients found that they had been spending a lot of money on arts sponsorships, but were finding it increasingly difficult to get customers along. Those customers were being targeted by so many companies for hospitality activities that they were losing interest.

Our client's answer was to drop most of their sponsorships and minimise their more standard hospitality activities. Instead, they committed to two large, invitation-only events every year. They concentrate on making these once in a lifetime experiences for their customers. In one instance, they worked with one of the country's top symphonies to create a private dinner and concert in a very non-traditional venue. They invested in fabulous set decorations and sensational food and drink, and a memorable evening was had by all. Was this costly? Yes. But it was far more powerful and cost effective than their old way of doing things.

Chapter 5

Getting the right proposals

How many proposals do you get in a year? What percentage of them really meet your needs? If you are like most companies, that percentage is very, very small.

Major corporations can receive hundreds, sometimes thousands, of sponsorship proposals every year, and can spend thousands of hours on evaluating their suitability. Whether you are part of a big corporation or not, you are probably spending far too much time evaluating proposals. Imagine how much easier and productive your job would be if you just got the right proposals in the first place.

In this section, we outline a very real and very simple method for getting the right proposals. We have been teaching this method for some time now, and we consistently hear the same thing: the number of proposals that companies receive drops by 50–75% and the quality of the proposals they do receive improves dramatically.

Tell sponsorship seekers what you need

This is not rocket science. If you want proposals that meet your needs, you have to be prepared to tell sponsorship seekers what those needs are. This does not mean that you need to spend every waking moment on the phone with sponsorship seekers, it just means that you need to have a mechanism in place to get that information across easily.

Proposal Guidelines

One of our favourite tools for sponsors is Proposal Guidelines. This is a short, external document that you provide to sponsorship seekers that concisely outlines a number of things:

➤ your general requirements from sponsorship, including any exclusions
➤ brand positioning

➤ an overview of the objectives you are trying to achieve

➤ target markets, by brand or product

➤ the information you need to make a decision on a proposal

➤ the proposal selection process

➤ the correct contact and address for submitting proposals.

If you use Proposal Guidelines religiously, you will find that sponsorship seekers who are not genuine prospects for your sponsorship will realise that and stop submitting proposals. On the other hand, genuine prospects will provide you with proposals that are customised, more partnership-oriented, more comprehensive, and more professional.

Sponsorship seekers want this information. They want to have the best possible shot at becoming partners with you. And if it isn't going to happen, they would much rather know before they have wasted their time and effort on presenting a proposal.

You can either put all of your brands on one document, or you can do separate guidelines for each brand or family of brands. Either way works fine. You also do not need to give away any confidential information in order for this to be a very effective tool.

We strongly recommend that you involve your Sponsorship Team in the development of your Proposal Guidelines. This will make sure that the team's needs and concerns are represented, and that the proposals you receive will be as comprehensive as possible.

Keeping your Guidelines current is paramount. They should be updated whenever your situation changes. Even if you aren't going through any major changes, do review and update them at least every six months.

Remember, the Proposal Guidelines is always going to be a working document. Do not have your Guidelines printed on a glossy brochure. Murphy's Law virtually ensures that they will be out of date as soon as they are delivered from the printer. If you need them in hardcopy, simply print them out on letterhead as they are required.

A Proposal Guidelines template is supplied on page 69.

Making them available

If your Proposal Guidelines are going to work, you need to ensure that it is easy for sponsorship seekers to get their hands on them, particularly because many of them won't know the proper area of your company to contact. You should be sure that up-to-date Proposal Guidelines are available through the following outlets:

➤ Internet site

➤ every brand group

➤ every regional office

➤ marketing department

> Sponsorship seekers want to know what you need.

Get your Proposal Guidelines into the hands of the first person that answers the phone.

➤ sponsorship department

➤ corporate/community affairs department

➤ PR department/agency

➤ ad agency.

The best approach is to put the Proposal Guidelines into the hands of the first person that answers the phone in each of these departments, so that when someone calls and says, 'Can I speak to someone about sponsorship?' that person can e-mail or fax the Guidelines to them straightaway or refer them to your Web site.

Do be sure that anyone who might field a call from a potential sponsee knows how to get his or her hands on the Proposal Guidelines to e-mail or fax it.

Case study: Capital Chilled Foods Australia

Capital Chilled Foods is the exclusive processor and distributor of the leading milk brand in their marketplace. As such a major and visible part of the corporate landscape, they receive a lot of unsolicited calls, e-mails, and proposals from sponsorship seekers. Most of these are inappropriate for their brands.

A few years ago, they started providing Proposal Guidelines to anyone making enquiries about sponsorship, and the difference that this succinct, two-page document has made to their business has been marked:

• nine out of ten contacts who receive their Proposal Guidelines don't bother to respond with a new proposal. After reviewing the Guidelines, they realise that their organisation just isn't a good match. As each proposal takes at least an hour to review, this saves an enormous amount of time

• making Proposal Guidelines available has very clearly positioned sponsorship by Capital Chilled Foods as a marketing investment, rather than a donation

• those that do take the time to think through the Guidelines and deliver an opportunity that is a bit different and meets their needs often represent excellent investments for Capital Chilled Foods.

Since they receive fewer proposals, they have to say 'no' less often. In some markets, this can be a big consideration.

Unsolicited proposals

You will continue to receive some unsolicited proposals that have not been prepared according to the Proposal Guidelines. Here is where you have to be strong. Do not read these proposals! Mail them straight back to the sender with a copy of your Proposal Guidelines and a letter inviting them to submit a new proposal. Within a couple of months of putting your Guidelines into place, word will have got round and you will be receiving far fewer of these uncustomised proposals.

A sample Proposal Guidelines Letter for unsolicited proposals can be found on page 72.

The bonus

Investing the hour or so that it will take you to create and implement your first set of Proposal Guidelines will undoubtedly have a positive impact on the number and quality of proposals received. But it also has another bonus.

The simple act of creating and disseminating Proposal Guidelines to your stakeholders makes a clear statement that sponsorship is changing within your organisation, that it is becoming far more objective and far more results-oriented. If you ask for your peers' input, to ensure that their needs are represented, which is strongly recommended, then this impact will be even greater.

> Proposal Guidelines also make a big impact internally.

Proposal guidelines template

 Guidelines1.doc

[*Sponsor*] receives dozens of proposals every year, many of which we reject because they do not adequately meet our needs. We have developed this document to make our requirements clear to potential sponsorship seekers, and to encourage the presentation of proposals that meet those needs.

General

➤ We will consider proposals in all categories except [*insert exclusions here*]

➤ We require sponsorship and sales (if applicable) exclusivity in the category of beer and pre-mixed alcoholic beverages

➤ We generally need a minimum of six months lead time

➤ Logo exposure is considered a bonus, but is not the primary goal of sponsorship

➤ We prefer to invest in sponsorships that carry out audience research during and/or after the event, including sponsor questions, and provide results to the sponsor

➤ We expect that our sponsorship partners will invest a minimum of 10% of the total value of the sponsorship to pro-actively maximise the sponsorship.

Core brand values/attributes

To assist you in understanding our positioning, here is an overview of our core brand values and attributes:

➤ 'What's Best About America' (tag line)

- an American icon product
- high quality
- relaxation with friends
- manly (full strength beers)
- 'Drink Responsibly' message.

Sponsorships must provide *at least* six of the following

These should be tied to both your overall objectives and key attributes/values and number 10–15.

- A natural link with our core brand values (see above)
- Provision of content for Internet site
- Mechanisms to add value to our target markets
- Naming rights to the event or any high profile sub-events
- On-site sales
- Access to existing databases
- Database-generating activities
- Provide opportunity for key customer hospitality ('What money cannot buy' activities are particularly good)
- Provide promotional main media time/space (logo exposure does not count)
- Access to athletes and other appropriate celebrities
- Product placement (using our product in a meaningful way as part of the event)
- Investment divided into an upfront fee plus a performance-based incentive.

To be considered, proposals *must* include the following

- Key details of the opportunity
- Overview of your marketing plan—including what is and is not confirmed
- List of sponsors who have committed to date
- A comprehensive list of benefits, including how they relate to us and our products
- Timeline, including important deadlines
- Credentials of your company and key subcontractors (publicist, event producer, etc.).

Process for consideration

- All proposals are reviewed by the sponsorship manager to assess suitability, feasibility, and resources required (human and monetary)

➤ Recommended proposals are presented to [*title*] for approval

➤ Sponsee is notified of the disposition of the proposal within [*number*] weeks.

Target markets, by product

Do not give away anything confidential, but you should name the products and their key markets. The more specific you are the better.

Hawk Beer	Males, 18–30, manly, sports- and socially-oriented, active
Light Hawk	*Primary*: Women 18–34, single, active, capable, independent, tomboy-ish, somewhat fashion conscious
	Secondary: Designated drivers, responsible, socially-oriented, active
Raven Ale	Males 25+, upscale, status- and quality-oriented, highly brand aware
Raven Special	Up-market bars, pubs, and restaurants, available East Coast only
Mad Vulture	Males and females, 18–24, single, music and fashion-oriented (pop culture), party/rave-oriented, not generally alternative types. Introducing new flavour in October 2002

Proposal submittal details

insert full contact details

Be proactive

Getting the right proposals doesn't stop with simply improving the proposals that arrive in your mailbox. You have to identify properties that may be strong partners and request proposals from them.

Your strategy should have identified potential sponsees for consideration. Don't wait. Make contact straight away, even if it might be a year or two before you are ready to work with them (although it is only fair to tell them that). And don't worry, asking them for information and a proposal does not obligate you.

A letter that you can use to request a proposal is supplied on page 73.

> Requesting a proposal does not obligate you.

Proposal guidelines letter

Letter1.doc

26 June 2002

Mr Tom Darling
Executive Director
National Gallery of Contemporary Art
PO Box 123X
SYDNEY NSW 2001

Dear Mr Darling

Thank you for your invitation to participate in the 10th Annual Contemporary Art Awards. We have recently developed a set of Sponsorship Guidelines that outline our sponsorship marketing objectives, requirements, and areas of interest. I enclose these Guidelines for your review.

I encourage you to study these guidelines prior to submitting sponsorship proposals to Latrobe Bank. Of course, you are welcome to resubmit a proposal regarding the Contemporary Art Awards if you believe there is a fit once you have reviewed the Guidelines.

Yours sincerely,

Susan Golding
Marketing Manager

Proposal request letter

 Letter2.doc

23 February 2002

Mr Declan O'Keefe
Marketing Manager
Hartford Flames Football
PO Box F2000
HARTFORD CT 06101

Dear Mr O'Keefe

I am writing to express preliminary interest in sponsorship of your team and request a proposal from Hartford Flames Football. We are particularly interested in your young athlete development programs and other family-oriented initiatives.

I have enclosed our Proposal Guidelines. Bullseye Stores values the creation of win–win partnerships and we encourage you to review these Guidelines to get an understanding of what we need to achieve through sponsorship, as well as the information we require in order to move an opportunity forward.

Please provide a preliminary proposal by 8 March, as we would like to discuss it at our next Sponsorship Team meeting. We will contact you within a week of that date. If you have any questions on this, do not hesitate to give me a call.

I look forward to hearing from you.

Sincerely,

BRIDGET WAGNER
Regional Marketing Director

Chapter 6

Evaluating proposals

Do not read the
back page of the
proposal first.

Once you define
what you want to
achieve, evaluation
becomes far easier.

When evaluating proposals, most sponsorship managers do the same thing first: they flip to the back page of the proposal to see how much it costs. If it sounds like a bargain (or at least doesn't make their hair stand on end), they might look at the rest of the proposal. This might be common, but it is absolutely the wrong way to go about it.

Some sponsorships cost an extraordinary amount, but may be worth every penny. Some cost a lot, but have almost no real value to your company. Conversely, a bargain is only a bargain if it delivers on objectives and connects with your target market. Buying a sponsorship just because it's cheap makes about as much sense as buying shoes two sizes too small because they're on sale.

Once you have an understanding of what you want to achieve and who your target markets are, and you have determined where you want your sponsorship portfolio to be, proposal evaluation will become quite an objective process.

We recommend that you first evaluate a proposal against a number of strategic areas, including:

➤ whether and to what extent the opportunity will deliver against objectives

➤ whether it fits with your brand

➤ whether it fits your target market(s)

➤ whether it can deliver benefits that will add value to your consumer and trade relationships

➤ whether you are likely to get broad internal buy-in for the sponsorship

➤ the professionalism and expertise of the sponsee.

We call this phase 'The Wringer'. Only after you determine whether or not the sponsorship is a strategic fit can you address other issues, such as feasibility and financial requirements. We have developed a comprehensive tool called the Proposal Evaluation Criteria that sets all of this out for you. It is found later in this chapter.

Most of what you need to know to evaluate proposals well will have already come out of your strategy process. There are a few additional sponsorship selection skills and tools that might also be helpful, such as the '5-and-2' rule, how to match unique attributes, and assessing the ability of the sponsee to deliver what it promises.

The 5-and-2 rule

We have created something called the 5-and-2 rule, which is very useful for keeping sponsors focused on what they are trying to achieve. We believe that a strong sponsorship will have both of these attributes:

1. the ability to achieve at least five different objectives
2. promotional buy-in from at least two different business areas within your company.

If you have a sponsorship that will deliver on these two things, the likelihood is high that you will achieve an even higher number of objectives and that even more of your stakeholders will want to get involved.

Five objectives

In your Sponsorship Strategy, you outlined a broad menu of appropriate objectives. Each of these objectives flows naturally on from overall marketing objectives for the brand.

To ensure that you are hooking into the power of sponsorship, it is imperative that each sponsorship meets at least five of your objectives. This will:

➤ provide multiple channels for creating a connection with the customer

➤ foster more creative thinking

➤ create additional channels for getting the trade involved

➤ involve various business units (sales, trade, research, media, etc.) more deeply in the unique values that sponsorship brings to the marketing mix

➤ position sponsorship as a key part of the marketing portfolio (which it certainly should be)

➤ promote a more expansive, creative view on what sponsorship can do for your company

➤ create a stronger and more obvious value-bond with the sponsee.

Two stakeholders

As we have already discussed, sponsorship doesn't work if it is run in a vacuum. It should be heavily integrated with your current marketing activities, acting as a catalyst to make them work more effectively.

To that end, it is imperative that, before you commit to a sponsorship, you have a commitment from at least two different divisions or business areas to use the sponsorship in their marketing plans.

These could include:

➤ brand marketing

➤ public relations

➤ trade relations

➤ sales

➤ research

➤ loyalty marketing/CRM

➤ Internet

➤ merchandising

➤ human resources

➤ ad agency (usually in conjunction with brand marketing)

➤ customer service

➤ consumer affairs

➤ corporate or public affairs.

Their commitment must be substantial—just whacking a logo onto the Web site doesn't count. If they don't see this as something that will add excitement or value to the target market, then anything they do will look like a token gesture. You need real commitment. If you can't get that kind of commitment from at least two stakeholders, then do not invest in the sponsorship, because it will underperform and cost you too much every time.

Matching unique attributes

While you shouldn't make your sponsorship decision based upon what your competitors are doing, you do need to be aware of their effect on your sponsorships and the results you achieve.

Whatever business you are in, chances are that you share a number of key attributes with your competitors. An important aspect when selecting sponsorships is to ensure that you are connecting it with your brand's uniqueness, not all the ways that you are the same as your competitors.

One way to look at this is to draw up a simple continuum, with your company on one end and your key competitor(s) on the other. For each brand, list the things that make you different from one another, not the attributes that you share. Then plot where on that continuum the potential sponsorship naturally sits.

Sponsorships should align with your brand's *unique* attributes.

If the sponsorship sits on your end of the continuum, your life will be much easier. If it sits at the other end, it is not necessarily a bad investment, you just need to accept that it will be more difficult for you to make it work than it would be for your competitor. You will need to promote what might be a less obvious link to one of your unique attributes, which has the potential of seeming contrived.

We have drawn a very simple continuum using the two largest airlines in Australia, Ansett Australia and Qantas, in the period leading up to the Sydney 2000 Olympic Games (Figure 6.1). Both are excellent airlines. Both have extensive domestic schedules. Both offer very similar services at virtually the same price. The major area that they diverge is that the brands have very different personalities. Qantas owns the 'Australian' positioning, while Ansett was about individualism. In addition, Qantas has an extensive international schedule while, at that time, Ansett relied heavily on relationships with other carriers to create their international network.

Ansett invested a lot of money to be the airline sponsor of the Sydney Olympics, but making it work for them was never going to be easy, because it was clearly a more natural fit with Qantas. The 2000 Olympics were big, international, and brashly Australian—almost an exact fit with Qantas's unique attributes.

Figure 6.1 Sponsoring an event that is naturally aligned with your competition can be difficult

Ansett Australia
Tagline: 'Go your own way'
Song: 'My Generation'
Attributes:
Limited international schedule of their own
Celebrating the individual
Businesslike

Qantas Airways
Tagline: 'Spirit of Australia'
Song: 'I Still Call Australia Home'
Attributes:
Australia's primary international airline
Australian icon
Kangaroo on tail

**Sydney
Olympic
Games**

Understanding the sponsee's capabilities

Once you have received a proposal in which you are interested, there are five questions that you can ask that will highlight the sponsee's commercial orientation and understanding of your needs, or their lack of it:

➤ How did they arrive at the fee?

• Right answer: It is based upon the value of the package.

• Wrong answer: Because we needed $X to . . .

➤ How many other sponsors have they approached or are they approaching?

- Right answer: Fewer than 12.
- Wrong answer: More than 20.

➤ How were those potential sponsors selected?

- Right answer: Because they were most closely matched with what we have to offer and our audience.
- Wrong answer: Because we thought they had a lot of money.

➤ How many hours per week will they be devoting to sponsor servicing?

- Right answer: Between 5 and 10 hours or more (depending upon the size and complexity of the sponsorship).
- Wrong answer: What's servicing?

➤ What is their sponsorship expertise?

- Best answer: At least three years in commercially-oriented sponsorship.
- Okay answer: New to it, but a member of the sponsorship association, attending workshops, reading books, networking furiously.
- Wrong answer: None, with no plans for education.

Proposal evaluation criteria

 Evaluation1.doc

Sponsee: ....

Contact name: ....

Contact phone: .... Fax: ....

Date submitted: ....

Step 1—The Wringer

All sponsorships under consideration for investment by [sponsor] must meet the following criteria. It should be noted that most proposals will not make it through this phase.

Absolute requirements

➤ Must be a psychographic fit with key target market(s), as determined by research

➤ Must be able to achieve a minimum of five objectives, as outlined in the Sponsorship Strategy and on our Proposal Guidelines. Check all that apply:

❐ [List your menu of objectives]

➤ Must have buy-in from at least two business areas. Check all that apply:

❏ [*List business areas*]

➤ Must have the provision to directly involve or add value to customers and potential customers

➤ Must have the ability to be a catalyst for marketing activities. Check all that apply:

[*This list is an example only.*]

❏ Above-the-line advertising	❏ Web site content
❏ Loyalty program	❏ Other Internet activities
❏ Database generation	❏ New product launch
❏ New customer acquisition	❏ Product demonstration/sampling/display
❏ Sales promotion	❏ New product test marketing
❏ Media promotion	❏ Research
❏ Retail promotion	❏ Direct or on-site sales
❏ Trade promotion	❏ Networking
❏ Employee promotion	❏ Merchandising (POS, etc.)
❏ Shareholder promotion	❏ Shareholder publications
❏ On-pack promotion	❏ Employee publications
❏ Web site promotion	

➤ Must take place predominantly in [*location*]

Pluses

➤ Should be a natural value and/or attribute fit. List applicable shared attributes

....

....

....

➤ Should have ample public relations interest

Exclusions

➤ Must not be controversial or divisive

➤ Must not violate state or federal lottery/gambling laws

➤ [*List any other exclusions*]

In addition, the following must be taken into account as an indicator of the professionalism and understanding of the potential sponsee:

➤ Was the sponsorship opportunity professionally presented?

➤ Does the proposal include all information necessary to make an investment decision?

➤ Was the sponsee provided with Proposal Guidelines? If so, were those Guidelines followed?

Step 2—Feasibility

If a sponsorship makes it through the above Wringer, it must be feasibility-checked against resources and timelines.

Human resources

➤ Approximately how many hours will it take to plan and maximise this sponsorship?

➤ How many hours per week will it take to implement this sponsorship?

➤ Is this within the capabilities of internal human resources?

➤ If not, is there the budget to outsource all or part of this function?

Timeline

➤ Is there adequate time to maximise this sponsorship within a standard timeline (six months+)?

➤ If not, is it worth accelerating the timeline to participate (minimum three months)?

Step 3—Financial

If we have got this far, it must be a pretty good opportunity.

➤ How much is the sponsorship fee?

➤ If the sponsorship achieves all of the objectives set out above, would it be worth that amount to our company?

➤ Is this within current budget constraints?

➤ If not, can we access funds through other budgets (product marketing, sales promotional, new product launch, etc.)?

➤ Can we negotiate an incentive package to reduce up-front costs?

➤ Can we negotiate a package that reduces cash costs in return for non-cash contribution?

'Let's meet' letter template

 Letter3.doc

15 January 2002

Mr Floyd Farley
Executive Director
National Humane Society
PO Box 40
Toronto ON M9C 4V2

Dear Mr Farley

Thank you for your proposal to sponsor the National Humane Society.

We have reviewed your proposal and I would like to meet with you to discuss aspects of the cause-related marketing program you have outlined.

In particular, we are interested in exploring ways in which Kate's Premium Pet Foods can get involved with database-building and merchandising opportunities. Kate's Premium Pet Foods will be launching a loyalty program in late 2002, and your project meets many of our marketing needs.

We would also like to review your current membership structure and any market research you might have done on this group. While your proposal indicates that over 350 000 people a year contribute to the National Humane Society, you have not indicated the size or quality of your database.

Please provide me with more details about your database, merchandising program, and any market research you might have. If you telephone my assistant, Werner, he can arrange a mutually convenient time for us to meet.

I look forward to hearing from you.

Sincerely,

KATE W. RANNER
President

Saying 'No'

Almost everyone hates saying no. There are support groups for it, books about it, and every time we overcommit ourselves we kick ourselves over it. Unfortunately, when you work in sponsorship, you will find yourself saying no to many more sponsorship opportunities than you accept.

Many sponsors simply send out an 'all our funds are currently committed' letter. This might get sponsorship seekers off your back, but it isn't doing anyone any favours. The best thing to do is to tell them why the proposal is being rejected and provide them with a current copy of your Proposal Guidelines, so they can try again another time. This approach will show that you are partnership-oriented and not just blowing them off.

The good news is that if you use your Proposal Guidelines religiously, you will get a lot fewer proposals and have to send far fewer rejection letters.

Rejection letter template

 Letter4.doc

24 July 2002

Ms Veronica Kronfeld
Marketing Director
British Rugby Federation
22a Great Peter Street
LONDON SW1P 3NQ

Dear Ms Kronfeld

Thank you for your invitation to participate in the British Club Rugby Awards.

Unfortunately, we are unable to sponsor the Awards this year as our Sponsorship Strategy for the next 18 months concentrates on local community programs in regions where production factories are located.

I enclose our Sponsorship Guidelines, outlining our specific sponsorship objectives and target markets. Should you have any programs that meet our objectives and areas of interest, I encourage you to forward a proposal.

We wish you every success for the Awards.

Yours sincerely,

JAKE TALLIS
Sponsorship Manager

Chapter 7

Negotiation

Never limit
yourself to what is
offered in the first
proposal.

If you believe a sponsorship has merit, at some point you will need to stop talking about its potential and start getting into specifics.

Negotiation is the process of refining a partnership until all parties are satisfied that their interests are being served. This is called negotiating to win–win. If you have approached the whole selection process in an objective-oriented way, negotiation should be relatively straightforward.

Whatever you do, never limit yourself to what is included in the first proposal. There is no harm in negotiating for any number of more useful or creative benefits than those found in 'the package'. And, most sponsees are very open to incorporating non-cash benefits such as contra or promotion into your fee in place of part of the fee, so long as the benefits will assist them to achieve their objectives.

The tools and skills found throughout this chapter will help you to think more broadly when creating a partnership, while ensuring that you don't lose sight of the fact that you aren't the only organisation that needs to achieve objectives. The better partner you are, the better your sponsorship will be.

Understanding your position

The first thing you need to do is understand your position. What benefits do you need and want? And what benefits can you offer in return? You are not in a position to negotiate anything until you know these things.

What benefits do you need/want?

In order to understand what sponsorship benefits will have value to your brand, undertake an inventory of everything you could possibly utilise. Make a list of every promotional and marketing opportunity that could possibly be of value to you, your trade, or your target markets. Please note that this should be a big list. Think of everything—get creative.

If you know your objectives, determining the specific benefits that can help you achieve them will be easy. Our suggestion is to get together with a number of people across several departments and brainstorm everything you could possibly utilise from a sponsorship—any sponsorship. This will achieve three very important things:

1. It will get you and your Sponsorship Team thinking very broadly about the potential for sponsorship in your organisation.
2. It will create a good understanding of what different departments want from sponsorship (often very different than you would think!).
3. It will create a checklist that will ensure you negotiate every benefit of value to you that you possibly can.

Once you have this master list—your Negotiation Checklist—working through individual opportunities becomes far simpler. During negotiation, you can trade benefits that have low value to you for those that have higher value. Often, you can get additional benefits just by asking, because many benefits that have a high value to you are very easy and inexpensive for a sponsee to deliver. In other cases, you might work with the sponsee to restructure the sponsorship altogether. It is extremely doubtful you will ever get everything on your Negotiation Checklist from one sponsorship, but you will probably get more than you think.

Whichever way you use it, having a Negotiation Checklist will stop you unnecessarily limiting your options out of habit or just because you can't think of anything creative off the top of your head. Have it handy when you look through proposals and have it with you as you go through the negotiation process.

A generic Negotiation Checklist is attached here to get you started.

> Using your
> Negotiation
> Checklist will keep
> you open-minded.

Negotiation checklist

 Negotiation1.doc

What follows is a generic Negotiation Checklist. This is a starting point for taking inventory of everything you could possibly want from a sponsorship. You will probably not get all or even most of these items, but it creates a menu from which to develop counter proposals and win–win relationships.

Sponsorship types

➤ Naming rights sponsorship (perceived 'ownership' of the event)
➤ Presenting sponsorship

➤ Naming rights or presenting sponsorship of a section, area, entry, or team

➤ Naming rights or presenting sponsorship of a day, weekend, or week at the event

➤ Naming rights or presenting sponsorship of an event-driven award, trophy, or scholarship

➤ Naming rights or presenting sponsorship of a related or subordinated event

➤ Major sponsorship

➤ Supporting sponsorship

➤ Official product status

➤ Preferred supplier status

Exclusivity

➤ Category exclusivity among sponsors at or below a given level

➤ Category exclusivity among sponsors at any level

➤ Category exclusivity in event-driven advertising or promotional media

➤ Category exclusivity as a supplier or seller at the event

Licence and endorsements

➤ Use of sponsee logo(s), images, and/or trademark(s)

➤ Merchandising rights

➤ Product endorsement

Contracts

➤ Discounts for multi-year contracts

➤ First right of refusal for renewal at conclusion of contract

➤ Last right of refusal for renewal at conclusion of contract

➤ Performance incentives

Venue

➤ Input in venue, route, and/or timing

➤ Use of sponsor venue for launch, main event, or supporting event

On-site

➤ Sampling opportunities

➤ Demonstration/display opportunities

➤ Opportunity to sell product on-site (exclusive or non-exclusive)

➤ Coupon, information, or premium distribution

➤ Merchandising

Signage

- Venue signage (full, partial, or non-broadcast view)
- Inclusion in on-site event signage (exclusive or non-exclusive)
- Inclusion on pre-event street banners, flags, etc.
- Press conference signage
- Vehicle signage
- Event participant uniforms/pinneys/number tags
- Event staff shirts/caps/uniforms

Hospitality

- Tickets to the event (luxury boxes, preferred seating, reserved seating, or general admission)
- VIP tickets/passes (backstage, sideline, pit passes, press box, etc.)
- Celebrity/participant meet and greets
- Event-related travel arrangements, administration, and guide/chaperone (for consumer prizes, VIP, or trade incentives)

Information technology

- Provision of content for sponsor Internet site
- Provision of Web 'events' for sponsor Internet site (e.g. chat with a star, Webcast)
- 'Signage' on event Internet site
- Promotion or contest on event Internet site
- Links to sponsor Internet site from event Internet site
- Naming rights (perceived 'ownership') to event Internet site
- 'Signage' or promotion on event CD-ROM
- Licence to produce an event-oriented CD-ROM for promotion or sale

Database/relationship marketing

- Unlimited access to event-generated database(s) for direct marketing follow up
- Opportunity to provide inserts in event-oriented mailings
- Rental of event database for one-off communication
- Opportunity to run database-generating drawing or contest on-site
- Opportunity to run database-generating drawing or contest on-site as a requirement for attendee admission

Public relations

➤ Inclusion in all press releases and other media activities

➤ Inclusion in sponsor-related and media activities

➤ Public relations campaign designed for sponsor's market (consumer or trade)

Ancillary or supporting events

➤ Tickets or invitations to ancillary parties, receptions, shows, launches, etc.

➤ Signage, sampling, etc. at ancillary parties, receptions, shows, launches, etc.

Other promotional opportunities

➤ Custom-design and administration of media promotions

➤ Custom-design and administration of sales promotions (consumer and trade)

➤ Sell-in to trade of sales promotions

➤ Design, production, and distribution of POS

➤ Design of on-pack promotion, liaison with factory (packaging and distribution)

➤ Securing and administration of entertainment, celebrity appearances, etc.

➤ Provision by sponsor of spokesperson/people, celebrity appearances, costumed character etc. to enhance association

➤ Proofs-of-purchase for discount admission

➤ Proofs-of-purchase for discount or free parking

➤ Proofs-of-purchase for premium item (on-site)

➤ Mail or phone-in proof redemption

➤ Opportunity to provide prizes for media or event promotions

➤ Couponing/advertising on ticket backs

➤ Discount admission coupons for customers (distributed in-pack or POP)

Media profile

➤ Inclusion in all print, outdoor, and/or broadcast advertising (logo or name)

➤ Inclusion on event promotional pieces (posters, fliers, brochures, buttons, apparel, etc.—logo or name)

➤ Ad time during televised event

➤ Event-driven promotional radio or television schedule

➤ Event-driven outdoor (billboards, vehicle, public transport)

➤ Sponsor/retailer share media (themed display ads, 30/30 or 15/15 broadcast)

➤ Ad space in event program, catalogue, etc.

Research

➤ Access to pre- and/or post-event research (quantitative or qualitative, attendees or target market)

➤ Opportunity to provide sponsorship or industry-oriented questions on event research

Sell-on

➤ Right for sponsor to on-sell sponsorship benefits to another organisation such as an associated company or retailer (this is always pending sponsee approval)

➤ Right for retailer sponsor to on-sell sponsorship benefits to vendors in specific product categories

Contra

See the Inventory of Assets on page 90 for more contra ideas.

➤ Opportunity to provide equipment, services, technology, expertise, or personnel useful to the success of the event in trade for part of sponsorship fee

➤ Opportunity to provide appropriate media or promotion in trade for part of sponsorship fee

➤ Opportunity to provide media at sponsor-contracted discounted rates in trade for part of sponsorship fee

➤ Opportunity to provide access to other discounted services (printing, travel, etc.) in trade for part of the sponsorship fee.

Production

➤ Design and/or production of key sponsor events (hospitality, awards, etc.)

➤ Hiring and/or administration of temporary or contract personnel, services, and vendors for above

➤ Logistical assistance, including technical or creative expertise

Cause tie-in

➤ Opportunity to involve sponsor's preferred charitable organisation or cause

➤ Donation of a percentage of ticket or product sales to charity

Media production

This is generally only an issue if the event is run by a media company.

➤ Production of event-driven broadcast or print advertising

➤ Production of event-driven video for promotion, training, or documentation

Vesting

Please note, taking an equity stake is not very common. If you do it, be sure to get qualified legal advice.

➤ A portion of overall net profits

➤ A portion of gross revenue

➤ A portion of proceeds from a part of the event (ticket sales, concessions, parking, exhibitors, etc.)

What can you provide?

When it comes to how sponsors pay for the benefits provided, most needlessly limit themselves to cash and/or product. In reality, anything that you have or have access to that will reduce sponsees' expenditure or increase their value to other sponsors, customers, or media, has value and should be considered as part of your offer. This is often referred to as contra or in-kind.

Attached is a generic Inventory of Assets. This is a starting point for taking inventory of everything that you could possibly bring to the table in a sponsorship negotiation. Again, you will probably not use all or even most of these items, but it creates a menu from which to make an offer that provides a high degree of value to a sponsee while minimising your cash investment.

Remember, at the same time many of these items are maximising your sponsorship, they are benefiting sponsees by achieving their objectives, increasing their value to other sponsors, or saving them money.

Inventory of assets

 Negotiation2.doc

Promotion

➤ Media promotion

➤ Promotion of sponsee through retailers

➤ Promotion of sponsee on-pack, in POS, or through other merchandising

➤ Promotion in internal employee communication

➤ Promotion to customers (mailings, magazine, newsletter, Web site, etc.)

➤ Sponsee signage on sponsor building

Media

➤ Access to heavily discounted media rates through sponsor's media buyer

➤ Tags on existing advertising

➤ New advertisements profiling sponsee

➤ Providing a limited media schedule (probably shared with the sponsor)

Creative

➤ Creative work for the sponsee done by sponsor's advertising agency or in-house graphic department

People

➤ Provision of celebrity for event endorsement or appearances

➤ Donation of employee for a fixed-term assignment (full or part-time for set number of weeks/months)

➤ Employee volunteers to augment on-site staff

➤ Access to in-house experts and subcontractors (public relations, media planning, research, etc.)

Infrastructure

➤ Office space

➤ Office equipment or services

➤ Event equipment or services

➤ Access to discounted subcontractor deals (printing, mailing, etc.)

Other contra products or services

➤ For use as prizes, incentives, or giveaways

➤ To add value to other sponsorship packages

Travel

➤ Access to discounted airline or hotel deals

➤ Contra travel or hotel (if sponsor is in travel business)

Different approaches

There are many different approaches you can take to negotiating or renegotiating a sponsorship. Some of them will encourage a partnership-orientation while ensuring you get what you need from the investment. Others will do the exact opposite. If you want to be sure you get the most from your sponsorships, carry out the negotiation right and it will set the stage for a fruitful partnership.

Refining the offer

This approach is appropriate if the adjustments are quite minor, rather than structural, including:

➤ the benefits package outlined in the proposal is close to what you need, requiring only minor modification

➤ the payment structure needs addressing (e.g. incorporating contra- or performance-based incentives).

If this is the case, we recommend discussing your needs with the sponsee to determine if some benefits can be exchanged for benefits that will be of more use to you. Use your Negotiation Checklist.

You should also discuss the sponsee's wider objectives. Chances are you may be able to offer them product, promotional, or infrastructure contra that will meet their needs and lower your cash investment. You may also be able to provide them with access to a market that they would find difficult or expensive to reach on their own; for instance, through on-pack promotion of their event.

Restructuring the offer

Negotiate
face-to-face if
at all possible.

If you see a lot of potential in a sponsorship proposal, but it requires more modification than just refining the current offer, you might want to consider restructuring it. This will be most useful if any of the following are true:

➤ you are interested in a different level or type of sponsorship

➤ you want to take a larger or more comprehensive role

➤ you want to structure a sponsorship that goes across multiple related organisations, not just the one that approached you (e.g. across national, state, and local governing bodies)

➤ you want to bring a partner into the negotiation (i.e. retailer, associated company, or other strategic partner).

In this case, you should outline, in general terms, what you have in mind and request a meeting. Although it is possible to completely restructure a relationship without being in the same room, maintaining a partnership-orientation through a more complex negotiation is far more likely if you discuss it face to face.

A good place to start the meeting is if both organisations restate their objectives and target markets. This will ensure that the meeting stays on equal footing, with the needs of both parties taken fully into account. You might find it useful to bring your Proposal Guidelines and request similar information from them.

From there, you need to work together to determine the opportunities, challenges, and potential issues, and come up with a mutually agreeable partnership.

Workshopping

When you are negotiating a restructure, bringing together a selection of stakeholders from each organisation and workshopping it can be extremely effective.

We suggest the following course of action:

➤ both organisations should agree that they will approach the process with a 'why not?' attitude, keeping them open to new ideas

➤ both organisations should share their overall objectives, target markets, needs, and any other relevant information

➤ parallels should be drawn between those factors for each organisation

➤ discuss the level and type of sponsorship that would be most effective for both organisations. Do not be constrained by any set levels or types that the sponsee may have already in place

➤ discuss the specific benefits that both sides can provide to best meet each other's goals, including any cash component (remember, cash is only one benefit a sponsor can provide)

➤ discuss any potential stumbling blocks and how these could be addressed.

➤ agree on the components, who will document this in a written proposal (either side can do it, not just the sponsee), and the timeframe.

If you handle the negotiation this way, be aware that it might be a learning process for sponsees. Even if they are not used to it, however, most sponsees welcome a partnership-oriented approach and will often use these skills with their other sponsors in future.

Workshopping can also work very well with a less drastic, refinement-type of negotiation. In that case, you will most likely concentrate more on the promotional and other maximisation aspects of the program.

> Both organisations should approach a negotiation with a 'why not?' attitude.

Arrogance will get you nowhere in a sponsorship negotiation.

Case study: Ski Chevy

Chevrolet, a division of General Motors in the United States, has developed a partnership with 14 of the country's top ski resorts, which they use to anchor cold weather promotions for their range of sport utility vehicles (SUVs).

They choose top ski resorts that pull a large proportion of their market from their local/regional area (i.e. they are not solely tourist-oriented). This allows for strong dealer participation in the regions where these resorts are located. Then they negotiate for a range of benefits, including season lift tickets for provision to SUV buyers, display for several SUVs at each resort, and content for their excellent destination Web site, www.skichevy.com.

The most interesting thing about this deal

is how they have paid for it, which is primarily in contra. They provide vehicles to the ski resorts, which is fairly standard stuff, but they also negotiate promotional contra. Instead of running a standard SUV media campaign during the colder months, Chevy incorporates promotion for each of the ski resorts in their core geographic markets. As these resorts don't generally have the budget for big media campaigns, this has extremely high value for them.

In addition to sponsoring resorts, Chevy is also a sponsor of the US Ski Team and the US Snowboarding Team, adding additional credibility to their relationship with the sport and those participating in it, and creating lots of opportunities for cross-pollination.

For more info, check out www.skichevy.com.

Putting the screws in

This approach is common, but very counterproductive. Many sponsors believe that since they have the money, they are in the driver's seat and they should be able to dictate the terms of an agreement. The number of sponsorships out there that have been negotiated this way is testament to the fact that sponsors can often get away with it. The small fraction of those sponsorships that are working well for the sponsors is testament to the fact that undermining the partnership-orientation of a relationship spells disaster nearly every time.

There is no such thing as a win–lose sponsorship. Whoever is the 'winning' party—you or the sponsee—may benefit from that initial thrill of victory, but sponsorship can only work well when both parties are achieving their objectives and adding value to each other. A relationship that starts out win–lose will work out lose–lose in the end. It is only by treating a sponsee as a partner that you will gain full access to the power that sponsorship can offer.

Bidding wars

Over the past few years, there has been a trend towards the eruption of bidding wars between direct competitors for the most desirable investments, with the sponsees being the willing benefactors and often instigators of the activity. This has resulted in a number of things:

➤ it has inflated the price of many events past where they are cost-effective

➤ it has created even more pressure for these overpriced sponsorships to perform

➤ it has shifted the focus away from investing strategically to one-upping the competition

➤ it has often created the requirement for the payment of additional, *sponsee-controlled* leverage funding.

The end result is that some sponsorships have become less strategic, more expensive, more adversarial, and have less opportunity for an effective leverage program. If you have lost a sponsorship like this to the competition, you can only console yourself that they probably overpaid.

The ideal situation is that your company will become a preferred partner for sponsorship in your category, but this approach will not always work, particularly if you are dealing through a broker.

When slugging it out with a competitor, you have three appropriate options:

1. If the sponsorship is a current or potential strategic performer, as determined by your Evaluation Criteria, then it should be negotiated to a reasonable rate. If required, additional funds could be sought from other budgets, such as Loyalty marketing/CRM or sales, assuming you can negotiate appropriate benefits to make it worth their while. The rate must be commensurate with the projected performance against multiple objectives.

2. If the sponsorship is not a strategic performer but does offer significant direct or indirect sales, it becomes a strictly mathematical equation based on the cost of sale. In this case, any investment should be made from the sales budget.

3. If the sponsorship is never going to be a strategic performer and it is not cost-effective as a sales exercise, then don't sponsor it, even if that means that the competition will get it.

| Negotiation issues

Whichever approach you decide to take, there are a few things that you should take into account when you enter a negotiation.

Rules of thumb

There are a few negotiation rules of thumb that will make your role in the negotiation process vastly easier.

Negotiate peer-to-peer

Sponsorship-seeking organisations are full of people who are supposed to sell sponsorship, but can't actually make a commitment until they have gone back to their boss or board for approval. This is unacceptable and wastes your time. If you are capable of and prepared to say 'yes', so should your sponsee counterpart.

Know your bottom line

It is easy to get caught up in the moment and lose sight of what you are trying to achieve. No matter how much you want a sponsorship, if the sponsee can't offer the benefits that will allow you to achieve your objectives, you need to walk away. Likewise, if the sponsorship fee is too high for the likely benefit to your company, then don't take it.

Be prepared to walk away

If at some point in the negotiation, it starts to become adversarial or looks like becoming win–lose, then it is time to thank your counterpart and walk away. This is a far better outcome than pushing the point and ending up with a less effective sponsorship.

Also, don't ever enter a negotiation with the mindset that you *need* to do the deal. Your counterpart will see this and may well take advantage of it. We have seen situations where the sponsee has figured this out, made an excuse to cut the meeting short, and then promptly called the potential sponsor's competition. The next thing the sponsor hears from the sponsee is that one of its direct competitors is interested.

Structuring payments

It is reasonable that fees above a given amount (commonly around $15 000–$20 000) be paid in instalments. One common way of doing this is to pay one-third upon signing of the agreement, another third two to three months out, and the final instalment around two weeks out from the event.

When structuring a multi-year agreement, keep in mind the following things:

➤ if the event is new and will likely grow more valuable as time goes on, you may want to structure fees to reflect larger payments in later years

➤ if the event has a long track record of delivering the goods, you may elect a flat-payment structure

➤ if the event is new and you are to be the key sponsor who is the 'perceived owner' of the event, you *may* be asked to pay a larger fee in the first year to assist in underwriting the infrastructure. Keep in mind, though, that there should be a dramatic drop in fees in future years to make up for your up-front investment.

Never negotiate from a position of need.

Performance-based fees

We are in favour of fee structures that incorporate a component that is performance-based. This creates an incentive for the sponsee to deliver as promised—to go that extra mile—and most sponsors see this as a refreshing departure from sponsees that take the money and run.

Instead of paying $10 000 cash for a sponsorship, you could pay:

$8000   Up-front payment

$2000   If exit polls reveal over 30% increase in propensity to buy your product

$2000   If over 2000 people participate in database generating activities

This would cost you a total of $12 000 instead of the original $10 000, but the sponsee would be more closely tied to helping you achieve your objectives. In our opinion, this is a very strong strategy.

Case study: Sandbox.com

Sandbox.com, an online gaming site, brings the term performance-based fees to a whole new level.

For their sponsorship of the MS Society, Sandbox.com paid nothing. That's right, nothing. The MS Society will receive all or part of its $500 000 fee only when someone wins Sandbox.com's $1 million or $100 million jackpots. With nearly 7 million members when this book went to press, it is reasonable to expect that this payment is a real possibility.

In return for their commitment, Sandbox.com has gained a very forward-thinking partner and is receiving introductions from the MS Society to potential site advertisers and partners, as well as promotion in the MS Society's magazine.

Sales-based fees

Sometimes a sponsor will want to tie all or a portion of the sponsorship fee to sales. As much as we all understand that the bottom line for many sponsors is sales, it is unfair to put that kind of responsibility on a sponsee.

Sponsorship provides many of the influences that lead to sales, including promoting loyalty, changing people's perceptions about a brand, educating people about the benefits, and enhancing the brand's positioning. But selling the product is something that sponsees do not implicitly control, so it is unfair to ask them to take that risk.

The line blurs somewhat when you negotiate for on-site sales. On-site sales are directly proportional to the size of the audience and amount of exclusivity granted. If you are the beer sponsor of a basketball team, and they have a winning season or a great promotional program and their attendance goes up by 35%, you will sell more beer. Some companies elect to provide a bonus to the sponsee for increased sales, some for increased attendance. Unless the beer is flat or overpriced and no one buys it, the net result should be approximately the same.

Exclusivity

There is only one rule of exclusivity: the more exclusivity is granted, the more valuable it is.

There are three types of exclusivity—sponsorship, signage (venues can sometimes sell conflicting signage), and sales. You can be granted exclusivity across any or all of these areas.

Most exclusivity is granted on the basis of categories, and is often referred to in contracts as 'category exclusivity'. This usually refers to the category of business that your company is in, for example, airline, carbonated soft drink, ice cream or automobiles. You can request an extension of exclusivity across a wider range of categories, but be aware, it will come at a significant additional price because it will prevent the sponsee from being able to sell sponsorships in those categories affecting their bottom line. An example of this would be if Pepsi were granted sponsorship and sales exclusivity across categories such as: carbonated soft drinks (their true category), non-carbonated soft drinks, sports drinks, fruit juices, fruit- and iced tea-based drinks, flavoured milk, and water.

Reporting

Most sponsors don't address reporting during negotiations, but the best way to ensure that a sponsee submits the regular reports that you need to assess the sponsorship's progress is to discuss it during negotiation. Agree to what the reports will cover and the frequency that they will be submitted.

Quantification and evaluation

During negotiation is also the best time to discuss both how the results of the sponsorship will be quantified by your company, as well as how sponsee performance will be evaluated. If a sponsee knows up front how the sponsorship will be quantified and evaluated, it reinforces your objectives and makes clear to them what is important to you.

For more information on quantification and evaluation, as well as why they should be evaluated separately, see Chapter 12—Quantification starting on page 149.

Renewals

Do determine at what point you will begin discussing the contract renewal. You don't

The more exclusivity you get, the more expensive the sponsorship is likely to be.

want to be two months from a major event and unsure whether or how you will be involved. Set a renewal negotiation period that will provide your company with the time it needs to implement the sponsorship program, and the sponsee with enough time to find another sponsor in case your relationship doesn't go forward.

In addition, if it is predicted that an event will grow substantially during your contract, you could end up facing a large jump in fees at renewal time. One option is to negotiate a cap on the amount a sponsorship fee can rise at renewal—for instance, 20%—when you are negotiating your initial contract.

Accommodating shifting needs

If your brand is not mature—that is, it is either in its adolescence or infancy—it is likely that your needs will shift significantly within the timeframe of a multi-year contract. You have two choices:

1. If you can predict your future needs, negotiate for a shifting set of benefits from one year of the contract to another.

2. If you can't predict your future needs, you can negotiate an 'objective review process', during which you can discuss your changing needs with the sponsee and the sponsee will do its best to accommodate those needs.

    Most of the time, you will be able to predict those needs.

Special notes for retailers

A number of retail sponsors are working with their vendors to create comprehensive and multi-faceted sponsorship programs. Some of these involve the retailers passing on benefits of the sponsorship to their vendors. Some bring their vendors into the sponsorship relationship, so the suppliers become sponsors in their own rights.

Whichever way they do it, this type of sponsorship has a track record of working very well for both the retailer and the suppliers involved. The key to making this possible is negotiating from the start for the right to pass on benefits and/or bring on board sub-sponsors.

Negotiating with a broker

Selecting the right sponsorship can be a daunting task. Negotiating the right benefits to help you achieve your marketing objectives can be even more difficult. Drop a sponsorship broker into the mix, and it can be very easy to put a great sponsorship opportunity into the 'too hard' basket.

Brokers, or agents, are hired by sponsorship-seeking organisations to assist them in

> Your needs may change. Be sure to negotiate for some flexibility in benefits.

Some brokers are great, others are cowboys.

securing sponsorship. In exchange for assistance in packaging and selling sponsorship, they receive a commission, generally between 15 and 40% of the gross sponsorship fee, including contra. Brokering happens most often in the area of sport, but there are brokers who work in virtually every area.

There are some exceedingly professional sponsorship agencies and brokers—those who work closely with the sponsee to fully develop their skills, marketing plan, and what they have to offer. They then work with both the sponsor and sponsee to engineer long-term win–win relationships. They consider it their duty to follow through to ensure that the sponsorship is implemented to exceed expectations. These brokers are worth their weight in gold to both sponsors and sponsees.

On the other end of the spectrum are agencies or brokers who have the 'take the money and run' approach. They have little to do with sponsees, do not know or care about their needs, and rely on the shotgun approach to sales—hoping against hope that someone out there is interested. By the time the reality of the sponsorship sets in for their client or the sponsor, they are out of the picture. Unfortunately, people like this represent some really good opportunities.

The most important thing to keep in mind when working with a broker is that the partnership being developed is between you and the sponsorship seeker, not you and the broker. Even if the broker is going to be involved in the ongoing maintenance of your sponsorship, the ultimate responsibility for delivering on your investment lies with the sponsee.

It is clearly in your best interests (and theirs) if the sponsorship seeker is involved every step of the way, including in key meetings. This will ensure that they understand your objectives and audience, as well as what will be expected of them as a partner. It is not uncommon for brokers to promise benefits that a sponsorship seeker either doesn't understand, doesn't control, or simply cannot deliver for the negotiated fee.

Doing your homework

Before you start any negotiation, you will need to do your homework, because working with a broker is often far more complicated than working directly with a sponsorship seeker. A few well-placed phone calls will provide you with a lot of information.

What is the going price for the sponsorship?

A lot might have happened since the proposal first hit your desk. If the broker is having a hard time selling it and time is growing short, the sponsorship may have been offered around at a discounted price. It may also have been offered at a discount price to companies being targeted by the broker for some larger initiative. If you know this, then you know the bottom line.

How have other negotiations for this event gone?

If a potential sponsor didn't sign on because it couldn't agree on terms, that's fine. It happens. If, however, the negotiations broke down because of a rift between the sponsorship seeker and the broker, or because the broker had a conflict of interest, proceed with extreme caution.

Are sponsors of their other events happy?

This is a simple question, the answer to which will speak volumes about the approach and professionalism of the brokers. It might also let you in on some of their negotiating techniques (telling someone that a direct competitor is moments from signing a contract is popular).

Check the Web sites for the broker and their events. The likelihood is that you will know somebody within at least one sponsoring company. Give them a call. Take notes.

> Be sure your broker has no conflicts of interest.

Case study: Negotiation gone wrong

Although this is a true example, the situation was so acrimonious that we are electing to use false names for both the companies and the event.

One example of a brokered negotiation that went horribly wrong is when Mikado Motors agreed with a broker to terms for naming rights of the Singapore Champion's Tennis Tournament.

The broker, who had been trying to negotiate a deal on the same event with Jupiter Motors (brokers often negotiate with competing companies right up until the contract is signed),

fouled the deal late in the game. Jupiter was unhappy about losing the event to Mikado and decided that it wanted to sponsor the tournament to such an extent that it threatened legal action and to pull out of other, larger deals with that broker. The broker, knowing on which side their bread was buttered, sided with Jupiter and tried to tell Mikado to get lost.

Luckily, this ploy didn't work, but it cost a lot in legal fees for Mikado to get what it believed it had already achieved through agreement with the broker.

Questions to ask the sponsee

You also need to ask several questions of the sponsee. Do not commit to a brokered deal unless you are satisfied with the answers to the following.

Who will be handling the sponsorship servicing—the sponsee or the broker?

Some properties contract their agency or broker to handle servicing, and if they are good, this can be a real plus. Otherwise, you are probably better off working directly with the sponsee on the implementation of your investment.

If it is the sponsee, what is their commitment to sponsorship servicing?

The answer here is critical. Servicing sponsorships is time consuming and requires expertise. It should not be handled by someone who is already overcommitted or who has no expertise or authority within the sponsee's organisation.

Does the sponsee understand all aspects of the proposed deal?

It is important that the sponsor and sponsee understand each other. You would be surprised how many sponsees never see the proposal or the deal until it is their turn to sign a contract. This is another sign of a broker who is more interested in the commission than in building long-term relationships.

Does the sponsee understand what you are trying to achieve—your objectives and target markets?

Again, this is often not communicated to the sponsee by the broker. Be prepared with a briefing document so that the sponsee understands your goals.

Chapter 8

Contracts

When you enter into an agreement to sponsor an organisation, it is always with the hope that everything will go as planned and there will never be another reason to look at the contract. Unfortunately, sometimes things do go wrong, so it is imperative that you understand the issues.

Types of agreements

Always, always have some sort of written agreement in force. The more formal the agreement, the more likely it will be complete and legally binding. In order of desirability, these are the types of agreements you could have:

➤ legal contract drawn up by a solicitor, bearing the signatures and company seals of both organisations

➤ legal contract adapted from a template drawn up by a solicitor, bearing the signatures and company seals of both organisations. In the Appendix we have included a comprehensive Sponsorship Agreement Pro Forma that has been created for this book by Allens Arthur Robinson. It can also be found on disk

➤ legal contract adapted from a template drawn up by a solicitor, bearing the signatures of both organisations

➤ letter of agreement outlining all the points of agreement, including benefits, communication, and payment dates, and signed by both organisations

➤ confirmation letter outlining the benefits and payment dates. Either the sponsor or the sponsee could produce it. This is not desirable and should be avoided as it does not offer the structure and protections of a contract.

Determine at what level you need a letter of agreement or a contract. Often a letter of agreement, signed by both parties, will be used for sponsorships valued under a certain amount, such as $20 000. Above that amount, a full contract will be required.

A contract pro forma is a very useful tool that can be utilised in several ways:

➤ as the basis for your agreement

A contract pro forma will save you time and money.

➤ as your first pass at a legal contract, which can then be given to a solicitor for fine tuning (saving you a considerable amount in legal fees)

➤ as a reference so that you are aware of possible issues and legal considerations.

We do not recommend using the pro forma as the basis for your agreement unless you have a lawyer check the agreement prior to entering into it.

Who should provide the contract?

Common sense says that you should always try to provide the contract, because in so doing, your needs will be looked after. For larger contracts, this is definitely the way to go.

For smaller agreements, it depends largely upon how bureaucratic and au fait your corporate legal department or firm is with sponsorship. If they understand sponsorship and can write a contract that stays in keeping with the spirit of win–win, they're a great asset and you should definitely use them. Otherwise, our suggestion is to ask them to develop a pro forma, as outlined above, which can be customised by you for specific programs.

Your legal department will not want to hear this, but for smaller contracts, it is nearly always quicker and more straightforward for the sponsee to develop the contract (although this can vary widely from one sponsee to another). If you go this route, be sure that your lawyers have a look at any agreement before it is signed.

Resolving problems

When structuring an agreement, always try to include a series of steps for resolving any conflicts that might arise. You only move onto the next step when what you have already tried has not worked. The four basic steps are, in order:

➤ Discussion—This means having a meeting with the express purpose of coming to a resolution that is agreeable to both parties.

➤ Mediation—This involves getting an independent arbiter to mediate discussion without making a decision.

➤ Arbitration—This involves getting an independent arbiter to hear both sides and make a decision.

➤ Litigation—A long and usually expensive foray into the legal system.

Servicing plan

Every contract should include as an attachment a sponsorship servicing plan, provided by the sponsee, which should include:

Always include problem resolution in your contracts.

- ➤ contact name and details of your key contact for the sponsorship
- ➤ critical dates (art deadlines, launches, etc.)
- ➤ communication plan (how often the sponsor and sponsee will liaise, whether it will be by phone or in writing, and what information will be included)
- ➤ other information, dates, etc.

First and last rights of refusal

These very important parts of any sponsorship contract are often overlooked or misunderstood. They have to do with your rights at renewal time and can be critical if you want the best possible opportunity to continue the investment.

First right of refusal

Having first right of refusal ensures that, as incumbent, you have the legal right to renew an agreement before any negotiations take place with another company for the same or similar sponsorship rights. The right to renew could specify the terms of the renewal, including price and sponsorship rights, or may involve extensive negotiation of some or all key terms of the agreement.

As a general rule, the more tightly the renewal terms are specified in the original agreement, the more likely that the first right of renewal can be enforced. The risk of specifying terms up front is that the market conditions and other matters relating to the time of the original agreement may change significantly, making the true worth of the sponsorship substantially higher or lower than the contracted renewal price.

Last right of refusal

This right ensures that, no matter what another company offers for a sponsorship or other rights that are similar to your original agreement, you will have the opportunity to match or better it. If they up the ante again, you will have the opportunity once again to better it. This can lead to a bidding war, but not always. It is better to risk the war and choose whether you want to fight it than not to have the opportunity to retain an event that you want. Last right of refusal is very common in television broadcast rights agreements and top level sports sponsorships.

Blackout dates

You can also nominate a period during which the sponsee cannot discuss sponsorship of their event with any of your direct competitors. This usually runs up to and through

> It is better to risk a bidding war and choose whether you want to fight it than not to have the option at all.

your nominated renegotiation window, giving you the best chance at creating a win–win partnership without other potential sponsors clouding the air.

In most cases, you should ensure that you at least have first right of refusal. There are instances when this may be less of an issue, such as if a sponsorship is a short-term, tactical activity, you may not be interested in renewing. If a sponsorship is of a one-off event, there is no need to address rights of refusal at all.

Please note: We have defined these terms to give you some understanding of their meaning, but these are legal terms with often complex ramifications and, therefore, should not be entered into without the advice of a qualified sponsorship lawyer.

Corporate/brand image

➤ Ensure that your sponsee provides you with the right to proof all printed material, all media releases, and anything that includes your name, acknowledgment, and logo.

➤ Ensure that you have a clause ensuring that the sponsee agrees to use its best endeavours to present positive media for the organisation and its activities.

Insurance

➤ Ensure that insurance responsibilities (event insurance, public liability, professional indemnity) are detailed in the agreement.

Transfer of contract or benefits to a third party

➤ Can the rights of either party be transferred to a third party?

➤ Can benefits be on-sold to a third party?

➤ Are there limits to the types or amount of benefits that can be on-sold?

➤ Are there limits to the types of organisation to whom the contract or benefits can be on-sold or transferred?

Dispute resolution

➤ Have you ensured that a dispute resolution process is included in the agreement?

Payment

➤ What is the agreed fee for the property?

➤ When and how will it be paid?

➤ Is there contra involved? Specifics must be detailed.

➤ Any performance-based fees should be detailed.

Contract checklist

Before signing anything, ask yourself all of these questions:

The obvious, but frequently overlooked

➤ Is the agreement dated?

➤ Does the agreement clearly state who the agreement is between?

➤ Have you ensured that the party with whom you are entering into an agreement controls the rights you are purchasing? You would be surprised how often benefits are promised by a sponsee which doesn't directly control them.

➤ Over what period of time is the agreement valid?

➤ Have you ensured that the details of the sponsorship are confidential?

Benefits

➤ Is each and every benefit to *both parties* included within the contract?

➤ Is the level of exclusivity included?

➤ Are naming rights or presenting rights artwork and acknowledgment lines specified within the agreement?

➤ Are any additional costs for agreed benefits (e.g. signage production) outlined within the contract?

➤ Are all costs associated with enhancing the sponsorship (e.g. buying additional tickets) outlined within the contract?

Reporting and evaluation

➤ Have you ensured that the timing, type, and frequency of reports is included in the agreement? A completed Servicing Plan is a plus.

➤ Have you ensured that your Sponsorship Evaluation Criteria has been outlined?

➤ The frequency of meetings outlining all aspects of the sponsees activities that might affect the property should be included in the agreement.

Renewals

➤ Have you set a date or window for starting renewal negotiations?

➤ Have you set a cap on how much a sponsorship fee can rise at renewal?

➤ Have you included first right of refusal?

➤ Have you included last right of refusal (if applicable)?

Sponsorship agreement pro forma

Included in the Appendix is a Sponsorship Agreement Pro Forma that was developed specifically for us by Lionel Hogg, Partner of Allens Arthur Robinson. The full agreement can also be found on disk.

This sample agreement may be a useful starting point for a sponsorship agreement. However, it is very general because it is impossible to draft a document that accounts for all situations or for legal differences in all countries.

Ideally, it should be used as a template that is completed by the sponsee and sponsor and then given to a lawyer to check the drafting, change it to suit the law of the relevant place and better outline the rights of the parties. This will ensure that the agreement process is collaborative and will probably cost you far less than securing a lawyer to draft an agreement from scratch.

Warning

This document is provided as a sample only and is not a substitute for legal advice. You should seek the advice of a suitably qualified and experienced lawyer before using this document.

In particular, you or your lawyer should:

➤ check the law in your jurisdiction—make sure this agreement works there

➤ check for changes to the law—law and practice might have altered since this document was drafted or you last checked the situation

➤ modify wherever necessary—review this document critically and never use it without first amending it to suit your needs as every sponsorship is different

➤ beware of limits of expertise. If you are not legally qualified or are not familiar with this area of the law, do not use this document without first obtaining legal advice about it.

How this Agreement works

The Agreement assumes that there are standard clauses that should be in every Agreement and special clauses needed for your sponsorship. The standard clauses that should apply all of the time are called the 'Standard Conditions'. The parts that relate to your specific sponsorship are the 'Schedules' and the 'Special Conditions'.

The Schedules and the Special Conditions have precedence over the Standard Conditions. In other words, what you insert is more important than what is already written. This is why it is vital to use a lawyer or know what you are doing.

Read the Agreement

Before doing anything, read the Agreement and see how it might apply to your situation. There might be Standard Conditions that are unsuitable. There might be new conditions you need to add. Do not assume that the Agreement is right for you.

The sample agreement is for an *exclusive* sponsorship for the relevant sponsorship category.

Complete the Schedules

You should complete each Schedule following the guidance notes in that Schedule.

For example, Schedule 23 is called 'Sponsor's termination events'. The guidance note tells you to see clause 9.2. You should read clause 9.2 and understand the circumstances in which the sponsor has a right to terminate the agreement. You should then insert in Schedule 23 any other circumstances peculiar to your sponsorship (e.g. the sponsor might want to terminate the agreement if the team being sponsored loses its licence to play in the major league or if the contracted lead performers for the musical withdraw their services).

Add Special Conditions

The Special Conditions (at the end of the Schedules) enable you to insert other conditions that are not dealt with by this sample agreement.

Changing Standard Conditions

You should *not* change the Standard Conditions without consulting a lawyer. The Agreement is drafted as a package and changing the Standard Conditions might have an unintended, domino effect on other terms.

If you have to change the Standard Conditions, do so by adding a Special Condition, such as, 'clause 18 of the Standard Conditions does not apply'.

Sign the Agreement

The parties sign and date the document on the last page. Make sure that the person with whom you do the deal is authorised to sign.

Finding a lawyer

You should consult a lawyer practising in your jurisdiction and experienced in sponsorship matters. If you don't have a good sponsorship lawyer, there are a number of sports law organisations around the world that can provide a referral, or you can contact Allens Arthur Robinson in Australia.

Although you may not be a sporting organisation, these associations will be a great source for referrals, as sponsorship law skills are quite transferable across sponsorship genres.

Full contact details for a number of these organisations can be found in Appendix 2.

If you have questions about the pro forma agreement

If you or your lawyer have questions about the Sponsorship Agreement Pro Forma, you are welcome to contact its author:

Lionel Hogg, Consultant

Allens Arthur Robinson

PO Box 7082 Riverside Centre

Brisbane Qld 4001 Australia

Phone: (61-7) 3334 3170

Fax: (61-7) 3334 3444

e-mail: lionel.hogg@aar.com.au

Part 3

maximisation
and
management

Chapter 9

Maximisation

> When you invest in a sponsorship, you are investing in opportunity.

> Maximisation, activation, and leverage all mean the same thing.

When you invest in sponsorship, you are investing in opportunity. A well-selected sponsorship may be a wonderful way of connecting with your target market, but unless you make that connection relevant, creative, and use it to add value to your relationship, that connection won't be made.

The things you do—promotions, advertising, employee programs, the Internet, etc.—to create that relevance and those relationships with your target markets is called maximisation.

Some people call it maximisation, some leverage, others activation. They all mean the same thing and we use the terms interchangeably. Whatever you call it, you will not achieve your objectives unless you do it. Yes, it costs money (but probably not nearly as much as you think). Yes, it takes time. But, if you are not prepared to take these steps, you should not be in the business of sponsorship, because there is nothing a sponsee can give you that will achieve your objectives without your active participation.

But, we have no money for maximisation!

Does this sound familiar?

1. Your portfolio is basically spent out.
2. You have very little in the way of leverage funds.
3. Your stakeholders believe that the only way to get more out of a sponsorship is to increase leverage funding.
4. There is no more money in the budget that can be redirected towards sponsorship.
5. The portfolio is not performing.

To some, this situation might look hopeless. To us, it looks typical, and far from hopeless.

Going back to the Get Real Rule introduced in Chapter 2, many of the best sponsorships have the smallest leverage budgets because they use sponsorship as a catalyst. The following strategies will help you to get the most from your sponsorships while keeping your costs reasonable.

Using your Sponsorship Team

Although your Sponsorship Team should be involved throughout the sponsorship process, its members will really come into their own when they work together to maximise a sponsorship. This is the case for a number of reasons:

➤ the members' expertise across different fields creates a very holistic and creative approach to maximisation

➤ team members are often looking for ways to make their own marketing activities more effective. Sponsorship can often be a catalyst to achieving their objectives more effectively

➤ people in a group work off each other, improving and expanding good ideas. In our experience, a group is always more creative than one person working alone

➤ finally, maximisation is one of the most fun parts of sponsorship. If your group does this part, they will usually stay interested and excited even when their sponsorship roles aren't as attractive.

> A sponsorship will not achieve your objectives without your active participation.

Brainstorm exercise

This exercise is a simple and straightforward way to get some great maximisation ideas out of your Sponsorship Team. It doesn't seem like much, but in our experience, it not only results in far better sponsorships, it also serves to open the minds of your Sponsorship Team.

First, provide everyone with a Brainstorm Brief (template attached), and let them review it. Then, ask these three questions, in this order, one at a time:

1 What could we do to create more impact around this sponsorship without spending any extra money?

This question forces your group to be resourceful. It is also fostering true integration, because you are positioning the sponsorship as a catalyst. Remind your team members that they all have budgets and are trying to achieve the same objectives. Ask them whether or not this sponsorship would make any of their planned activities more effective, more impactful, or less expensive.

2 What could we do to create more impact around this sponsorship if it had no budget constraints whatsoever?

The second question is about the big idea. The funny thing is that, once everyone has got done shouting out how they would buy a blimp or give a car to everyone who buys the product, the ideas tend to be not only feasible, but relatively inexpensive. Generally, the only difference between the good ideas generated from this question and the ones generated from the first question is that these ideas might need some seed funding from the sponsorship budget to get them started. Keeping your team focused on your objectives is the difficult part here. Just keep reminding them what you are all trying to achieve.

3 How would each of you quantify the results of your involvement?

This question is about making your job easier. In order to manage sponsorships well, you do need to have a good working knowledge of all aspects of marketing. You don't, however, need to be an expert in all of them. But, having you do all of the quantification is asking you to be just that. A publicist should be assessing publicity results. The CRM manager is best placed to quantify loyalty activity. Around your table you have a group of people who each have the expertise and resources to easily set targets for their participation and quantify results against them. Now is your chance to use this resource.

> Don't overburden your team with details. Keep your Brainstorm Brief succinct.

Brainstorm brief template

 Brainstorm1.doc

This document has been developed to provide the important information about a sponsorship without burdening your team with too much and hindering the creative process. When you do your own Brainstorm Brief, try to maintain that balance.

Overview

Product: Cabana Premium White Rum, emphasising newest product in the line, Cabana Citria (citrus flavoured).

Target markets: Primary—Urban professionals, 25–35, $50 000 plus household income, high disposable income, renters, new foreign car buyers, single, aspirated, early adopters (trend setters), active, social, drink outside the home, music lovers.

Secondary—Urban professionals, 25–40, DINKs, home buyers, new foreign car buyers, established careers, socially active both in and out of the home, $70 000 plus household income, art lovers.

Tertiary—Managers/owners of urban bars, pubs, and licensed restaurants, particularly those populated by the primary and secondary markets (trendsetters).

Objectives: 1. Increase trial of Cabana Citria by trendsetters

2. Educate trendsetters to multiple uses of Cabana Citria
   (cocktails, summer coolers, entertaining)
3. Increase penetration of Cabana Citria into key bars, pubs, and
   restaurants

Hot Jazz in the Summertime

Melbourne Tourism has created a nine-day festival of jazz that will be featuring the best
of national and overseas jazz talent in both normal and unconventional settings. It starts
the third week of January and takes in Australia Day celebrations.

Other major sponsors include Sony Music, Volvo, Channel 10, Crown Casino, and
the Southbank retail and entertainment precinct. Sony Music is bringing out a selection
of their top jazz artists and has indicated that one or more of them could be available
to participate in promotions.

In addition to a comprehensive promotional schedule on Channel 10, a strong schedule
in *The Age* newspaper and complementary radio has also been negotiated. Starts 2 January.

This is a three-year sponsorship. The annual sponsorship fee is $100 000.

Major benefits

➤ Major sponsorship of the festival
➤ Naming rights sponsorship to *Art Fusion*—a jazz series taking place in art galleries
  and spaces around Melbourne
➤ Tickets to all major events
➤ Featured alcoholic beverage and the only spirits available at all festival-controlled
  venues
➤ Sponsorship exclusivity in the category of alcoholic beverages
➤ Opportunity to host private parties/receptions
➤ Program advertising
➤ Logos on everything, signage, publicity, etc.

| Leverage activities

There are hundreds of activities that you could do to leverage your sponsorship. We
discuss a number of them across the next several pages. What we offer here is a sample,
so please use this as a guide. You need to make your leverage program relevant to your
audience, relevant to your brand, and creative enough to capture people's attention. In
short, make your program your own.

Don't copy your
competition. Make
your leverage
program your own.

Loyalty/CRM

Although these marketing areas are listed in no particular order, we have put loyalty marketing first because it is such a terrific fit with sponsorship's new emphasis on connectivity.

You could use sponsorship to provide your members/loyal customers with exclusive access to:

➤ members-only merchandise

➤ members-only invitations to events, launches, special days, celebrity appearances

➤ members-only discounts to events, parking, transport, merchandise

➤ members-only opportunities to participate in the event in some way

➤ members-only promotions

➤ special seating

➤ priority ticketing

➤ customised gifts (e.g. a birthday card signed by a star player).

Case studies: Loyalty marketing

BMW uses their relationship with James Bond films to reward loyalty in a way that money just can't buy—by inviting BMW owners to star-studded Bond film premières around the world.

IN the US, Southwest Airlines uses sponsorship to create surprise rewards for their top business fliers. They believe that these no-strings-attached, once-in-a-lifetime experiences, such as a trip to the NHL All-Star Game, create a sense of loyalty that is far beyond the standard frequent flier program.

STILL in the travel mode, Holiday Inn found through research that their predominantly male customers are 74% more likely to watch university basketball than the average male. They used their sponsorship of the NCAA to give customers *4000* tickets to the NCAA Final Four tournament. (For you non-basketball types, this tournament is the holy grail of university basketball.) Travellers could enter at check-in, and could even trade in frequent stayer points for more entries.

ENGENDERING loyalty doesn't always mean giving people free stuff. When the Rolling Stones did a blockbuster 28-city US tour in 1997, their sponsor, Sprint, provided all of their long distance phone customers with an opportunity to buy tickets before they went on sale to the general public.

Database generation

There are literally dozens of ways to generate database information around a sponsorship, including:

➤ ticket sales

➤ contests

➤ competitions

➤ toll-free numbers

➤ trial offers

➤ discount offers

➤ test drives

➤ coupons

➤ registrations

➤ point of sale

➤ kids' pages

➤ fan clubs

➤ Internet site

➤ sales receipts

➤ credit card sales

➤ information inquiries

➤ membership programs

➤ warranties

➤ welcome cards

➤ exit/entrance surveys

➤ post-event research

➤ product registration.

Case studies: Building databases and memberships

PONTIAC used a sponsorship of the first US series of 'Survivor' (remember Richard?) to launch their new SUV, the Aztek. They leveraged this, in part, by creating 'The A-List Adventure Contest', an on-line essay contest that served to strengthen their positioning, build a database, and get closer to their potential buyers by getting those buyers closer to Survivor. Twenty winners were chosen and then hosted on a six-week adventure trip of a lifetime.

BANK of America sponsored the Oakland Athletics baseball team, which includes access to database information from the team's fan cards. Fans filled out a questionnaire to get their cards, which they swiped at games to build points for discounts, merchandise, etc. Bank of America used this data to develop customised communications for each market segment.

THE US Air Force Reserve took a novel approach to recruiting when it sponsored a Quake II computer gaming tournament. The heavily customised program targeted exactly the right people and reinforced the Air Force's heavy technological slant and emphasis on teamwork. It provided a strong platform for recruitment and drove traffic to the Reserve's Web site.

EVEN organised religion is getting into the act. In North Carolina, the United Methodist Church used sponsorship of two car racing teams to raise the profile of the church while gaining access to the large motorsport audiences in their region for information distribution.

Internet

The Internet is changing so fast that it is a temptation not to list ideas in this section, in case we look silly and out of date in a year's time. Here are a few ideas. Be aware that you should be keeping abreast of new developments and thinking about how you could use them with sponsorship to connect better with your marketplace:

➤ run a promotion on the sponsee's site

➤ have a hot link from the sponsee's site

➤ run a promotion on your own site

➤ use the sponsorship to provide content for your site

➤ access sponsorship-related celebrities to contribute to your site

➤ access sponsorship-related celebrities to do live chats on-line

➤ provide downloadable event or merchandising discount coupons on your site

➤ provide downloadable coupons redeemable for sponsorship-driven premiums

➤ Webcast all or part of the event live on your site

➤ carry clips of the event on the site

➤ create a forum for reviews and comments about the event

➤ have event information on your site (e.g. easily printable maps, rules)

➤ feature tips, rules, and other information

➤ have event merchandise available on your site

➤ create ways for grassroots sportspeople, artists, humanitarians, etc. to participate or feature their work on the Web site

➤ let people vote for something or have their say about an issue on your site.

Case study: Pepsi.com

Many have tried, but we've never seen a better sponsorship-driven corporate site than Pepsi.com. Pepsi has used their major sponsorships of properties as diverse as motor sport, music, baseball, and big budget movies to create a content-driven destination site that appeals to several key target markets.

From a Q&A forum with Faith Hill to motor racing games to Britney Spears' tour diary to soccer skills coaching, this site has the goods. Check it out for yourself (www.pepsi.com).

Above-the-line advertising

There are companies and ad agencies that believe that sponsorships and advertising don't mix. That isn't the case, but it's not an easy mindset to break. If your brand people and ad agency are more open-minded, however, there are many ways you can use sponsorship to create impact through above-the-line advertising:

➤ create new advertising featuring key elements of a sponsorship

➤ use sponsorship-oriented celebrities, images, or sounds in more general advertising (e.g. using an associated celebrity as a spokesperson)

➤ creating a public service commercial, melding advertising messages with sponsorship-oriented information (e.g. a sports drink company using athletes to show the proper way to stretch before exercise)

➤ do sponsorship-related pull-throughs on existing adverting

➤ tag the end of existing advertising

➤ do any of the above and run the ad in conjunction with the sponsee's own advertising.

Case studies: Above-the-line

IN 1998, baseball enjoyed a home run derby, pitting two of the sport's best hitters against each other in an emotional race to break the single season home run record. When Mark McGwire broke that record, Major League Baseball sponsor MasterCard quickly created a 'priceless' ad that baseball fans still remember. The tear-inducing closing line of the ad was, 'The official card of Major League Baseball and believer that records were made to be broken'. Very nice.

WESTPAC, Official Bank of the Sydney 2000 Olympics, decided against using hackneyed glory shots of their sponsored athletes in their advertising, and instead humanised them, with great results. In the lead-up, they used one of Australia's top swimmers, Susie O'Neill, in a series of ads where young athletes took her on and beat her. Unfortunately for Susie, their sports were archery, fencing, and synchronised swimming! During the Olympics, Westpac continued with this charming and approachable style by celebrating their athletes' medals with ads featuring the athletes' families making an absolute mess of the sport, then proclaiming, 'I don't know how she [or he] does it'.

PLAYING off of the one-on-one rivalry running through tennis, Heineken used their sponsorships of the sport to create witty radio spots that highlight the super-premium positioning of their beer. One spot featured two men trying to one-up each other on the topics of money, jobs, and women, with a tennis match being played and won in the background. The tagline: 'Heineken—Proud sponsor of the US Open and grudge matches everywhere'.

FEDEX, the Official Express Delivery Service of the NHL, cemented their investment with a sensational television ad built around the Detroit Red Wings' recent Stanley Cup win. The crowd is chanting 'we want the Cup', the team is standing on the ice at Joe Louis Arena waiting for the Cup and looking confused. Meanwhile, the Stanley Cup has been delivered to an equally confused Bolivian villager named Jose Luis Arena. Of course, that never would happen if they used FedEx. If you want to see it, check out www.adcritic.com.

Media promotions

One of the most prevalent ways of supporting a sponsorship is through media promotion. This is a big area and we've devoted a lot of space to it.

Generally, media promotions are created with one or more media partners. You provide them with co-ownership of the promotion and usually a paid schedule, and they provide several times that investment in media value. This can be an extremely cost-effective way of connecting with your target markets.

Rather than list all of the ways you can do media promotions, which would fill the whole book, we are providing you with a number of tips and tools to help you get it right.

Who should create the promotion?

Generally speaking, you are much more likely to achieve your goals if you create the promotion rather than the sponsee or media partner. Read 'Eight steps of promotional media' section on page 122 for some hints.

Do you go to one or more media outlets?

If you have determined that you can achieve your objectives with either of two competing media outlets, our suggestion is that you brief them both on the promotion, and ask them to come back to you with a package that meets the brief.

If you have determined that there is only one medium outlet that will suit your needs perfectly, you should negotiate closely with it to create a partnership. Do not let the outlet hold you to ransom, though—you can always walk away and rethink your approach for a different type of media.

How much value should you get?

If your proposal is structured correctly (see 'Eight steps of promotional media' on page 122), you should be receiving far more value than the amount you are paying. Below, we have outlined some typical value-to-cost ratios and what the values include. The media partner will be able to provide the specific value-to-cost analysis for you.

MEDIA	TARGET VALUE TO COST RATIO	VALUE INCLUDES
Television	3:1 to 8:1	<ul><li>Paid spots</li><li>Bonus spots (confirmed)</li><li>Bonus spots (space-available)</li><li>Promotional spots (co-branded by the television station)</li><li>News coverage</li><li>Other editorial coverage (lifestyle, sporting, or news-magazine programs)</li><li>Ad production</li><li>Use of an on-air personality for endorsement, appearances, voice-overs, or as a spokesperson</li></ul>
Radio	3:1 to 10:1	<ul><li>Paid spots</li><li>Bonus spots (confirmed)</li><li>Bonus spots (space available)</li><li>Pre-recorded promotional spots (co-branded by the television station)</li><li>Live promotional spots</li><li>Live liners (very short promotional spots)</li><li>News coverage</li><li>On-air interviews</li><li>Remote broadcasts</li><li>Ad production</li><li>Use of an on-air personality for endorsement, appearances, voice-overs, or as a spokesperson</li></ul>
Newspaper	3:1 to 8:1	<ul><li>Paid advertising</li><li>Bonus advertising (confirmed)</li><li>Bonus advertising (space available)</li><li>Insertion of program, poster, or other promotional material that you supply</li><li>Printing and/or design of program or poster</li><li>Special supplement (can often be used as the official program)</li><li>Advertorial coverage</li></ul>
Magazine	2:1 to 5:1	<ul><li>Paid advertising</li><li>Bonus advertising (confirmed)</li><li>Bonus advertising (space-available)</li><li>Special section</li><li>Insertion of program, poster, or other promotional material</li><li>Advertorial coverage</li></ul>
Outdoor	2:1	<ul><li>Paid advertising</li><li>Bonus advertising</li></ul>

Is there any downside to media promotions?

Sometimes. If you work with, say, one radio station, it will provide much greater value for your investment if you agree not to work with any other radio stations. This could severely limit the amount of people in your target market that you can reach. In that case, you have two choices:

➤ offer paid and promotional exclusivity to the one radio station and get maximum value from it. Use other types of media to get the reach you need

➤ offer promotional exclusivity, but not sales exclusivity, explaining that in order to achieve your objectives you need greater numbers than it can deliver alone. You will probably get less value from it as a result

Eight steps of promotional media

Promotional media buying is very much the same as any other kind of marketing transaction. It's part science, part street smarts, part creative, and lots of common sense. Here are nine easy steps to make the task easier.

1 Set your objectives for media

Establish your specific goals. What are you trying to do? Know what you want to accomplish, who you want to communicate with and how much you have to spend before you begin the media-buying process.

2 Target your media correctly

As with above-the-line media, the key to success is to choose the media partner(s) who will deliver the largest portion of your target market for the least amount of money. For instance, the number-one radio station may deliver you 115 000 listeners in your target market, but you will pay to reach its total audience, which might be many times your core audience.

On the other hand, if you select a lower-rating radio station, magazine, television program, etc. where *its* core market is *your* core market, the likelihood is:

➤ you will spend less money to reach more of your core audience with less media waste

➤ its listeners/readers/viewers will be more receptive to your marketing message.

3 Understand why media run promotions

Media competition for the attention of consumers is increasing exponentially, and the fact is that most media are virtually interchangeable with others, in terms of content.

In addition to making a sale to you, most media want one or more of the following things from a media promotional opportunity:

➤ to create a point of difference from their competition through the creative use of promotions (remember, most media are competing with other very similar media for the same audience). This will attract more listeners/viewers/readers and make them more attractive for advertisers. Creative is the key word here—if it looks or sounds like every other enter-to-win promotion in the marketplace, it isn't worth anything in a media negotiation

➤ to increase the profile of their shows, personalities, stars, etc.

➤ to create new advertising vehicles or other revenue generators.

Helping media make money

There are a lot of ways that you, as an event sponsor, can help your media partners to make money, and get yourself a better promotional deal in the bargain:

* create a promotion that has room for a co-promoter and let the media partner sell this in to one of their advertisers. As long as the product is complementary to yours, and you retain perceived ownership of the promotion, this can work really well

* if you have a print partner, you could work with them to create an event handbook or program and let them sell advertising in it. This could appear in their publication (also a circulation-driver) or be available at the event, on- or in-pack, or through your trade

* if you have a television partner, you could work with them to develop a special about the event (and your role in it). Then they can sell advertising around it. This can be expensive and is not for everyone

* you can provide exclusive access to an event-related celebrity for an appearance. If they are a big enough celebrity to expand their audience, they can sell more advertising

* bring one of the other sponsors into the promotion with you so they get two buys instead of just one.

If you opt to let a media organisation bring in one or more promotional partners, be sure you have the right to approve them. You don't want to end up creating an opportunity for your competition to get involved.

4 The more creative the better

Think outside the square, push the envelope, think laterally—whatever you call it, it is about thinking creatively.

Make your promotion relevant to the audience—really think about what this audience is interested in, what they want, then give them that and more.

Make your promotion creative. Sure, everyone wants a vacation, but open any magazine and you could enter five different contests to go to a beach resort, and with discount travel packages in every newspaper, most people know that's just not that big

Broadcast media terminology

Homes Using Television (HUT)

A measure of the percentage of homes who are viewing TV at a given time.

People Using Television (PUT)

A measure of the percentage of all people who are viewing TV at a given time.

Rating

A measure (expressed as a percentage) of viewers watching TV within a specific demographic. Ratings are also called TARPs (see below).

Target Audience Rating Point (TARP)

Measure of audience level at a given time on TV. This is expressed as a percentage of the potential audience available of a given demographic.

Example: If there are 1 million adults aged between 25 and 39 in your market and 250 000 of them see your advertisement then you have reached 25% of the potential audience and the spot would have a TARP of 25.

Gross Rating Points (GRPs)

A summary of all TARPs on a TV schedule and can also be referred to as total TARPs.

---

a deal. Be sure what you offer is special—go to the extra effort to make this something that they could not do without you.

5 Involve your advertising agency

This is really your call, but we strongly suggest that you utilise the creative resources of your ad agency to ensure that what you promote to your target media is fully developed and creatively executed.

6 Negotiate for control of scheduling

Many media partnerships provide promotional schedules at their discretion. This is of absolutely no value to you. If you can't match your markets with programs and publications that deliver the ads, the sponsorship is of little value to you. It doesn't matter how many bonus ads you get, if they happen at 3.00 a.m. or during inappropriate programming, it won't work.

Negotiate for time slots in programs that consistently deliver the ratings and target market you are seeking. Negotiate for newspaper and magazine placements in sections that have proven circulation and the readership profile you need.

7 Never pay more than your volume rate

There are some media that will tell you that, since they are giving you a lot of unpaid promotion, the buy must be made at rack or casual rates, even if you are a regular advertiser who normally gets a substantial discount. This is a load of rubbish.

If you structure your promotional offer correctly, you are actually doing them a favour—you are helping them to create a strong point of difference and paying their costs to do it. You should never pay more than the rate negotiated by you or your media buyer for the paid portion of the deal.

8 Keep your ear to the ground

Make time to meet and network with people in the media industry. These people are approachable. Learn the lingo, read industry publications and use your contacts to find out about media buying. If there is a promotional media campaign that you feel has been particularly successful or innovative, contact the organisation and arrange to discuss the campaign with the relevant people.

Keep your ear to the ground on how radio, television and newspapers are performing. Listen to the radio and keep an eye out for industry trends, new programs and industry developments. Become an active media watcher. It is not possible to be good at sponsorship and not watch television, listen to commercial radio, and read newspapers.

Media promotions worksheet

 Promotions1.doc

This worksheet is designed to assist you with the planning and valuation of your promotional media campaign.

Total media budget

	Cost	Value
Television	....	....
Radio	....	....
Newspaper	....	....
Magazines	....	....
Outdoor	....	....
Total	....	....

Breakdown by media

Television

Campaign to commence X/X/XX and conclude X/X/XX.

Total cost: $XXX

Total value: $XXX

Value to cost ratio: X:1 (target between 3 and 8 to 1)

	Dates	Number
Paid spots	....	....
Bonus spots (freebies)	....	....
Promotional spots	....	....
Production	....	....
News coverage	....	....
Celebrity/on-air personality appearances	....	....

Radio

Campaign to commence X/X/XX and conclude X/X/XX.

Total cost: $XXX

Total value: $XXX

Value to cost ratio: X:1 (target between 3 and 8 to 1)

Broadcast media terminology *(Cont.)*

Often, your media plan may state that you will purchase, for example, 250 TARPs per week. This figure is an expression of GRPs and will be comprised of a number of separate advertising spots.

Impacts

Impacts are an expression of the total audience you reached in thousands. In the above example, instead of referring to the spot as delivering 25 TARPs, you would say that it delivered 250 000 impacts.

Cost Per Tarp (CPT)

The cost of reaching 1% of your audience—calculated by taking the capital cost of your advertising spot divided by the number of TARPs it delivered. In the above example, had the spot cost $10 000 the CPT would have been $400.

Average Audience

Refers to the estimated audience over a stated period of time. (You may see this for the telecast of an event you have sponsored.) The period of time can vary and the result is usually expressed in thousands.

Audience Share

This is often quoted by TV networks to express the percentage of people using television that watched the particular programme or event.

Broadcast media terminology *(Cont.)*

Remember—it only refers to the percentage of those watching any TV and not the potential of a demographic. You can have a TARP that is different to the share figure.

Reach/Coverage

Percentage of total potential audience reached over a given period of time. The schedule of 250 TARPs may have reached 50% of your potential audience.

Frequency

Refers to how many times, on average, people have seen the advertisement. Reach × frequency will equal total TARPs e.g. the schedule of 250 TARPs reaches 50% of the audience, 5 times on average (50 × 5 = 250). Frequency is often measured in 'bands'. These numbers will often be quoted as being 1+, 2+ or 3+ which refers to people who have 'been reached' one or more times, two or more times, or three or more times. Using the same example, our schedule has reached 50% of the audience 1 or more times or 50% 1+.

FTA

Free to air TV—a collective descriptor for 7, 9, 10, ABC and SBS—as opposed to Pay TV.

	Dates	Number
Paid spots	....	....
Bonus spots (freebies)	....	....
Pre-recorded promotional spots	....	....
Live liners (short, live promotions)	....	....
On-air interviews	....	....
Remote broadcast		
Celebrity/on-air personality appearances	....	....

Newspaper

Campaign to commence X/X/XX and conclude X/X/XX.

Total cost: $XXX

Total value: $XXX

Value to cost ratio: X:1 (target between 3 and 8 to 1)

	Dates	Size
➤ Paid advertising	....	....
➤ Bonus advertising (confirmed)	....	....
➤ Bonus advertising (space available)	....	....
➤ Program insertion (you supply the content)	....	....
➤ Supplement (often used as program)	....	....
➤ Advertorial coverage	....	....

Magazine

Campaign to commence X/X/XX and conclude X/X/XX.

Total cost: $XXX

Total value: $XXX

Value to cost ratio: X:1 (target between 2 and 5 to 1)

	Dates	Size
Paid advertising	....	....
Bonus advertising	....	....
Advertorial supplement	....	....
Insert	....	....
Other	....	....

Outdoor

Campaign to commence X/X/XX and conclude X/X/XX.

Total cost: $XXX

Total value: $XXX

Value to cost ratio: X:1 (target 2 to 1)

	Dates	Location
24-sheet	....	....
Supersites	....	....
Taxis	....	....
Buses—inside	....	....
Buses—outside	....	....

Sales promotions

A sales promotion is any activity for which buying (or sampling) a product is a requirement of participation. Sales promotions can be run or promoted through on-pack, in-pack, point-of-sale, point-of-purchase, media, the Internet, or through database marketing.

Most sponsorship-driven sales promotions are a simple 'enter to win' or 'buy this and go into the drawing'. They work, to some extent, but tend to really miss the point. Sponsorships are about what people care about. Hook into that, and you will connect with your audience.

Here are a few ideas. You could:

➤ connect the entry mechanism to the sponsorship (e.g. to enter a drawing having to do with a sponsorship of the Guide Dogs, you have to submit a photo of yourself and your dog)

➤ rather than a contest entry, create an event or program only accessible to people who have proofs-of-purchase

➤ if you have a prize, make it a once-in-a-lifetime kind. A vacation at a cheesy holiday resort just doesn't do it anymore.

We could go on and on, but really, what you want to do is to create something that will interest and connect with your target market, then require them to buy the product (or take a test drive, etc.) to participate. The more creative you are, and the more it is connected to the consumer's needs and wants, the better it is likely to work.

Print media terminology

Circulation
The total net paid sales of a specified publication. Most publications in Australia have their circulation independently audited.

Readership
The total number of people reading a particular publication according to a given definition. For Sunday newspapers, for example, the sample are shown a masthead and asked whether they have read or 'looked into' the paper last Sunday.

Average Issue Readership
A person who reads or 'looks into' any issue of a publication within a specified time period.

Pass on Readership
Readership of a given publication by persons other than the purchaser of that publication (also called 'Secondary Readership').

Readers Per Copy
The result of dividing an estimate of a given publication's readership by an estimate of its circulation: e.g. Circulation of 205 000, Readership of 365 000 + Readers per Copy = 1.8.

RHP
Right hand page (generally more valuable than a left hand placement).

EGN
Early general news.

Case studies: Sales promotions

DIET Coke sponsored the UK release of the movie, *Bridget Jones's Diary*, by commissioning Helen Fielding, the author of the book on which the movie is based, to write a sequel chapter. This chapter was only available in 12- and 24-can packs of Diet Coke. They supported this big idea with ticket promotions, where winners were invited to attend their local première.

CAUSE-RELATED marketing is another type of sales promotion, and Procter & Gamble have used this strategy to build their brands across both emerging and mature Asian markets. They partnered with UNICEF to create an organisation called 'Open Minds'. The overall theme is about improving the lives of children. Of course, P&G realised that would mean different things in different countries, so they gave their country managers the flexibility to select a cause that was relevant and appropriate. Once arranged, 1–2% of sales—many millions of dollars, to date—is donated to that cause, with most P&G regions instigating additional fundraising activities and many employees donating money and time to the cause. As cause-related marketing is relatively new in the region, it has created a strong point of difference for P&G products, helping them to achieve many sales and branding goals. For more information, check out www.open-minds.org.

Cross-promotions

Cross-promotion is the general term for creating a promotion in partnership with one or more other organisations that benefits all involved. These could include:

➤ sponsor cross-promotion—a cross-promotion with another sponsor of the event

➤ non-sponsor cross-promotion—a cross-promotion with an organisation that is not related to the event

➤ retail promotion—a cross-promotion with one or more retailers of your product or service.

Sponsor cross-promotion

As sponsors of the same event, you already have something in common. You are also probably interested in the same marketplace (or at least portions of the same marketplace). It makes perfect sense that sponsors can get together to create cross-promotions that support both sponsorships—saving both parties money while doubling the communication base.

It should be noted that some sponsees go to great lengths to keep their sponsors apart, afraid that they will compare notes on benefits and costs. Do not let this deter you. If the sponsee will not facilitate a meeting, go directly to the other sponsor. After all, if your investments work better, you are more likely to remain sponsors, and the sponsee needs to recognise that.

In order to create a cross-promotion with another sponsor, you both need to be quite open about your sponsorship. We suggest you both provide the following information at the initial meeting:

➤ scope of your sponsorship (in general terms, and usually leaving out your expenditure)

➤ your target markets

➤ your objectives for the sponsorship

➤ any sponsorship-driven activity that has already been planned.

The more your target markets and objectives are matched, the more likely it is that a good cross-promotion will result.

Once you have shared this information, you can either brainstorm ways that you can work together, or you can simply put forward a proposal for discussion.

Cross-promoting with non-sponsors

Sometimes it makes sense to develop cross-promotions with companies outside of the circle of event sponsors. Going this way provides you with a lot of freedom in selecting your cross-promotional partners and can gain some excellent results. You must, however, be aware of some potential areas for conflict:

➤ non-sponsors can use cross-promotions as a means for ambushing their competition, such as Adidas partnering with event sponsor Powerade, when Nike is among the other event sponsors. The deal may be a great idea, and your intentions may be honourable, but you could be caught up in controversy. Some companies don't care about controversy, but if yours does, be careful

➤ sponsees can also get touchy about cross-promotions with non-sponsors, as they may believe that the non-sponsor is getting the benefits of sponsorship without paying a fee. Do two things: check your contract to ensure that you are not specifically prohibited from doing this type of promotion, and be sure that the benefits delivered to the sponsee through the cross-promotion are greater than their perceived loss

➤ media can also be a problem. If an event has an official media partner, and you do a media promotion with a competitor, there are likely to be some noses out of joint, although that rarely stops it from happening.

Retail cross-promotions

Involving your retailers and/or distribution system is often a key element in fully

Retailers are more
concerned with
store traffic than
selling your
product.

maximised sponsorship programs. Retail cross-promotion can add weight to other sales promotional activity and can serve to communicate the marketing message powerfully at the point of purchase.

On the side of the retailer, a powerful cross-promotion can serve to drive store traffic and sales, as well as to create a point of difference from the competition. In order to achieve this for the retailer, you must be willing to share perceived ownership of all or part of your sponsorship. You will also have much better success at selling in this concept if a component of the sponsorship program actually takes place at their premises, such as celebrity appearances, events, registrations, etc. Also effective can be providing the retailer with naming rights or presenting sponsorship of a sub-event.

Exclusive or non-exclusive?

Due to the fact that retailers are usually looking for a point of difference from their competitors, it is much more likely that you will achieve a successful retail cross-promotion if you work exclusively with one retailer.

It is not impossible to work with multiple retailers, but their level of support will probably be lower. In this case, it is usually more effective to create a retailer incentive program around a sales promotion instead.

Accessing retail promotional funds

Often, a manufacturer or service provider will provide its larger retailers with promotional funding, such as case allowances. These funds are to be used by the retailers to promote the product in conjunction with their stores. Unfortunately, most of the time the funds lie dormant in a bank account and are never used for the intended activity.

Accessing these accumulated funds to augment sponsorship is an art form in highly developed markets, such as the US and parts of Europe, but is just starting in many other markets.

The key to accessing these funds is to create a retail cross-promotion where the retailer takes a great degree of ownership of the program and pride in their involvement. When it comes to how they will pay for their involvement, you can then point out that this type of activity qualifies for use of promotional funds that have already been provided to them by your company, effectively costing the retailer nothing.

Trade promotions

Running a trade promotion is really about one thing: sales. It is about incenting your trade to do the things that lead to selling more of your product. There is any number of ways to do this, including:

- ➤ sponsorship-driven incentives based upon incremental sales, wholesale commitments, specials, displays, and/or use of in-store merchandising
- ➤ in-store activities, such as celebrity appearances or other sponsorship-driven activities
- ➤ entries into a contest for bigger prizes based upon incremental sales, wholesale commitments, specials, displays, and/or use of in-store merchandising
- ➤ display contests for sponsorship-driven prizes
- ➤ providing the trade with a sponsorship of a portion of the event.

Case study: Oscar Mayer Rookie League

Many years ago, we had the opportunity to work on this very effective sponsorship, and even now, we believe that it demonstrates some of the best thinking in trade promotions that we have seen.

Oscar Mayer, an American manufacturer of hot dogs and lunch meat, had a long association with baseball and wanted to do two things: create more grassroots impact among kids and their mothers; and create real promotional buy-in by key individual retailers.

They identified the Rookie League concept as a real winner. Similar to Little League, Rookie League was a baseball league for pre-teens, with one major difference. At that age, pitching is a problem. Either the pitcher is so good no one can get a hit, or he is so inaccurate that no one can get a hit. Another problem was that kids with less apparent ability were being stuck in positions where they had few chances to participate. So, Rookie League replaced the pitcher with a pitching machine and rotated positions every inning. It was a hit with both parents and kids.

Selling the Oscar Mayer Rookie League to retailers was easier than anticipated. Individual stores were each 'given' a team in their local area. The teams were provided with store logo branded uniforms and the store was provided with a big team photo, merchandising material, and a faxed weekly update of team results. The stores got right into it, proudly displaying the team photo in the stores. Some of them even hosted barbecues and fundraisers for their teams. The key for Oscar Mayer, however, was the displays. Their products had increased displays, prominence, and specials in virtually every store, resulting in unprecedented incremental sales for the season.

Oscar Mayer was ahead of their time in addressing the functional and emotional needs of both their consumer and trade markets, and reaped the benefits.

Hospitality

Think about this for a minute . . . All those people that you invite to your hospitality events, how many of your competitors are inviting them to the same or similar events? How many companies in other categories are trying to schmooze those same VIPs? And how different is your hospitality experience to any of the others?

Chances are that your key customers and VIPs are also a lot of other companies', and they get invited to more events, receptions, launches, and skyboxes than they can

> Don't bore your trade with the same old hospitality activities.

Your key
customers are
people, not
companies.

shake a stick at. The answer is not to stop doing hospitality, but to do it better than anyone else. The answer is to stop thinking 'this is how hospitality is done' and to start thinking about what these people—and they are people, not companies—really want and try to incorporate those things into your hospitality program.

➤ Do they want to spend quality time with their families?

➤ Do they want to spend time with their heroes and get autographs and photos?

➤ Do they want a once-in-a-lifetime experience?

➤ Do they want to participate in the event in some way? Do their kids/grandkids?

➤ Do they like special merchandise?

➤ Would they rather do something big and wonderful once or twice a year, or be invited to something smaller several times a year?

Whatever you do, make it special. Take the extra time, spend the extra money, but make your hospitality program stand apart from other companies. If you don't, you run the risk of becoming just another free ticket to something.

Case studies: Hospitality

THE Discovery Channel, a major sponsor of the Panda exhibition at the Washington National Zoo, realised that, in order to capture the attention of their key corporate clients and contacts, they would have to offer something really different in the way of hospitality. They realised that what these busy corporate executives needed was more quality time with their families, so The Discovery Channel arranged for these clients and their families to have a unique behind the scenes Panda viewing, complete with special children's activities.

ONE large building products company used their sponsorship of the country's elite Institute of Sport to entertain their key clients in a way that was the exact opposite of how most VIP programs are run. They flew their clients to the Institute, where they partook in two days of fitness and health testing, as well as top-level training in a variety of sports. The clients enjoyed being trained by the best in the country, something none of their other suppliers had done for them.

Public relations

Public relations is often an important part of sponsorship programs and is an art form all of its own. We offer the following suggestions:

➤ do not focus on your logo or your name, focus on getting your marketing message to your target market

➤ understand that all media are not equal. One spread in a national magazine could be worth dozens of smaller placements, and a photo showing your logo is worth much less than one that actively promotes your marketing message

➤ do not rely on the sponsee's public relations program to do the job for you. It may or may not be able to add value to your program through PR, but often even the best intentions register barely a blip in media. Design and run your own program for your target market

➤ do not rely on a press release to get your story picked up. You have access to all the interest that a sponsorship can bring: use it and use it creatively.

New product launch

Sponsorship can be an extremely powerful way to launch a new product or launch an existing product to a new target market. If you select an appropriate sponsorship, there are numerous ways in which you can make that product more relevant to your target market:

➤ hold the media launch at the event. You will have a built-in audience and increased interest and relevance, making it more media-worthy

➤ do product sampling, demonstration, or display at the event

➤ host a trade launch event around the event, introducing it to your key trade in style and providing them with a 'what money can't buy' experience while you're at it

➤ create a sales promotion, driving consumers to try the product in exchange for event-inspired benefits

➤ create a trade promotion that provides event-driven incentives for the trade to provide displays, shelf space, and/or promotion for your product

➤ develop a database of potential consumers

➤ conduct research using the attendees.

Case studies: New product launch

IN 2000, American Express launched the Blue Card in the United States. The Blue Card is a 'smart' credit card aimed at the younger, technology savvy consumer. American Express chose a Cheryl Crow concert in Central Park, New York City, for the launch of the new card, selling advance tickets exclusively to new Blue Card holders. The concert sold out in three hours. Blue was launched as the hip, 'have to have' credit card.

DISCOUNT retailer, Target, is a major sponsor of the Washington Monument's restoration project in Washington DC. To coincide with the launch of its new Michael Graves housewares line, Target commissioned internationally-renowned designer Michael Graves to design the illuminated scaffolding system that will surround the monument throughout the two-year restoration project. Sponsorship of the reconstruction project ensures Target of a national platform for promotions while indirectly promoting Target's newest line of housewares.

WHEN Labatt Ice beer was launched in the UK, gaining credibility with the 18–21 year old urban groover target market was going to be critical. Research showed that their favoured charity was the Terence Higgins Trust, so Lebatt sponsored major club events across the UK, raising money for the AIDS charity through beer, merchandise, and ticket sales. As the cause is so relevant to this group and the brewer guaranteed a minimum donation of £40,000, a number of key celebrities jumped on board to endorse the beer, giving the brand even more appeal to this hard-to-target audience.

Employees

As powerful as sponsorship can be for communicating with consumers, it can be just as powerful for communicating with your employee base. It can help you to increase their knowledge, improve morale, increase productivity, or add value to the people who make your company what it is. Within a larger sponsorship portfolio, it is not above the realm of possibility to select a sponsorship specifically to achieve employee-based objectives.

When looking at promoting your sponsorships internally, be sure to think about what is important to your employees. If involving their families in an employee promotion will net better results, then do it. There are no hard and fast rules here.

Some suggestions:

➤ merchandising, usually done to employees at cost

➤ employee perks (merchandise, tickets, appearances, etc.)

➤ product knowledge programs

➤ incentive programs

➤ volunteer programs, creating fun ways for your employees to become materially involved in the sponsorship

> a contest for an employee to travel to a major event to be the company 'representative'
> family day at the event, where employees and their families get to go for free
> entertainment, exhibition, or celebrity appearance at your site
> involving employees in sponsorship-driven advertising or PR.

Let the employees choose?

Some companies involve their employees in the actual selection of one or more of their sponsorships, giving them a range to choose from and then adopting the top one (or several). This creates a great deal of ownership of the sponsorship by employees, who will then be especially receptive to communication built around it. This is particularly effective around the sponsorship of causes.

Case study: Australia Post

Australia Post was a sponsor of the 1996 Australian Olympic Team, competing in Atlanta, and, in addition to a number of consumer and business activities, used this sponsorship to anchor several staff initiatives, including:

* product knowledge competition—Australia Post had introduced a number of products to compete with new expedited delivery entrants to the marketplace, but soon realised that a lot of their employees didn't fully understand the new products. This competition raised the level of product understanding, requiring a perfect score for an entry to go into a draw for a trip to the Atlanta Games. Product knowledge rose by over 60% as a direct result of this promotion

* Olympic Postie competition—with hundreds of athletes at the Games, there would be a lot of fan mail to deliver to them. Australia Post held a competition to search for the ultimate Postie, who would have the honour of representing the company in Atlanta. Entrants had to demonstrate both outstanding knowledge of and patriotism for both Australia and Australia Post

* merchandise—Australia Post partnered with Team sponsor Adidas to produce a line of authentic athletic wear—much of it the same as the Team would wear—that carried the Australia Post logo along with the Australian flag and Olympic Rings. This merchandise was offered at wholesale price to Australia Post employees, who purchased hundreds of thousands of dollars worth in the lead-up to the Games

* Olympic Job Opportunity Program—in addition to sponsoring the Team, Australia Post also employed twelve high-profile Team members, providing them with an income and flexible hours in the lead-up to Atlanta. They had all kinds of jobs. Some even delivered mail! In addition to the promotional opportunities created by this program, having these athletes employed alongside the regular workforce was a real morale-builder. They also won six medals—two gold, two silver, and two bronze.

An employee survey showed that the impact of this sponsorship on their performance and commitment to their jobs was at least 15 points higher on every aspect than for Australia Post's sponsorship of the 1992 Olympic Team. The Olympic Postie delivered 250 000 pieces of mail to Australian athletes in Atlanta.

Shareholders

Shareholders are increasingly factoring into maximisation programs, with many companies using sponsorship to communicate with and add value to them. How or if you decide to use this option will depend upon a number of things, including:

➤ the number, size, and longevity of your shareholders

➤ shareholder confidence

➤ the ease with which you can communicate with them

➤ whether stockholders are focused on something else (e.g. a takeover).

Cross-pollination

Finally, we have cross-pollination. Cross-pollination is when a sponsor uses two of their sponsorship investments together to create something that is more effective, interesting, or newsworthy, such as:

➤ running a promotion driven by a non-cause sponsorship, with the financial beneficiary being a cause that you also sponsor

➤ having an athlete or other celebrity from one of your sponsorships as a spokesperson or participant in another.

These are the two most common ways of doing cross-pollination, but they are by no means the only ways. Use your imagination. Put a hockey team together with a flower show. Put a motor racing team with an art gallery. If it will interest your marketplace, do it.

Case studies: Cross-pollination

PEARL Vision used cross-pollination to great effect when they sponsored the American tour of *The Buddy Holly Story*. Already a great fit with both their target market and their product (who could forget Buddy's glasses!), they decided to make it even more relevant by involving one of their other sponsorships, New Eyes for the Needy. In addition to a number of other promotions, they offered consumers discount tickets to the show when they donated their old glasses at their stores.

DOG food manufacturer, Alpo, sponsors Operation Bass, North America's largest fishing tournament group, because of the strong connection between fishing and dog ownership. They extend the reach to families by running fishing-themed carnivals at local Wal-Marts during tour stops. During these carnivals, they also involve another of their

programs, the Great Dog Connection, a project that works with local animal shelters to place homeless pets with families.

MAJOR American retailer, Sears, brought together two of their major sponsorships, the WNBA and the National Alliance of Breast Cancer Organisations, to create an on-going program of breast cancer awareness and prevention. The basketball players create interest for younger women at a time when they need to learn about this disease, while Sears anchors a cause-related marketing campaign to raise money for NABCO.

GENERAL Mills puts a lot of stock in cross-pollinating. Their sponsorship of the LPGA included a major cross promotion with another of their sponsees, the American Heart Association, while their sponsorship of a NASCAR team also promotes their Boxtops for Education initiative.

Keeping a sponsorship fresh

Sponsorships, like most other things, have a natural lifecycle (see Figure 9.1). It has now been widely accepted that it takes around three years before a sponsorship delivers maximum returns. Before that, it may be delivering well on objectives, but it takes a bit of time for a sponsorship to develop a life of its own.

At around seven years, a sponsorship will generally start to decline. This is not necessarily the death knell for the relationship. It may be time to move on, but if the sponsorship is still relevant to your target market, you might be better off simply restructuring your approach to freshen it up.

Figure 9.1 Sponsorship's natural lifecycle

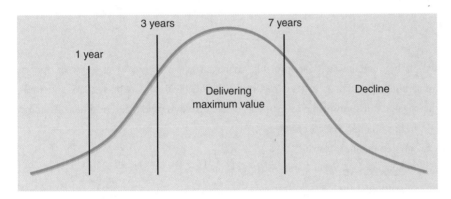

The simplest way to freshen up a sponsorship is to go right back to the drawing board. Go at it as if it was a brand new sponsorship, using your team to create entirely new ways to use it to achieve your objectives.

Take this step before the sponsorship goes into decline. Freshen up your sponsorships while they are still going strong. Preventing a sponsorship from declining is far easier than resuscitating it once it is failing.

Shifting needs

Just as you should negotiate for shifting needs, you also need to maximise for shifting needs. Your objectives might change from time to time, particularly as a brand moves through its own lifecycle. If you see that your sponsorship activities are no longer meeting your goals, it's time for a rethink.

Chapter 10

Sponsorship management

We know, we know . . . sponsorship management isn't nearly as sexy or fun as maximisation, but it is just as important. Luckily, with the right systems and tools, managing your sponsorship investments doesn't have to be difficult or time consuming.

In this chapter, we cover:

➤ implementation plans

➤ managing your relationship with the sponsee

➤ reporting

➤ managing subcontractors.

Implementation plan

Implementing a sponsorship, and all the associated leverage activities, will be made infinitely simpler if you have a plan of action.

The Implementation Plan defines what you and the sponsee want to achieve and how you are going to manage the sponsorship. Every sponsorship, regardless of its size or value, requires its own plan. It does not have to be a tome, but every plan should include:

➤ an overview

➤ a situation analysis

➤ a list of objectives

➤ strategies to meet those objectives

➤ objective-based performance indicators that will be used to measure the success of those strategies (work with your team to determine these)

➤ target markets

Objectives must be SMART—Specific, Measurable, Achievable, Results-oriented, and Time-bound.

➤ action list/timeline/accountability

➤ budget

➤ an evaluation strategy.

We have included an Implementation Plan template to get you started.

Implementation plan template

 Implementation1.doc

Overview

In the overview, include details on the overall aims and objectives of the sponsorship Implementation Plan. Briefly outline the strategies that will be undertaken to meet the objectives.

Situational analysis

In the situational analysis, give a brief overview of where the sponsorship is at in its contract (e.g. *year 2 of a three-year commitment*), who the key contacts are, and any major issues that might affect the sponsorship.

If the sponsorship is ongoing, outline the past history of the sponsorship, as well as recommendations and tactics that will be undertaken to improve and refocus the sponsorship.

Sponsorship objectives

In dot points, detail the objectives of the sponsorship. Objectives must be SMART—**S**pecific, **M**easurable, **A**chievable, **R**esults-oriented, and **T**ime-bound. A detailed list will assist both you and the sponsee to keep tabs on the marketing opportunities available.

Target audiences

Who are you trying to reach with this sponsorship? Who will it affect? Your list might include staff, target markets, the sponsee organisation and its members/fans/database, your senior management, media, and ticketholders.

Sponsorship benefits

Include a list of all benefits that have been included in the sponsorship contract, as well as a list of other benefits that have been agreed to verbally or in writing.

Evaluation

The sponsee and you should work together to determine how you will measure the success of the sponsorship program. Detail how the sponsorship will be evaluated against objectives and how the sponsee relationship will be evaluated.

Action list

Detail every leverage activity, event, key date, report, meeting and every aspect of the provision of benefits and information you have been promised. Next to each item, indicate the timeframe and person responsible.

Budget

Indicate all costs, above and beyond the already budgeted marketing activities, that are required to make this sponsorship happen. Be sure to cost management of the sponsorship, as well. Time is money.

Managing the relationship

Although sponsees are generally getting much more professional in the way they do business, you will probably still find yourself managing the process at one time or another. The following should help.

Sponsor Information Kit

In your first meeting with the sponsee once the contract is signed, we suggest you provide a kit to them, which contains the following items:

➤ details and an overview of responsibilities for all key contacts, including after-hours contacts if any part of the event takes place outside of normal working hours

➤ a restatement of your objectives for this sponsorship, your target markets, core brand values, etc. You might find it easiest to provide them simply with your Implementation Plan, however you should omit financial and other confidential details

➤ how the sponsorship and sponsee performance will be evaluated

➤ a template for written sponsee reports, showing the information you need, as well as the dates and format in which you want to receive them (i.e. by e-mail on the first of every month). A Reporting Template is attached

➤ artwork, including any guidelines, PMS colours, etc.—bromides and on disk

➤ any other information or materials that will streamline the sponsorship process.

Exchanging information kits can save a lot of headaches later.

Sponsee Information Kit

We also suggest you request a Sponsee Information Kit from your partners, including:

➤ their plan for implementing your sponsorship (they should have one)

➤ contact details and an overview of responsibilities for all key contacts, including after hours details

➤ key dates and deadlines

➤ updated list of sponsors and media partners, including their contact details

➤ all parameters for materials (ad and banner sizes, colours, etc.)

➤ artwork, including any guidelines, PMS colours, etc.—bromides and on disk.

Regular meetings

No, having a beer with a sponsee in the skybox does not count! You need to hold regular meetings with the sponsee from inception of the contract right through to the conclusion. This will ensure that the sponsee is aware of your situation and goals at all times, and keeps you on top of developments, opportunities, and potential trouble spots.

As for timing, we find bi-weekly meetings to be very beneficial. Under no circumstances should you go longer than a month between meetings.

Written updates

If you only have time to meet monthly, then you should definitely request a mid-month written update from your sponsee—just a concise report of where the sponsorship is, noting anything that is currently outstanding. Tell the sponsee from the outset the information you will need, so there is no confusion.

We have provided a simple Reporting Template that you can provide to sponsees. It will help guide them in the preparation of their monthly reports, so that they provide the information that is important to you.

Put everything in writing

This is important. If it is in writing, then there is no excuse if something does not get done, addressed, or checked.

Every time you meet, someone needs to take notes and confirm all action items, including responsibilities and timelines, in writing. When you talk on the phone, fire up your e-mail while you are still on the line so you can quickly send an e-mail confirming your conversation.

Also, if something needs doing between meetings (and it always does), be sure to put that in writing as well. It does not need to be formal, just a quick fax or e-mail will do.

> Having a beer in the skybox is not a meeting.

Education

Even though keeping sponsees' skills up to date isn't your responsibility, assisting them in this area is clearly in your best interest.

We have recently seen a number of companies invest a small amount of time and money in training for their sponsees, with terrific results. In addition to clarifying what is expected of the sponsees as partners, the skills imparted tend to change the entire flavour of the relationship. The sponsorship becomes more objective-oriented, more partnership-oriented, and as a result, far more fruitful.

Finally, increasing a sponsee's expertise will help them to secure, retain, and have better relationships with other sponsors. As these are virtually always major challenges for sponsees, making an investment that will help them to achieve their larger objectives will add a great deal of value to your relationship.

> Investing in sponsee education is a high leverage activity.

Reporting template

 Report1.doc

[Sponsorship name]

Report date:	
Report period:	
Report prepared by:	

Contracted benefits provided to [*sponsor*] during the month of [*previous month*]:

Added-value benefits provided to [*sponsor*] during the month of [*previous month*]:

Overview of activities to be undertaken by [*sponsee*] during the month of [*upcoming month*]:

Cash payments or contra to be provided during the month of [*next month*]:

Key dates, meetings, and activities for upcoming month(s):

Opportunities/issues to address:

Subcontractors

While many sponsorships can be fully managed and implemented in-house, there are likely to be times when you will bring in or involve outside help. Managing subcontractors can be very easy, and it can be very hard. Your best bet for getting a good result with a minimum of headaches is to do the following:

➤ provide a strong brief at the beginning of the relationship

➤ include them on your Sponsorship Team for any pertinent meetings

➤ give them a copy of your Implementation Plan

➤ be sure they get copies of any reports provided by the sponsee

➤ keep them in the loop if anything changes.

We have attached a Subcontractor Brief template. This is an example of the type of information you should provide to a subcontractor early in the relationship. It can also be very useful as a tender document for competitive pitching. The template shows a publicity brief, but this is only an example. This template could be modified to reflect a number of different types of subcontractors or agencies.

Subcontractor brief template

 Subcontractor1.doc

I. Objectives

A. Strong media relations campaign that communicates the brand message of [*message*] around the launch of [*sponsor's*] sponsorship of [*event*]

B. Coverage across all media, with emphases on the following areas:

1. [*List target markets–be specific*]

2.

3.

C. Close contact with media to ensure the best possible coverage and story angles

II. Guidelines of operation

A. Your responsibilities for the media launch are:

1. Creating, mounting, and tracking a top-quality publicity campaign across all media

2. Working with [*sponsor/advertising agency/other*] to create an effective media kit

3. Producing all creative input and administrating the media launch to the following rough guidelines:

Timing: XXX

Location: XXX

Theme: XXX

Featuring: [*athletes/artists/politicians/other*]

4. Developing a guest list and invitations (in conjunction with the above). Invitees will include:

    (a)   Media

    (b)   Major customers

    (c)   Cross-section of [*sponsor*] staff

    (d)   Event VIPs [*athletes, artists, representatives, etc.—be specific*]

    (e)   Politicians [*be specific*]

5. Co-ordinating photo opportunities, interviews, and other special requests as they pertain to publicity

6. Full and accurate accounting of expenses and fees

B. Timetable

1. Preliminary publicity plan to [*sponsor*] by [*date*]

2. [*Sponsor contact*] to open lines of communication between publicist and sponsee when publicity plan is approved

3. [*Date*], publicist to enact publicity plan and begin campaign (to magazines, television, and other alternative media that need longer lead times)

4. The launch is planned for [*date, time*]

C. Communications

1. We will expect weekly updates on publicity progress, including a list of placements, confirmation of clips, and responses to invitations

2. We will include [*publicist*] on all pertinent sponsorship communications

3. Specific requests for information, both ways, should be put in writing

III. [*Sponsor*] resources

A. Information available:

1. Implementation Plan

2. Biographies of all VIP athletes

3. Examples of 2001 tour materials

4. Background on [*sponsee*]

5. Budget

B. Information to be confirmed:

1. Athletes available for launch

2. Clients/staff to be invited

   C. Materials currently available:

      1. Sponsorship artwork

      2. Above-the-line ads

      3. Logo artworks

      4. Photos of VIP athletes in action

      5. Video portraits of VIP athletes

      6. [Sponsor] and [sponsorship specific] banners

   D. Materials in development:

      1. Web site

   E. The sponsorship team:

      Although there are many other people involved in this sponsorship, these are the key contacts:

      1. [Name, title, company]. [Specific responsibility]. [Phone/fax/e-mail].

      2. [Name, title, company]. [Specific responsibility]. [Phone/fax/e-mail].

IV. Celebrities available

      1. [List all talent available]

      2.

      3.

      4.

V. Budget

There will be an absolute ceiling of [budget] for all costs associated with this campaign, which cannot be overrun.

If an opportunity exists to extend the impact of the sponsorship through additional publicity activities, these will be discussed and approved before authorising any additional expenditure.

VI. Evaluation will be based on:

   A. Weight of the campaign and effectiveness in communicating our marketing message

   B. Impact and innovative style of media launch

   C. Management process and communication

VII. SOURCE

   [Name, title, company, details, phone, fax, e-mail]

Chapter 11

Salvaging a bad situation

The move toward multi-year sponsorship contracts has been, on the whole, very positive. But, one of the most challenging things about sponsorship now is that if you decide an investment isn't working for you and it's not going to, you might be stuck with it for another couple of years. If this is the case, you have a few choices. You can:

➤ renegotiate

➤ make your benefits work harder

➤ on-sell benefits

➤ stop throwing good money after bad.

Renegotiate

> **Most sponsees are open to renegotiation.**

If a sponsorship is well enough matched that it could achieve a lot more strategically than it is, but the menu of benefits negotiated is inappropriate, it's time for renegotiation. Sponsees are usually far more receptive to renegotiation that you would think. They want your sponsorship to work, because if it works, then you will renew and their lives will be easier and their income more stable.

Our suggestion is to approach this problem as you would a first-time negotiation and hold a workshop with the sponsee. See Workshopping on page 93.

In order of desirability, these are the three ways you can renegotiate benefits:

1. Trade benefits that are not required for more appropriate benefits.

2. Upgrade the benefits in return for an increase in contra.

3. Upgrade the benefits at extra cash cost.

Making benefits work harder

If you've got a stack of benefits that aren't providing much value, and the sponsee isn't open to renegotiation, you could get your existing benefits to work harder. This really only works if the audience is right, although the event's positioning doesn't have to be perfect.

IF YOU HAVE THIS . . .	YOU COULD USE IT LIKE THIS . . .
An overabundance of signage and logo exposure	* Incorporate a marketing message, so that every time someone sees the logo, they understand your brand and its positioning better * Provide some or all of these benefits to a retailer, key customer, trade, or other VIP partner. You may not need awareness, but they might. You could also give them away as part of a trade incentive program
A hospitality box that you have a hard time filling and/or it's exactly the same experience as all of your competitors' boxes.	* Make the box a unique experience through theming, celebrity appearances, etc. * Invite your VIPs with their children * Use it as a prize in a consumer drawing, contest, or other promotion * Provide it (on occasion) to key customers, retailers, trade, or other VIP partners so they can entertain their customers
Participation in a media launch that is unlikely to be newsworthy	* Use your other sponsorships to get one or more athletes, artists, or other newsworthy people to the event on your behalf. It doesn't matter if they don't quite 'fit' with the event—that often makes it even more newsworthy
As part of your larger, appropriate sponsorship, you also receive sponsorship of a smaller sub-event, and it's either a dud or not a good fit	* Provide this sub-event sponsorship to a VIP partner that is a more appropriate sponsor * Totally rework the event so that it is more appropriate/interesting/fun * Cross-pollinate it with another of your sponsorships to create something that captures the imagination of your audience

On-selling benefits

If you are stuck with an event that is completely wrong for your brand, and the sponsorship has more than a year or two to go, one of the best options can be to on-sell some or all of the benefits to another company. Most sponsees are relatively open to this, so long as you agree not to bring in a company that conflicts with an existing sponsor, and they get to approve it before the sale.

Leveraging a bad
sponsorship is
never a good idea.

Stop throwing good money after bad

If the sponsorship is all wrong for you and none of the other options are open, by all means, stop throwing good money after bad! Do not maximise it. Do not waste any time on it. Do not promote it in any way. If you do, you will simply be pushing your brand away from its strategic course.

This is a hard choice, but one that should be used more than it is. Many companies believe that if they have a sponsorship, they are duty bound to leverage it in some way. If the sponsorship is strong, of course it should be maximised. If, however, the sponsorship is an unfortunate hangover of a previous bad decision, just leave it alone.

Chapter 12

Quantification

Companies have tried almost everything to effectively quantify the results of their sponsorships—from counting dollars to assigning points. None of these methods has ever proved to be wholly satisfactory because they are either too subjective or they are measuring the mechanisms, such as media coverage, rather than the results.

Defining objectives

Objective-based quantification is the most useful trend for quantification since sponsorship began. The basis of this type of quantification is that it's all about objectives, and if your objectives are SMART (Specific, Measurable, Achievable, Results-oriented, and Time-bound), they should be quantifiable.

Each objective should be laid out specifically.

Not

1. Increase sales
2. Develop database
3. Gain publicity
4. Demonstrate 'good corporate citizenship'

Instead

1. Create incremental sales of 10% over the benchmark of $240 000 per week during the six-week promotional period, as determined by retailer case commitments.
2. Develop a database of no fewer than 2500 qualified prospects, as determined by salary level, age range, professional status, and current insurance products owned. A profile of acceptable ranges is attached.
3. Gain a minimum of 10 high-level and 15 medium-level publicity placements, as determined by the Media Evaluation Model, over the six-week promotional period. An overview of the target market indicators and marketing messages is attached.

4. Increase over the six-month promotional period: (a) public opinion on our company's professionalism (from 45% positive to 64%), (b) commitment to Canada (from 12% to 35%), and (c) propensity to buy (from 22% to 36%), as determined by responses to our annual public opinion survey. A profile of the target markets is attached.

Your Sponsorship Team is your best resource for both developing objectives and quantifying results against them.

Once the objectives have been fully developed, the question you must ask yourself and your Sponsorship Team is, 'If these objectives are achieved, will you consider this sponsorship to have been a success?' If the answer is no, then the objectives need to be further developed or extended.

Generally speaking, fully developed objectives not only quantify key aspects of the sponsorship, but are indicative of wider success across all of the much more difficult to quantify areas.

Quantification mechanisms

Below, we have outlined a number of quantification mechanisms. This is just a sample, because your company will no doubt have its own mechanisms in a number of areas.

➤ Sales—new customer, loyalty sales, incremental sales, up-selling
  • Retail figures
  • Scanner data
  • Case commitments
  • Sales promotion participation
  • On-site sales
  • Coupon redemptions
  • Profit margins

➤ Target market perceptions/behaviour
  • Quantitative research (against benchmarks)
  • Qualitative research (against benchmarks)

➤ Database/loyalty marketing
  • Number and quality of people joining the database
  • Loyalty activity
  • Sales promotion participation
  • Participation in added-value programs
  • Merchandising

➤ Internet
- Participation in e-promotions
- Participation in Web events
- Number of e-coupons downloaded
- Number of e-coupons redeemed
- Number and quality of site member registrations
- Hits
- Click-throughs
- Time spent on site

➤ Media
- Number and quality of media placements
- Media promotion of marketing message

➤ Sponsorship impact
- Entrance/exit surveys
- Target market surveys

➤ Employees
- Product-knowledge contest results
- Incentive program results
- Awareness and attitude surveys
- Merchandise program sales

➤ Key customers
- Incentive program results—long and short term
- Relationship-building opportunities

➤ Retailers
- Number and quality of retail displays
- Number of newspaper specials
- Preference/attitude surveys
- Relationship-building opportunities
- See 'Sales', above

Media evaluation

Although we are strongly in favour of evaluating results rather than mechanisms whenever possible, public relations is one of those areas where evaluating the mechanism can be helpful in refining and targeting the message.

There are literally dozens of ways to evaluate the results of your sponsorship-driven publicity campaign. Some organisations equate logo time or space in unpaid media coverage to the same amount of time or space at commercial rates. Often a sponsor will multiply that figure by 5–30% to gain a figure that is more representative of the true impact. Some sponsees literally collect a stack of clippings, whether they have anything to do with the actual sponsorship or not, and then present them to the sponsor without realising that few of them are of any value.

What we have come up with is a Media Evaluation Model that brings unpaid media coverage straight back to objectives. Each piece of media coverage is rated based on the two major criteria for sponsorship success:

➤   the success in communicating the sponsor's marketing message(s)

➤   the success in reaching the target market(s).

This means that you must tell the sponsee exactly what you are trying to communicate and who exactly you are trying to reach with this message. Discuss this upfront with the sponsee.

Each aspect is rated on a scale of 0–10. The levels at which each score is reached must be determined and agreed with the sponsor prior to commencing the sponsorship. We often use the following.

Marketing message

0 = No mention of the sponsor whatsoever (it doesn't matter *how* good the coverage of the sponsee)

4 = *Maximum* number allocated to logo exposure or simple sponsor mention (it will usually be lower)

6 = *Minimum* number allocated to communication of the sponsor's marketing message

Target markets

This will be based upon the portion of the defined target marketplace that is reached with that communication. Keep in mind that if an article, for instance, appears in a publication that reaches only 5000 people, but they represent 80% of your target audience, that is more valuable than an article appearing in a mass market newspaper that reaches only 15% of your marketplace.

Given this, we suggest that one way of determining a score for Target Markets will be to give 1–2 points for each 10% of your total target market reached.

Plotting the results

When you multiply the scores for each result, anything that scores under 16 total should be considered to be of little or no value to your brand. Anything that scores between 16 and 36 is of medium value. And, anything that scores above 36 should be considered to be of high value to your brand.

This can be graphically represented on a chart, which will look something like Figure 12.1.

Figure 12.1 Plotting relative media values

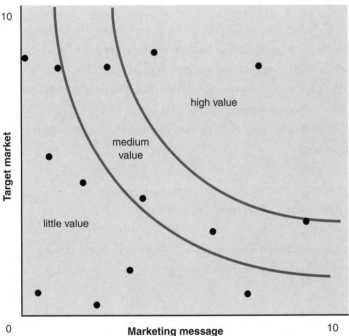

So . . . what's a 100?

Let's say that a milk bottler for a local area sponsors the local football team. The marketing message is 'Milk for Health & Fitness'. The marketplace is demographically wide, but geographically targeted. Imagine after a particularly great game, the local daily newspaper runs a front-page photo of a great tackle with the milk bottler's logo clearly shown, and the headline, 'They Must Be Drinking Their Milk'. That is a 100.

Chapter 13

Portfolio management

It would be wonderful to think that, if you put in the effort to make all of your sponsorships deliver 100%, your portfolio would be as good as it can be. Unfortunately, this isn't always the case. Sponsorship portfolios need management as a whole, not just as a collection of individual sponsorships.

There are a number of activities that you must undertake to be sure your portfolio is performing to its best:

➤ auditing

➤ balancing

➤ identifying opportunities for umbrella sponsorships

➤ information sharing.

In addition, you need to know how to exit a sponsorship that isn't working for you so that any potential downside is minimised.

Auditing

An audit looks at each of your sponsorships individually, assessing a number of things, including:

➤ Is the sponsorship, and specific benefits, provided appropriate for brand and target market needs?

➤ Is it fully maximised and delivering against objectives? If not, what would it take to make it work?

➤ Are your internal stakeholders interested and bought in?

➤ Is it cost and time effective to implement?

The audit is often the first place we start when assessing a company's sponsorship situation, and should be incorporated into your Sponsorship Strategy.

There are three rules to follow when you carry out a sponsorship audit.

1. It must be consistent

The same criteria must be applied to every investment, regardless of type. You will need a tool that is both stringent and flexible, understanding that different sponsorships have different objectives.

Our favourite tool for carrying out an audit is the Evaluation Checklist found way back in Chapter 6. Even though this tool was designed primarily for evaluating new opportunities, it is also an excellent and objective tool for evaluating existing investments.

2. It must be ruthless

This is no time for sentimentality. Your job is to achieve marketing objectives, not to waste money being nice. (There are, however, nice ways to exit a sponsorship—see our suggestions coming up later in this chapter.) And, just think about all of the fantastic things that you could do with the money and time freed up by getting rid of your unproductive sponsorships.

3. It must be fair

If a sponsorship isn't delivering and never has, before you drop it, look hard in the mirror. Is it a bad fit? Or has your company or brand let the opportunity languish? In many cases, the answer will be the latter. If it's your fault that the sponsorship hasn't done well, and it is a good fit, explore its potential before you walk away.

When assessing investments, we generally divide sponsorships into four categories:

1. Performing well, needing only minor adjustment.
2. Under-performing, but a strong opportunity worth re-working.
3. Under-performing, but not cost-effective to maximise (there is no use trying to make a silk purse out of a sow's ear).
4. No hope. Not performing and never will.

For sponsorships falling into categories 3 and 4, you should start to think about exit strategies. For advice on how to exit a sponsorship, see the section on Exit Strategies later in this chapter. If you've got investments sitting in category 3 that have a while before the contract is up, you should explore your options for making the most of the situation or even totally re-working it. You can find information on this in Chapter 11.

Your real opportunity to make a big difference in results lies with the second category. Turn your Sponsorship Team members loose and let them help you to recreate the investment into something that lives up to its potential.

Balancing

Balancing addresses your portfolio as a whole, ensuring that you are not overspending in one area while another goes unsupported. Areas of imbalance typically include target markets, objectives, geographic, and time of year.

Target market

You have, no doubt, prioritised your target markets for your brand(s). Balancing ensures that you have appropriate sponsorships with appropriate benefits for each of your most important target markets.

Some companies spend roughly the equivalent percentage of sponsorship funds that each market represents. This can work well for some brands, but others may want to target specific markets with a higher degree of activity. This is often the case where one target market is either very influential (opinion leaders) or growing fast.

Objectives

It is important to ensure that your portfolio represents a cross-section of your key objectives. If your sponsorship portfolio concentrates on only one or two objectives, a lot of opportunity is being wasted. For instance, if an ice cream company only sponsors so they can sell ice cream at events, they aren't fully maximising what could be great opportunities for adding value and creating relevance with their target markets.

Geographic

This is an area where there are many inconsistencies. Companies tend to do a number of things:

➤ overspend in their home city/state

➤ overspend on major metropolitan areas

➤ underspend on medium to small metropolitan areas and regional areas.

Sometimes there are geographic concentrations that make no rhyme or reason at all.

Try to ensure that your sponsorships are geographically reflective of at least the general geographic spread of your target markets. The exception to this is when a specific geographic area has a relatively high proportion of key consumers or trade, such as trendsetters.

Time of year

Represent your brand's sponsorship program on a timeline. Include promotional lead-ups to events, then take note if there are any major log-jams or gaps. Unless your product is seasonal, such as ice cream or snowboarding gear, you should address this as you move your sponsorship program forward. There are three main ways to address this:

1. Drop one or more sponsorships and invest in others that fill the gaps in your timeline.
2. Shift the specific activities you sponsor within the same organisation (e.g. if you sponsor an art gallery, involve yourself in exhibits that take place when you have less sponsorship activity in the marketplace).
3. Create promotions or other mechanisms, such as a destination Web site, which extend the impact of your sponsorships over a longer period.

Umbrella sponsorship

If you have a lot of sponsorships that are loosely connected, it may make sense to tie them together so that they gain some cohesiveness and function as one, larger sponsorship.

This is called creating a sponsorship 'umbrella'. Such umbrellas are built around a common theme—often a particular type of sponsorship; for example, youth sports, contemporary art, or music festivals.

There are a number of reasons why an umbrella strategy works well for a lot of sponsors:

➤ it presents a more consistent positioning and message to the consumer
➤ layering sponsorships in the same category is a terrific way to create local, personal relevance while maintaining the excitement and passion of the elite level
➤ it creates the opportunity for cross-pollinating between sponsorships
➤ it can allow for longer promotional periods
➤ it allows for economies of scale in maximisation efforts
➤ it works extremely well with ongoing loyalty marketing strategies and destination Web sites
➤ it creates perceived ownership of an entire category of event.

Using an umbrella strategy creates a situation where the strategically developed whole is far greater than the sum of the parts.

Case study: Starbucks

Starbucks Coffee has created an on-going sales promotion that ties together several of their sponsorships in their Southwest US region. When sponsoring a non-profit event or property, Starbucks invites both customers and employees to submit event-themed artworks. The winning works are then turned into coffee tumblers and sold in stores across the region, with $2 from every sale donated to the sponsee. They have used this overlay to leverage their sponsorships of properties as diverse as the AIDS Walk San Diego, the World-Famous San Diego Zoo, and the Sony ArtWalk.

Managing across brands and regions

Many companies have very similar sponsorship portfolios across regions or brands. Often, though, the level of information sharing across these areas is low.

Rather than reinventing the wheel every time, we recommend that regions and brands share information, such as:

➤ case studies (positive and negative)

➤ research results

➤ negotiation strategies

➤ new tools or systems developed

➤ opportunities to work together to create a more effective bargaining unit.

There are many ways that you can address this information sharing, but we have had success with our clients using one or both of these two strategies:

1. Develop a system of internal sponsorship reporting that focuses on objectives, strategies, and results. Distribute these reports semi-annually to all stakeholders.

2. Create a semi-annual think tank. All brands and/or regions could present an example of a sponsorship that is performing well against objectives, as well as one with which they are having trouble.

If your company is part of a multi-national group, we also strongly suggest that, for the same reasons, you are in regular contact with the sponsorship managers in other countries.

Exit strategies

Sponsorships do come to an end. Whether a sponsorship has reached the end of its natural lifecycle or your needs have changed, sometimes you simply have to walk away.

While some sponsees—often big sport—can easily replace your sponsorship with another, other sponsees can find it very difficult. Some sponsees will go so far not to lose your financial investment that they will threaten to take your 'abandonment' of them to the press.

Take heart. There are many ways to end a partnership without hardship, bitterness, or recriminations. We have outlined some of the key ways below.

Do not renew the contract

At the end of a contract, you always have the option not to renew. This is the simplest approach, and is often the most appropriate in a number of situations:

➤ the sponsee is seeking a significant increase in fees

➤ the sponsorship is short (three years or less)

➤ the sponsee is highly desirable

➤ the sponsee has been very difficult to work with

➤ the sponsee is not a cause.

In any of these cases, there might be some media coverage if you drop the sponsorship, but it is likely to be short term.

Causes are a bit of a special case, in that they usually have a large network of very passionately involved people who could take it personally if you drop the sponsorship unceremoniously. We don't suggest that you hang onto non-performing cause sponsorships, simply that it might be a better idea to ease your way out of them gradually, using one of the methods outlined below.

If you choose not to renew, we recommend you keep the following in mind:

➤ let the sponsee know as soon as you know that you will not be renewing the contract. This gives them the longest possible lead-time to find another sponsor

➤ continue to treat the sponsee as a partner right up to the end

➤ no matter what, do not badmouth them. You do not want to engage in a publicity war with an organisation that will most likely be seen as more sympathetic than your company.

Step out of the sponsorship gradually

Stepping out of the sponsorship gradually can be very effective if you are a major sponsor and replacing you is going to be difficult for the sponsee. This is particularly the case if you have been a long-term naming rights sponsor, because the sponsorship can be difficult to resell once your brand has become part of the lexicon around the event (e.g. the Molson Grand Prix and the Ford Australian Open).

We suggest the following process:

➤ tell the sponsee that you are planning to move away from the event at least 12 months before your current contract ends

➤ reassure the sponsee that you will not be leaving it high and dry and will continue to be involved at some level while they find another major sponsor

➤ negotiate a lower level sponsorship for 1–2 years. Do negotiate for exclusivity, because this protects you from having a competing brand take up the major sponsorship as soon as you step down.

The safety net you are providing should give the sponsee sufficient time to find a new sponsor, but if there are still major concerns, you could also assist it in its efforts (see below).

> If you are not going to renew, give the sponsee plenty of notice.

Helping a sponsee
is a very cost-
effective way of
exiting a
sponsorship.

Assist with sponsorship generation

If your relationship with a sponsee has been good, but you can't justify continuing with the sponsorship, a strong option is to assist it with generating new sponsorship. You could do any or all of the following:

➤ use your network to open some doors for the sponsee. You can't make promises, but you can get them in front of a few potential sponsors that they may have had difficulty accessing on their own

➤ educate the sponsee by providing workshop or conference tuition to ensure their skills are top notch

➤ hire a consultant on their behalf to assist them in bringing in new sponsors

➤ allow them access to some of your internal experts—PR, Web site design, etc.—to help improve their effectiveness.

These activities will have a large impact on the sponsee's future success, while costing you far less than renewing a sponsorship contract that isn't working for you.

Part 4

ambush
marketing
choosing not to sponsor

Chapter 14

What is ambush marketing?

Ambush marketing occurs when non-sponsors of an event create the impression that they are involved in the event—that they are sponsors—when they are not. An ambush can also occur when a small sponsor maximises its sponsorship so well that it seems as big or bigger than the higher level sponsors' investments.

As long as the ambusher does not actually claim to be a sponsor or use the logos or images of the sponsee, ambush marketing is legal.

Although any type of event can be ambushed, the biggest area for ambush is major sporting events, leagues, and competitions. World Cup Soccer, national sports leagues, and the Olympics are all examples of events around which ambushes regularly occur.

Controversy

Ambush marketing is controversial, there is no doubt about it. Some marketers think the practice is unethical or immoral, equating it to stealing or fraud. Others see it as just another marketing tool. Whichever side of the debate you take, you need to know three things:

1. Whether they partake in ambushing or not, most experienced sponsorship professionals agree that ambush is a strategic decision, not an ethical or moral one.
2. Calling an ambusher unethical or immoral isn't going to stop them doing it.
3. For the most part, the public doesn't care. There is already enough public cynicism about marketing, that even the biggest controversy over a sponsorship is unlikely to register a blip in the longer term. If the ambusher connects with people and the sponsor doesn't, it is the ambusher they will remember.

Types of ambush

There are a number of different types of ambush:

Strategic
An ambush that parallels the ambusher's larger marketing plan, with the aim being lasting, objective-oriented results of the calibre that can be achieved through sponsorship. The activity is often selected, maximised, and managed just like a sponsorship, but without a sponsee.

Media
An ambush that takes place primarily in the media, often with an ambusher taking up television rights for or a comprehensive ad schedule around the sponsored event.

Exposure
An ambush that revolves around getting a logo or marketing message into the event or in the media, such as 200 people wearing logo T-shirts seated behind the goal. Generally, the results are very short term, but this approach can be useful for new products.

Thorn-in-the-side
An activity designed primarily to annoy the competition. This is never a good idea.

Publicity
An activity designed to take the media emphasis off the event and/or specific sponsor. This may or may not involve the ambusher being identified. It could just be an unidentified publicity stunt (e.g. streaker).

Ambushing up
This is when a rightful sponsor of an event does such a good job utilising their sponsorship that they seem like a far bigger sponsor than they are.

Although strategic ambushes and ambushing up represent only a small fraction of all the ambush activity in the marketplace, they are the only types of ambush that are likely to provide lasting marketing returns.

The others are largely wastes of money. They are virtually all non-strategic and ignored by the public, with the only redeeming quality being the ambushers' ability to congratulate themselves over getting something—even something useless—for nothing.

> Don't ambush if your main goal is getting something for nothing.

Case studies: Ambush marketing

COCA-COLA had a virtual stranglehold on the elite levels of UK soccer, so Pepsi went for the grassroots, sponsoring the national Five-a-Side Championships, the country's largest amateur sports competition. In all, over 100 000 people on 15 000 teams compete for the right to play in the nationally televised final. Pepsi also sponsors soccer programming and uses soccer stars in advertising, further extending their link to the sport.

IN Australia, the two largest airlines, Ansett Australia and Qantas, regularly ambush each other. One memorable instance occurred when Qantas bought the television sponsorship of the pre-season football competition, which is sponsored by Ansett. The result was that when people turned on their televisions, they were treated to 'The Ansett Cup, brought to you by Qantas'.

ALTHOUGH Adidas was an official sponsor of the Women's Soccer World cup in the US in 1998, Nike's sponsorship of both the US team and several American stars threw a spanner in their marketing works. Adidas had the challenge of trying to showcase their sponsorship to an American audience without showing the American team, while Nike proactively maximised their sponsorships, and took the opportunity to launch the first signature soccer shoe line for women, with soccer superstar Mia Hamm.

NIKE was at it again in France, the site of the 1998 Soccer World Cup. While they did not sponsor the Cup, they did sponsor a number of top-ranked teams. They also invested heavily in a stunning ad campaign. The most visible thing they did, however, was to create 'Nikepark: The People's Republic of Football', a soccer-themed amusement park, presided over by French soccer legend 'President' Eric Cantona. With soccer-themed activities and player appearances, it really was a must-see for any fan.

Chapter 15

How to prevent an ambush

There are two ways to prevent an ambush from happening to you: legally and strategically.

Legal

The main problem with preventing ambush marketing is that most of the time, it is perfectly legal. The only time that it is not legal is if the ambushing company falsely represents that it is a sponsor, claims endorsement by the sponsee, or blatantly misleads the public into believing these things to be true.

The Sydney Olympics was better protected than any event in memory, with legislation widened to include a large number of inferences, but even then, it was not airtight. There were still a number of very successful ambushes.

The best way to protect yourself through legal channels is to ensure that ambush protection is written into the contract with the sponsees. At the very least, this stops them from selling sponsorship, vending rights, or signage to any of your competitors, and will compel them to protect your rights within the scope of any media or subcontractor deals. But this is still only a partial measure, because most ambushes have nothing directly to do with the sponsee.

Strategic

The best ambush protection you can possibly have is to fully maximise your sponsorship. This will get you 75% of the way to being ambush-proofed. If you have created a strong program of support for your investment, any activities mounted by your competition will look weak and stupid by comparison.

If you want to close that 75% gap even further, you need to do two things:

➤ learn to ambush—you can't protect yourself from something you don't

> Most ambushes are legal.

If you want to stop an ambush, you have to know how to ambush.

understand. Even if it is not something you will ever do, it is important to have this knowledge. See the section on 'How to ambush' starting on page 168.

➤ develop a plan to ambush yourself. You will spot your vulnerabilities and might even come up with some great ideas for maximising your sponsorship.

Ambush exercise

This is an exercise that is meant to help companies identify their vulnerabilities, as well as to determine what is and is not within their control. It is useful for a whole range of sponsorships, but will be particularly valuable for larger sponsorships and/or events.

This exercise can be done individually or, ideally, with your Sponsorship Team.

Setting the stage

In order to mount an ambush, pretend your fiercest competitor is willing to spend an equal amount to what your company is spending to maximise your legitimate sponsorship. In other words, your competitor is trying to get the benefits of the sponsorship by spending the maximisation budget, but not the fee.

Step 1

Pretend you work for your fiercest competitor. Write down every way that you could ambush your company within the allotted budget.

Ask yourself these questions:

➤ How can I use the event themes/attributes to connect better with my audience members and/or add value to their experience at or around the event?

➤ What could I do to create confusion about the sponsorship at or near the venue?

➤ What could I do to create confusion in the media (paid or unpaid)?

➤ What could I do to create confusion among our consumers?

➤ Who could I sponsor that will carry my branding and/or message right into the event?

➤ What could I do to steal the limelight from the event?

Spend an hour or so. Get creative. Get mean. Believe us, your competitors could be doing this for real.

Step 2

You are now back in your rightful position at your own company, and it is time to analyse your potential for being ambushed.

Break up your ambush ideas into the following categories:

Sponsor   Potential area of ambush that can only be controlled through strong activity by you, making the ambusher's efforts ineffectual.

Sponsee   Potential area of ambush that can be controlled or influenced by the sponsee. Cover these off with the sponsee.

Other   Potential area of ambush that can be controlled, but not by the sponsee. This could include use of nearby venues, venue signage, vending rights, participant sponsorships (not already counter-sponsored). Investigate these.

No control   Potential area of ambush that cannot be controlled, such as existing sponsorship of participants, overhead blimps, publicity stunts, etc.

Step 3

Analyse the ideas in the Sponsor group against your current marketing plan and ask yourself the following questions:

➤ Are there any holes in my plan?

➤ Adding together the potential holes, could they possibly form a cohesive ambush?

➤ How much would it cost and/or what would need to be shifted to block the potential for ambush?

➤ Is lowering the risk of ambush worth the expenditure?

Step 4—take action

➤ Discuss the Sponsee group with your sponsees and work out a plan to minimise risk. Keep in mind, you have probably thought of more gaps than they have

➤ Investigate the Other group and decide what actions you will take to protect yourself from ambush

➤ Adjust your own sponsorship plan, if necessary, to protect yourself from potential ambush. The extra benefit is that your sponsorship will be even better maximised

➤ Have a glass of wine and remind yourself that not everything is in your control—you can only do your best to protect the value of your sponsorship

Chapter 16

How to ambush

Although we are including a section in this book about how to do ambush marketing, we are not advocating this activity. Ambushing is not for everyone, but we cannot ignore the fact that many companies do it and some of them are getting very good results.

Your goals for this chapter are:

➤ if you are not involved in ambush marketing and have no plans to become involved, you will at least understand the medium enough that you can better protect yourself. You will also know how to identify whether an ambush is a real strategic threat or simply cosmetic

➤ if you are interested in ambush marketing for your brand, you will be more discerning, more strategic, and get better results.

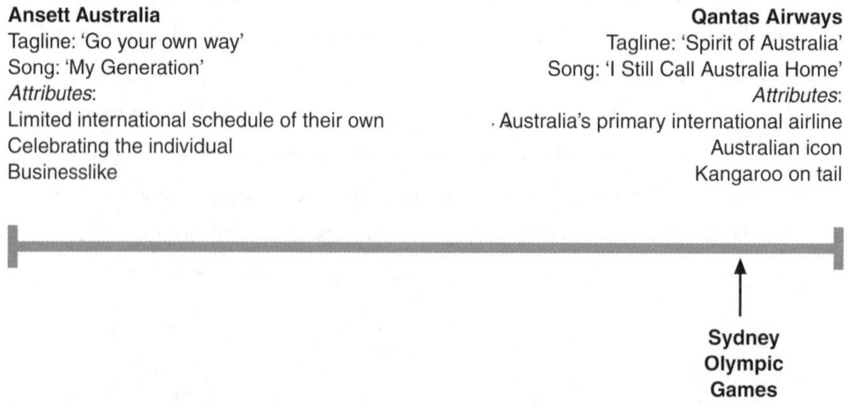

Figure 16.1 Attribute continuum

Natural vs. manufactured ambushing

One of the biggest indicators as to whether an ambush will work is how natural or authentic the activity is. The more natural the match between the ambusher and the event, the better it will work. In addition, the more authentic the connections between the ambusher and the event, the stronger the impression of alignment will be.

Ansett Australia
Tagline: 'Go your own way'
Song: 'My Generation'
Attributes:
Limited international schedule of their own
Celebrating the individual
Businesslike

Qantas Airways
Tagline: 'Spirit of Australia'
Song: 'I Still Call Australia Home'
Attributes:
Australia's primary international airline
Australian icon
Kangaroo on tail

Sydney Olympic Games

Let's have another look at the attribute continuum (Figure 16.1) from Chapter 6. As you will recall, Ansett Australia was the rightful airline sponsor of the 2000 Sydney Olympic Games, but the Olympics was a far more natural fit with Qantas' unique attributes.

This type of sponsorship not only makes it more difficult for the rightful sponsors to get the most from their investment, it also makes it very easy for their competitors to ambush them. In fact, if an event and a non-sponsor have a very close natural link, whether that non-sponsor embarks on any ambush activity or not, they are often incorrectly identified by the audience as having been a sponsor.

In addition, Qantas had the added benefit of authenticity. It had sponsored every Australian Olympic and Commonwealth Games team for 40 years before the Sydney Games. They also had longstanding relationships with a number of elite athletes—Olympic and otherwise. This combination of authenticity and natural fit is very hard to beat.

Most successful ambushes have a strong air of authenticity—such as a genuine connection with a sport—that will make the implication of involvement seem not only plausible, but probable. In sport, this is often accomplished by sponsoring athletes, teams, or governing bodies (such as state or national sports associations) during or in the lead-up to the event and ensuring that the maximisation efforts around these legitimate sponsorships imply a larger association with the sport or upcoming event.

The polar opposite of a natural ambush is one that is manufactured. This occurs when a non-sponsor, who is not at all a natural fit, tries to mount an ambush. They usually have a difficult time making this type of ambush work because not only are they trying to imply that they are involved in the event when they aren't, they also have to manufacture the affinity with that event that a natural, authentic ambusher already has. It is very, very difficult to achieve this without the ambush looking contrived, and if it looks contrived, it won't work.

In the lead-up to the Sydney 2000 Olympics,* there occurred one of the best examples of a contrived ambush we have ever seen. National Australia Bank was not a sponsor of the Olympic Games, nor had it been involved, at least in recent memory, in Olympic or other international sports. In fact, compared with other banks in the marketplace, it had a low involvement with sports of any kind. At the same time, the rightful financial services sponsor, Westpac, was doing a great job with its sponsorship of the Olympic Games.

> A successful ambush will always have an air of authenticity.

---

* Apologies for all of the Sydney Olympic references. They simply provide some of the best examples of ambush that we have ever seen.

Undeterred, National Australia Bank signed up a group of Olympic athletes, called them 'Team National', and used them across a range of marketing media. It looked contrived from the start—even the name lacked realism—with the result being that well before the Olympics started, Team National had faded from the marketing landscape.

Making it happen

There are a few rules of thumb that you will need to keep in mind if you intend to use ambush as a marketing tool.

Select your ambush strategically

The fact that ambush marketing is controversial draws some people and companies to it like a moth to a flame. They like ambushing because it is exciting and devious and they might get their names in the paper. While these things may be true, getting caught up in this mindset will do you no favours.

If your ambush activities are going to work, you need to be as objective and results-oriented as you are with your sponsorship program. Ambushing costs money, just like sponsorship. Before you move forward with any ambush activities, you need to ensure that it is right for your brand and that you are doing it for the right reasons.

Consider an ambush if . . .

➤ The sponsors aren't effectively maximising their investment, or haven't in the past
➤ The ambush opportunity is appropriate for your target market and will achieve multiple (at least five) marketing objectives
➤ You have ample time and resources to implement the activities
➤ You have buy-in across departments
➤ You have top level buy-in. Embarrassing your chief executive is never a good career move
➤ The ambush does not conflict with any of your existing sponsorships

Don't ambush if . . .

➤ The sponsor is fully maximising their investment, or has a history of it
➤ It's not a target market match
➤ It will not achieve more than one or two meaningful objectives
➤ You are just trying to annoy your competition
➤ You just want to get something for free (e.g. your logo on television)

Ambush marketing is not cheap.

➤ You want the excitement of doing something 'devious'

➤ Your senior management doesn't have the stomach for doing something potentially controversial

We recommend that you use your Proposal Evaluation Criteria found on page 78 when evaluating ambush opportunities.

Maximise and manage it just like a sponsorship

A strategically selected ambush should function exactly like a sponsorship, with the key exception being that you don't have a sponsee in the picture. You should go through the same processes to maximise, manage, and quantify your investments as you do with any sponsorship, including involving your sponsorship team. We have attached an Ambush Checklist. This is a starting place for you to think of ways you can work an ambush to get the best results against your objectives.

Go for impact

When developing your ambush program, keep two things in mind:

1. you are marketing head-to-head with a competitor using the same event

2. you are unconstrained by a contract and free to be as innovative as you like.

You need to be sure that your activities rise above the clutter of the event and your competitor, so be sure that whatever you do, it is impactful. If you were ever going to push the creative envelope, now is the time. Use humour. Use cleverness. Use arresting visuals or emotional hooks. Add value to your consumers in ways they wouldn't have imagined. This is no time to turn into a shrinking violet.

Be prepared for controversy

Not every ambush attracts the media's attention, but many of them do. Prepare for this possibility well before your activities become public. Sometimes it is better to let the controversy blow over. Sometimes it is better to answer your critics. Whatever the circumstance, be sure you have a plan in place.

Don't gloat

No matter how difficult you make things for the rightful sponsor and the sponsee, do not gloat. Gloating will only make you look spiteful and will undo any opportunity you ever had to present your ambush activity as a strategic business decision.

The public will accept a business decision. They have a much harder time accepting plain old nastiness.

> Treat an ambush just like a sponsorship, without the sponsee.

Ambush checklist

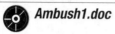 *Ambush1.doc*

The following represents a list of potential areas for ambush. This list is by no means exhaustive, but represents a wide range of potential weak spots that could be taken advantage of by an ambusher.

Strategic ambush opportunities are **marked with an asterisk***. These are the types of opportunities that will make up the backbone of a strategic ambush—that is, an ambush that will have a lasting effect on the audience. Generally, the more of these strategic opportunities taken up by an ambusher, the more effective the ambush will be. An ambush without any of these more strategic activities might have an effect, but it will usually be short term in nature and more likely to undermine the sponsor than to create a positive effect for the ambusher. The less strategic activities (no asterisk) are, however, very effective for reinforcing the more strategic activities, particularly at or near the event.

General

➤ Ambusher being more creative than the sponsor*

➤ Ambusher being more relevant to audience than the sponsor*

➤ Ambusher having more marketing weight than the sponsor

➤ Ambusher being a better, more natural match than the sponsor*

➤ Ambusher having a long history with the event, sport, or general sponsorship category

Consumer/trade hooks

➤ Creating a co-promotion with an existing event sponsor (e.g. Nike partnering with sponsor Optus at an Adidas-sponsored event)

➤ Creating themed promotions during the same period—media, sales, trade, retail, on-pack*

➤ Creating new event or program that makes the sport more relevant and/or accessible to the audience (e.g. hands-on festival of football across the road from a football Grand Final)*

➤ Sponsoring an existing event or program that makes the sport more relevant and/or accessible to the audience (e.g. state-wide junior football clinics)*

➤ Adding value to the experience of the event's venue and/or television audience*

➤ Purchase good tickets for the event—in a block, if possible—for use as prizes in a themed promotion (expensive from ticket brokers, but very effective)

Media

➤ Creating advertising that borrows from the theme of the sponsorship*

➤ Purchasing media time during a broadcast event

➤ Purchasing media time during a related television/radio program

➤ Running those themed ads during that media time*

➤ Purchasing media space in an event program or related print media

➤ Sponsoring a related television/radio program on a different station (e.g. 'The Footy Show')*

➤ Sponsoring columns, special sections, or other print media

➤ Using similar imagery to the sponsor

➤ Using similar imagery to the event*

On-site

➤ Creating and distributing to the audience merchandise that carries the ambusher's message into the event (e.g. sun visors)

➤ Providing special offers or bounce-back coupons on that merchandise

➤ Set up a display, sales, couponing, or sampling area near the event's perimeter (e.g. Mr Whippy's ice cream trucks)

➤ Purchase signage à la carte (for events that do not own venue signage rights)

➤ Strong external branding of the ambusher's skybox

➤ Upgrade the skybox to a larger venue on-site for the event

Event vicinity

➤ Having an on-the-ground presence near the event and/or at main routes to the event

➤ Doing promotions in nearby and/or related venues (restaurants, pubs, museums, retail outlets, etc.)*

➤ Buying up external signage in the event vicinity

Celebrities/athletes/participants

➤ Gaining endorsement by one or more participants in the event (e.g. athletes)*

➤ Having the endorsee carry the ambusher's logo or message into the event

➤ Using the endorsee for appearances (consumer or trade-based)*

➤ Using the endorsee to anchor promotion(s)*

➤ Using the endorsee in themed advertising*

➤ Using the endorsee to anchor related event(s)*

Publicity

➤ Announce a newsworthy initiative so that it corresponds or comes slightly ahead of the event (e.g. announcing a merger, float, groundbreaking new product, etc.)

➤ Create a publicity stunt that brings the spotlight onto the ambusher

➤ Create a publicity stunt that takes the spotlight off the sponsor (if a buxom woman streaks across a sports ground, odds are she is being paid by an ambusher)

➤ Hold a better event on or near the same day

Information technology

➤ Creating a destination Web site related to the event (e.g. same sport)*

➤ Provide opportunities to chat on-line with your contracted celebrities*

➤ Provide an e-mail box for sending fan mail (or umpire hate mail!)*

➤ Provide opportunities to participate virtually in the event in some way (e.g. post reviews, run a 'you be the umpire' promotion, etc.)*

➤ Provide themed electronic greeting cards, screen savers, etc. at your site

➤ Generate a database with purchasing/perception research via the Web site*

Database/loyalty marketing

➤ Create themed special offers or promotions for your key customers*

Trade/other VIPs

➤ Purchase hospitality space at the event

➤ Purchase great tickets for VIPs, and hold schmooze events at a fabulous venue nearby*

➤ Create a themed trade promotion*

Retail

➤ Themed POS/POP*

➤ Themed packaging*

➤ Other merchandising

➤ Retail co-promotion*

Conclusion

You've done it! You have completed *The Sponsor's Toolkit*, and we realise this is no mean feat. We were warned by our editor that we may have tried to put too much information in this one little book, but we believe that the more we provide, the more you will get out of it.

During workshops, we often joke that the reason we teach sponsorship is because we have made nearly every mistake there is to make in this business and we don't want our colleagues to make them too. While this is a bit of an over-simplification, it is also largely true. Over the years, and through plenty of learning experiences, we have found our way through the myriad of old-school thinking, myth, and misinformation to having a real understanding of how to identify and harness the true power of sponsorship.

Sponsorship has changed enormously in the past few years, and that level of sophistication is only going to increase. Our goal when writing this book was to provide you with an approach, a framework, and the tools to help you manage sponsorship better now, and to adapt to the inevitable changes in this medium as you move forward.

Like our workshops, this book is not just airy-fairy theory, but a proven and practical approach developed over 30+ combined years in the sponsorship business. We're not writers, we are sponsorship professionals. The tools we have provided are the tools we use. The strategies we recommend are an amalgam of strategies we have used across a wide variety of clients. And we really *do* believe that sponsorship is the single most powerful marketing medium available to a brand.

Even if you need some time to digest the full weight of *The Sponsor's Toolkit*, we are confident that you will see a significant and positive change in your sponsorship program as long as you keep these five things firmly in mind:

1. Your job is to connect with your target market, not with a sponsee.
2. To be a good sponsor, you have to do the right research, because it is only by knowing your target markets that you can successfully connect with them.
3. Invest only in a sponsorship that will achieve five or more objectives.

4. Take a team approach to selection, negotiation, maximisation, and quantification to make your sponsorship investments more effective and less costly.

5. Generating awareness proves that you exist—nothing more.

We do realise that our approach stands a lot of conventional thinking about sponsorship on its head, and that this is not always an easy sell internally. Our advice to you is simple: keep the faith and do the small things first. Create Proposal Guidelines. Start with a team brainstorm. Follow these steps and you will eventually get your sponsorship program where you want it to be, and probably faster than you think.

We would love to hear how this approach works for you and welcome your feedback. Information sharing is so vital to this industry as it shifts and changes, and we are certainly no exception. And don't stop with us. Share information and techniques with your colleagues and ask for the same from them. As the saying goes, 'knowledge is power'. That is certainly true in sponsorship. Our contact details can be found at the back of the book.

Writing *The Sponsor's Toolkit* has been a lot of fun for us and we hope you have fun with it. This is a wonderful, interesting, and infinitely malleable business. As challenging as it can be sometimes, those of us in the sponsorship business can count ourselves very lucky.

We wish you success with all your sponsorships!

Kim and Anne-Marie

Part 5

appendixes

Glossary

Above-the-line media	Traditional advertising venues—television, radio, newspaper, magazine, and outdoor. Also known as 'main media'.
Activation	The sponsor-generated activities that take place around a sponsorship and deliver most of the value of a sponsorship investment. Also called 'maximisation' or 'leverage'.
Advertising	Placing commercial messages in above-the-line media.
Advertorial	A favourable editorial, or editorial with a distinctly commercial slant, in a publication or on a program, purchased by a company for a fee. Generally, it must carry wording that clearly states it is a paid advertisement.
Agent	An individual or organisation that sells sponsorship properties on a commission or fee basis. Also known as a 'broker'.
Ambush marketing	When an organisation creates the perception that it is a sponsor of a property when it has not purchased the rights to that property.
Below-the-line advertising	Non-traditional advertising venues (anything that is not 'above-the-line'), such as sponsorship, publicity, sales promotion, relationship or loyalty marketing, coupons, database marketing, direct response, and retail promotions.
Brand marketing	Marketing activities with the primary goal of communicating the positioning, personality and non-functional attributes of a brand.
Broker	An individual or organisation that sells sponsorship properties on a commission or fee basis. Also known as an 'agent'.
Cause-related marketing	The practice of sponsoring a cause or other non-profit organisation, then linking an additional donation to sales of product, thereby creating a point of difference for the consumer. For example, 'For every can of Pups Dog Food sold, we will donate ten cents to the Guide Dog Society.'
Chairman's choice	Sponsorship investments made primarily on the basis of a senior executive's personal interests (e.g. sailing), rather than good business practice.

CIM

Customer Information Management. This is the area that controls and manages loyalty and database marketing activity. Can also be called 'CRM'.

Clutter

A term used to describe an overload of sponsor messages around one event. It is also used more generally to describe the massive amount of advertising and other marketing messages ever-present in today's developed society.

Contra

Products or services that are provided in lieu of cash in exchange for sponsorship rights. Also known as 'in-kind' or 'value in kind'.

Coverage

Media term referring to the proportion of the target market that has the opportunity to see or hear any one advertisement. It is expressed as a percentage of the total target market. Also known as 'Reach'.

Cross-promotion

When two or more organisations create promotional opportunities that benefit all partners.

CRM

Customer Relationship Management. The area that controls and manages loyalty and database marketing activity can also be called 'CIM'. CRM can also stand for 'cause-related marketing'.

Donation

An offering of product or cash that is given by a company without any anticipated commercial return. Also known as 'philanthropy'.

Early adopter(s)

A person or group of people who tend to try new things earlier than others and spread opinions about them. These people are very important to new products and brands and often attract a large percentage of early marketing budgets. Also known as 'trend setters' or 'opinion leaders'.

Exclusivity

Exclusive rights to sponsorship or on-site sales. Typically defined by the sponsor's category of business (e.g. 'exclusive automobile sponsor' or 'exclusive beer vendor').

Fit

The degree to which a sponsorship opportunity matches a brand's objectives, attributes, and target markets.

Frequency

Media term referring to the average number of times each member of a target audience receives an advertising message over the course of the ad campaign.

Grant

The provision of funds or material for a specific project generally not linked to a company's core business. The grant must usually be acknowledged by the recipient and generally must be acquitted. The grant is given on the basis of the need for the project rather than the promotional and marketing opportunities it might provide.

Image transfer
The process by which a sponsor associates itself with the core values and attributes of a sponsee, with the goal being to introduce or reinforce those attributes within its company or brand.

In-kind
Products and services that are provided in lieu of cash in exchange for sponsorship rights. Also known as 'contra'.

In-pack
The promotion of a sponsorship inside the sponsor's actual product packaging, e.g. a cereal box. Often done in conjunction with 'on-pack' promotion.

Launch
A public unveiling or announcement of the details of an event, program, or sponsorship, which is specifically designed to gain publicity. The launch often marks the start of the lead-up marketing program.

Leverage
The sponsor-generated activities that take place around a sponsorship and deliver most of the value of a sponsorship investment. Also called 'maximisation' or 'activation'.

Main media
Traditional advertising—television, radio, newspaper, magazines, and outdoor. Also known as 'above-the-line'.

Marketing message
The key message that an organisation wants to convey about its product or service through a sponsorship.

Marketing mix
A company's entire marketing program, made up of a 'mix' of marketing activities.

Maximisation
The sponsor-generated activities that take place around a sponsorship and deliver most of the value of a sponsorship investment. Also called 'leverage' or 'activation'.

Media sponsorship
An advertising package around a program or event generally consisting of paid and/or contra advertising, unpaid promotion and/or editorial support, and exclusivity.

Merchandising
The creation of promotional items around an event that will then be sold or given away. Merchandise can be produced and distributed by either the event, the sponsor, or both.

Naming rights sponsor
Basically the same as a principal sponsor, with the added benefit of the sponsor having their name added to the event name (e.g. the Blockbuster Bowl or the Tooheys Melbourne Cup). Also known as 'title sponsor'.

Narrowcasting
The opposite of broadcasting, that is marketing to a tightly defined group. Also known as 'niche marketing'.

Niche marketing
Targeting a group of people with a very tightly defined set of demographic and/or psychographic characteristics. Also known as 'narrowcasting'.

Offer

The proposal offered to a potential sponsor. Also known as the 'package'.

Official supplier

A (usually) low level sponsorship in which the sponsor either: (a) provides product or services to the event free or at a substantial discount, often not paying any additional sponsorship fee; or (b) pays a sponsorship fee to secure a guarantee from the sponsee that it will purchase the sponsor's product or service exclusively.

On-pack

The promotion of a sponsorship on a sponsor's actual product packaging. Often done in conjunction with 'in-pack' promotion.

On-selling

A sponsor reselling portions of the purchased sponsor benefits to one or more other companies. This is usually done with the full knowledge and approval of the sponsee.

Opinion leader(s)

A person or group of people who tend to try new things earlier than others and spread opinions about them. These people are very important to new products and brands and often attract a large percentage of early marketing budgets. Also known as 'trend setters' or 'early adopters'.

Outdoor

Literally, advertising that takes place outdoors, such as billboards, posters, and taxi or bus signage.

Package

The proposal offered to a potential sponsor. Also known as the 'offer'.

Packaging

Structuring the sponsor benefits and their relationship to the event and the sponsee.

Pass-through rights

The right for a sponsor to on-sell or give some of the sponsorship benefits to another company.

Perimeter signage

Banners and/or signs located near an event, but not inside the boundaries of the event itself.

Permission marketing

A relatively new term referring to the practice of asking consumers' permission before marketing to them. This technique is often employed in concert with loyalty or direct marketing activities.

Philanthropy

The voluntary giving of funds by foundations, trusts, bequests, corporation or individuals to support human welfare in its broadest sense.

POD

Point of Difference. An attribute that differentiates a product from its competitors. Sponsorship can often be a powerful point of difference.

Point of Difference

An attribute that differentiates a product from its competitors. Sponsorship can often be a powerful point of difference.

POS	Point of Sale. A display, signage, or promotional items produced for display with a product in the store and designed to create excitement and differentiate the product from its competitors.
Point of Sale	A display, signage, or promotional items produced for display with a product in the store and designed to create excitement and differentiate the product from its competitors.
Positioning	The personality of a brand, company, or event. Strong brand marketing is often focused on positioning.
Principal sponsor	The pre-eminent sponsor of any event or property, receiving the highest level of benefits and promotion.
Promoter	An individual or company who takes on some of the financial risk as well as responsibility for the marketing and promotion of an event in exchange for a portion of the profits.
Property	A generic term for sponsee.
Proposal	The sponsorship offer in written form.
Proposal Guidelines	A document produced by a sponsor that provides potential sponsees with information on the objectives, target markets, parameters, scope, and categories of sponsorship investments made by a company.
Public relations	Generating editorial media coverage, i.e. newspaper and magazine articles, television and radio coverage (generally in news, current affairs, or lifestyle programming). Also known as 'publicity'.
Publicist	A specialist in gaining editorial media coverage.
Publicity	Generating editorial media coverage, i.e. newspaper and magazine articles, television and radio coverage (generally in news, current affairs, or lifestyle programming). Also known as 'public relations'.
Quantification	Evaluation of the results of the sponsorship program.
Reach	Media term referring to the proportion of your target market that has the opportunity to see or hear any advertisement or advertising campaign. It is expressed as a percentage of the total target market. Also known as 'coverage'.
Reporting	The on-going process of a sponsee providing a sponsor with information regarding the performance of their sponsorship against agreed marketing objectives.
Sales promotion	Activities employed to encourage customers to buy a product or differentiate a product from the competition at the point of sale.

Sales sponsorship
A sponsorship that is entered into primarily to gain direct sales, e.g. a brewer sponsoring a festival in order to secure exclusive pouring rights, or a hotel chain sponsoring a touring stage show to guarantee all of those room bookings.

Segmentation
Defining different segments of a marketplace based upon demographics, psychographics, perceptions, and buying patterns.

Servicing
The process of the sponsee providing benefits to a sponsor, both what is agreed and additional benefits to assist them in achieving their objectives. Servicing also encompasses strong two-way communication between the sponsor and sponsee, as well as reporting.

Servicing Plan
A detailed plan that documents how a sponsorship will be serviced and implemented by the sponsee.

Signage
Signs that are specific to an event, such as banners, A-frames, and scoreboards. These can feature either sponsor or event messages, or both.

Sponsee
The recipient of the sponsor's primary sponsorship investment. Typically, sponsees will fall into the categories of arts, cause, education, community service, event, individual, Internet site, media, government, sport, or venue.

Sponsor
The organisation that buys sponsorship rights, packaged and granted by the sponsee.

Sponsorship
An investment in sport, community or government activities, the arts, a cause, program, individual, or broadcast that yields a commercial return for the sponsor. The investment can be made in financial, material, or human terms.

Sponsorship Audit
The assessment of each component of a sponsor's sponsorship portfolio against set evaluation criteria, usually leading to a readjustment of the portfolio.

Sponsorship Plan
A detailed plan that documents how a sponsorship will be implemented by the sponsor.

Sponsorship Policy
A document that indicates an organisation's philosophy and approach to sponsorship, including why it is involved, key influences to the sponsorship process, and any sponsorship exclusions or limitations.

Sponsorship Strategy
A formal document produced by a company or organisation that outlines the target markets, objectives for sponsorship, and specific strategies to achieve these goals. This document is usually closely linked to an organisation's marketing and/or revenue raising strategies. Generally, both sponsors and sponsees will have sponsorship strategies in place.

Sponsorship Team

A multi-disciplinary group of sponsorship stakeholders who have the responsibility for planning and implementing sponsorships. This group could include representatives from any number of areas, but often include management from the brand, sales, marketing, trade relations, PR, ad agency, CRM, and research.

Sticky marketing

A marketing activity that 'sticks', creating lasting changes in a market's perceptions or behaviours.

Target audience

The most appropriate audience for a particular product, service, or event. The audience can be made up of one or several target markets, which can sometimes be quite diverse.

Target market

A group of people who are likely purchasers of a product or service, or who are strong candidates for attending an event, and who share a similar demographic and/or psychographic profile.

TARP

Target Audience Rating Point. Media term referring to the percentage of the target market reached over the course of an advertising campaign. It is a gross measure, taking into account both reach (the number of people that a message reaches) and frequency. For example, if there are 15 million people in a target audience of males 18–34, and the marketer achieves 250 TARPs with its campaign, there would be 15 million × 250% = 37 500 000 times that men 18–34 heard/saw the marketing message.

Title sponsor

Basically the same as a principal sponsor with the added benefit of the sponsor having their name added to the event name, e.g., the Johnnie Walker Classic or Qualcomm Stadium. Also known as 'naming rights sponsor'.

USP

Unique Selling Point. The unique attribute(s) of a product or brand that often forms the basis of marketing activities.

Vendor

An organisation or company that sells a product or service at an event. This term is also used to describe a company that supplies a product to a retailer to sell (e.g. Kmart's vendors would include Black & Decker, Unilever, Coca-Cola, etc.).

Resources

There are many sponsorship resources available, and some are very good. This is a list of some we think you will find useful. We use many of these regularly ourselves.

Please note: We have accepted no compensation from these organisations, nor are we responsible for the content they provide.

Associations

The organisations listed here are a mix of sponsorship, marketing, and management associations. Whichever category they fall under, each of these organisations has made a commitment to provide quality education and resources to marketing and/or sponsorship professionals. There are some cases where we are not familiar with an organisation and have simply included their contact details.

Some of the marketing and management organisations do currently offer sponsorship education and/or resources. If your country's association(s) doesn't, we have found most are open to suggestions from members with regard to topics and good resources. Ask for the support you need if you're not getting it.

International
International Festivals & Events Association (IFEA)

The IFEA is aimed at events and festival organisers, although it does have some good resources for sponsors of these types of events. There are chapters in 36 countries. IFEA has conferences, publications, and even a certificate program. For details, contact IFEA, 2601 Eastover Terrace, Boise ID 83706, USA, (1-208) 433 0950, or www.ifea.com.

North America
American Marketing Association

This large association has a wide variety of publications, conferences, workshops, and symposiums available across the United States, although sponsorship does not feature heavily in its education program at present. For more information, see the AMA Web site on www.ama.org, or contact the chapter in your area. A full list is available on www.ama.org.

Association of National Advertisers (USA)

This organisation has a very strong educational program, including both workshops and conferences specifically for sponsors. The Association's publication, *The Marketer*, is available free on-line to members and non-members. Great on-line bookstore. For details, contact the Association of National Advertisers, Inc., 708 Third Avenue, New York NY 10017-4270, USA, (1-212) 697 5950, (1-212) 661 8057 fax, or www.ana.net.

Canadian Institute of Marketing

This association is well respected across Canada, with chapters and activities in major cities. Its quarterly publication, *The Marketing Challenge*, regularly covers sponsorship. Current and back issues are available free of charge to both members and non-members on the CIM Web site. For details, contact the CIM, 41 Capital Drive, Nepean, Ontario, Canada K2G 0E7, (1-905) 877 5369, (1-905) 702 0819, cim@igs.net, or www.cinstmarketing.ca.

Europe

European Sponsorship Consultant's Association (ESCA)

This association caters exclusively to sponsorship consultants. If you are a consultant doing business in Europe, it is probably worth a look. For details, contact the ESCA Secretariat, Tony Rudge, Marash House, 2–5 Brook Street, Tring, Hertfordshire, HP23 5ED, (44-144) 282 6826 phone/fax, or www.sponsorship.org.

Chartered Institute of Marketing (UK)

The Chartered Institute of Marketing is the largest marketing association in the world, with branches across the UK and the Republic of Ireland. It holds events internationally, not just in the UK. Its sponsorship resources are limited, but general marketing resources and networking opportunities are outstanding. For more information, contact the Chartered Institute of Marketing, Moor Hall, Cookham, Maidenhead, Berkshire, SL6 9QH, UK, (44-162) 842 7500, (44-162) 842 7499 fax, membership@cim.co.uk, or www.cim.co.uk.

The Marketing Society (UK)

This association holds numerous events around the country, as well as a star-studded annual conference. Members also get free access to magazines *Market Leader* and *Marketing Magazine*. For details, contact The Marketing Society, St. George's House, 3/5 Pepys Road, London SW20 8NJ, (44-208) 879 3464, (44-208) 879 0362 fax, info@marketing-society.org.uk, or www.marketing-society.org.uk.

Institute of Sport Sponsorship (ISS)

This organisation bills itself as 'The Sponsor's Voice' in the UK. For more information, contact ISS, Warwick House, 4th Floor, 25–27 Buckingham Palace Road, London SW1P 0PP, (44-171) 233 7747, (44-171) 828 7099 fax, info@sportsmatch.co.uk, or www.sports-sponsorship.co.uk.

Irish Management Institute

Although not specifically about marketing or sponsorship, this organisation has a good reputation for providing high-quality education to its membership and does provide some sponsorship education and resources. For details, contact the IMI, Sandyford Road, Dublin 16, (353-1) 207 8412, (353-1) 295 5150 fax, or www.imi.ie.

Marketing Institute of Ireland

The MII offers lots of marketing resources and networking. It also offers free subscriptions on-line to its bi-weekly marketing e-zine *M@rketPlace* to both members and non-members. For details, contact MII, Marketing House, South County Business Park, Leopardstown, Dublin 18, (353-1) 295 2355, (353-1) 295 2453 fax, or www.mii.ie.

Asia

Hong Kong Management Association

The HKMA is known for providing top-quality education and resources to businesspeople from Hong Kong and across the region. It has a Sales & Marketing Executives Club, providing great networking opportunities in the marketing field. For details, contact HKMA, 14/F Fairmont House, 8 Cotton Tree Drive, Central, Hong Kong, (852) 2526 6516, (852) 2868 4387 fax, hkma@hkma.org.hk, or www.hkma.org.hk.

Hong Kong Institute of Marketing

This is Hong Kong's pre-eminent marketing organisation, with a full complement of educational and networking activities. It also publishes *Asian Marketing Review*. For details, contact HKIM, Room 1902, 19/F AT Tower, 180 Electric Road, North Point, Hong Kong, (852) 2881 6682, (852) 2881 6057 fax, hkim@hkim.org.hk, or www.hkim.org.hk.

Marketing Institute of Singapore

The MIS is Singapore's key marketing body, with a membership of around 4500 professionals. Its involvement with sponsorship is limited, but it has other useful marketing programs. For details, contact the MIS, 51 Anson Rd, #03-53 Anson Centre, Singapore 079904, (65) 221-7788, (65) 223-8785 fax, or www.mis.org.sg.

Japan Marketing Association

The JMA has chapters in Kansai, Kyushu, and Hokkaido. For details, contact the JMA, Wako Building 3F, 4-8-5 Roppongi, Minato-ku, Tokyo 106, Japan, (81-3) 3403-5101, (81-3) 3403-5106 fax, jma02@jma-jp.org, or www.jma-jp.org.

Institute of Marketing Malaysia

For details, contact the IMM, PO Box 8086, Kelana Jaya, 46781 Petaling Jaya, Selangor Darul Ehsan, Malaysia, (60-3) 735 9677, (60-3) 735 9284 fax.

Indonesia Marketing Association

For details, contact the IMA, Wisma Dharmala Sakti, 5th Floor, Jl. Jenderal Sudirman Kav. 32, Jakarta 10220, Indonesia, (62-21)-251-2238, (62-21)-251-2248 fax, or markpjkt@indosat.net.in.

Institute of Marketing and Management (India)

For details, contact the IMM, 62-F Sujian Singh Park, New Delhi 110 003, India, (91-11) 469 9224, (91-11) 469 2874 fax, or immnd@vsnl.net.in.

Korea Marketing Association

For details, contact the KMA, 45 4-GA Namdaemoon-Ro, Chung-ku, Seoul 100-743, Korea, (82-2) 779-3581, (82-2) 752 6165 fax.

Marketing Association of Thailand

For details, contact the MAT, Lumpini Tower Building, 14th Floor, Lumpini Tower, 1168/21 Rama IV Rd, Sathorn, Bangkok 10120, Thailand, (66-2) 285-5987-88, (66-2) 285-5989 fax.

Australia/New Zealand

Australian Institute of Management

Although not specifically about marketing or sponsorship, this organisation has a good reputation for providing high-quality education to its membership. Great bookshop. For details, contact AIM, PO Box 112, St Kilda VIC 3182, Australia, (61-3) 9534 8181, (61-3) 9534 5050 fax, or www.aim.com.au. You can also contact the local AIM office in your capital city.

Australian Marketing Institute

The AMI regularly holds sponsorship-oriented functions and workshops and is a good source of general marketing information. For details, contact the AMI, PO Box 399, Carlton South VIC 3053, Australia, (61-1800) 240 264, (61-1800) 241 264, info@ami.org.au, or www.ami.org.au. You can also contact the local AMI office in your nearest capital city.

Australian Association of National Advertisers

The AANA is the peak body representing advertisers to government and media, but it also provides some great training courses and events. For details, contact the AANA, Suite 2, Level 5, 99 Elizabeth Street, Sydney NSW 2000, Australia, (61-2) 9221 8088, (61-2) 9221 8077 fax, help@aana.com.au, or www.aana.com.au.

Australasian Sponsorship Marketing Association, Inc. (ASMA)

ASMA is the sponsorship industry association for Australia, reaching into New Zealand, as well. Members receive a monthly electronic newsletter and discounts to a range of networking and educational activities. For details, contact ASMA, PO Box 71, Nundah QLD 4012 Australia, (61-7) 3630 4746, (61-7) 3630 4335 fax, or asma@ozemail.com.au.

Events & Sponsorship Association of New Zealand

This association is relatively new and has got off to a cracking pace. It is aimed primarily at sponsors, but also services sponsees. Membership includes a subscription to its monthly newsletter. For details, contact ESA, PO Box 105132 Auckland, New Zealand, (64-9) 377 4714, (64-9) 377 4715 fax, info@esa.org.nz, or www.esa.org.nz.

New Zealand Institute of Management

The NZIM is a very well-respected organisation with a wide variety of marketing courses, including the occasional sponsorship event. Excellent on-line bookstore. Chapters across New Zealand. For details, contact NZIM, PO Box 67, Wellington, New Zealand, (64-4) 495 8303, (64-4) 495 8302, national_office@nzim.co.nz and www.nzim.co.nz.

New Zealand Marketing Council

For details, contact Mr David Innes at the national office of the NZMC, Level 16, West Plaza Building, Corner of Albert and Franshawe Streets, Auckland Central, NZ, (64-9) 303 0485, (64-9) 303 0406 fax.

Africa

Institute of Marketing Management (South Africa)

The IMM is a very active association, with many events and training sessions around South Africa. For details, contact the IMM, PO Box 91820, Auckland Park 2006, South Africa, (27-11) 482-1419, (27-11) 726-3639, imm@icon.co.za, or www.imm.co.za.

Periodicals

International

IEG Sponsorship Report

This no-frills, bi-weekly newsletter is known for having the most current information, featuring the best and most successful ideas from across the industry, not just the big players. As a subscriber, you will gain access to an international directory of events, the *IEG Legal Guide to Sponsorship*, and numerous other publications. You can request a sample issue on-line. For more information, contact IEG, Inc., 213 West Institute Place, Suite 303, Chicago IL 60610, USA, (1-312) 944 1727, (1-312) 789 6488 fax, or www.sponsorship.com.

Ad Age Global

This is the international version of the very popular American marketing weekly, *Ad Age*. It does a great job of covering advertising and marketing in a truly global way, both in the publication itself and on-line. The company will provide a sample issue if you e-mail them. For details, contact *Ad Age Global*, 711 Third Ave, New York NY 10017-4036, (1-212) 210 0100, (1-212) 210 0465 fax, subs@crain.com, or www.adageglobal.com.

North America

Brandweek

Although similar in format to its sister publication, *Adweek*, *Brandweek*'s focus is squarely on brand marketing, with a big emphasis on below-the-line marketing activities. Sponsorship, sales promotion, relationship marketing, co-promotions—you name it, the magazine covers it and does it well. For more information, contact *Brandweek*, 1515 Broadway, 12th Floor, New York NY 10036 USA, (1-800) 722-6658 or (1-212) 536 5336, (1-212) 536 1416 fax, or www.brandweek.com.

PROMO

This publication bills itself as 'The Magazine of Promotional Marketing', and is very good. They also have a very complete Web site and a searchable archive of articles. For details, contact *PROMO*, PO Box 10587 Riverton NJ 08076-8587 USA, (1-800) 775 3777, (1-203) 358 5812 fax, or www.promomagazine.com.

American Demographics Magazine

This is a very good publication for American companies, and many of the articles will have just as much relevance to non-Americans. They have a top Web site, with the full text of many articles available. For details, contact *American Demographics*, PO Box 10580, Riverton NJ 08076-0580, USA, (1-800) 529-7502, subs@demographics.com, or www.demographics.com.

Marketing Magazine (Canada)

This is a well-respected marketing publication with strong marketing information for both Canadians and others. For details, contact *Marketing Magazine*, (1-800) 222-5029, marketing@indas.on.ca, or www.marketingmag.ca.

Sales & Marketing Management

This publication doesn't touch on sponsorship every time, but over the course of a year, it does have some excellent articles on the subject. It is well worth subscribing, particularly if your job description goes beyond sponsorship, because its coverage of other subjects is very strong. For details, contact *Sales & Marketing Management*, 770 Broadway, New York NY 10003-9595, USA, (1-646) 654 7259, service@salesandmarketing.com, or www.salesandmarketing.com.

Adweek

This is a very strong contender for the other major weekly advertising-oriented publication, *Ad Age*, and is a terrific complement to its sister publication, *Brandweek*. Subscriptions are available hardcopy or on-line. For details, contact *Adweek*, 1515 Broadway, 12th Floor, New York NY 10036, USA, (1-800) 722-6658. or (1-212) 536 5336, (1-212) 536 1416 fax, or www.adweek.com.

Ad Age

Ad Age is very advertising-oriented, but very complete in this regard. It has an excellent Web site with full articles available free. They provide a free sample issue if you e-mail them. For details, contact The *Ad Age* Group, Subscriber Services, 965 E. Jefferson Ave., Detroit, MI, 48207-3187 USA, (1-313) 446-0450, (1-313) 446-6777 fax, subs@crain.com, or www.adage.com.

Europe

Sport Business

This large format publication is so slick, it would be easy to jump to the conclusion that it is all flash and no substance. Fortunately, that is not the case. It is a very good resource with strong international coverage. Its Web site is excellent. For details, contact *Sport Business*, 205 Blackfriars Foundry, 156 Blackfriars Road, London SE1 8EN UK, (44-171) 721 7161, (44-171) 721 7162 fax, or www.sportbusiness.com.

Marketing (UK)

This is one of the UK's pre-eminent marketing publications. It comes out weekly and has a money-back guarantee. Its Web site is excellent and very complete. For details, contact *Marketing*, (44-208) 606 7500, marketing.online@haynet.com, or www.marketing.haynet.com.

Marketing Week (UK)

This is another top publication in the UK market. It is very comprehensive and covers sponsorship well. It has an excellent Web site. For details, contact Marketing Week, (44-171) 292 3711, or www.mad.co.uk/mw.

Marketing (Ireland)

This monthly consists mainly of snippets of news from around the region. While you are unlikely to get any in-depth coverage of sponsorship issues, it is certainly a good resource to keep you on top of the Irish marketing industry. For details, contact Marketing, 1 Albert Park, Sandycove, Dublin, (353-1) 280 7735, (353-1) 280 7735 fax, or e-mail cullen@marketing.ie, or www.marketing.ie.

IMJ (Irish Marketing & Advertising Journal)

Somewhat more comprehensive than Ireland's *Marketing* magazine, there seems to be more of a balance between coverage of above- and below-the-line activities. They have a great Web site. For details, contact *IMJ*, Unit T31, Stillorgan Industrial Park, Stillorgan, Co. Dublin, (353-1) 295 0088, (353-1) 295 0089 fax, imj@irishmarketingjournal.ie, or www.adworld.ie.

Asia

Asian Brand News

After the Asian currency crisis, many brands realised the need for strong brand building in the region, and that is the premise of this comprehensive, Asia-wide magazine. The Web site features current articles only, so check back often. For details, contact *Asian Brand News*, 6/F, Phase II, Ming An Plaza, 8 Sunning Road, Causeway Bay, Hong Kong, (852) 2577 2628, (852) 2576 9171 fax, askme@media.com.hk, or www.media.com.hk/brand_news/brand_news.htm.

Australia/New Zealand

AdNews

AdNews is a bit of a misnomer, because this Australian bi-weekly has recently taken a much broader and more comprehensive view on marketing. It is also incorporating some excellent sponsorship-oriented features. The Web site is limited, but offers short overviews of current stories. For details, contact Yaffa Publishing, 17–21 Bellevue Street, Surry Hills NSW 2010 Australia, (61-2) 9213 8290, or www.adnews.com.au.

The Sports Vine

This weekly publication is news-oriented and their coverage of sports business in Australia is very complete. *The Sports Vine* is published by B4B Sport and is available by e-mail only. For details, contact *The Sports Vine*, B4B Sport, Level 6, 228 Pitt St, Sydney NSW 2000 Australia, (61-2) 9867 4444, (61-2) 9267 1056 fax, or www.b4bsport.com.

B&T/Professional Marketing

B&T is a weekly, advertising-oriented publication, although it does cover marketing in a larger sense as well. *Professional Marketing* is its monthly sister publication, and is more in-depth. *B&T* subscribers receive it for free. *B&T* has a good Web site. For details, contact Reed Business Publications, Locked Bag 2999, Chatswood DC NSW 2067 Australia, (61-2) 9422 2999, (61-2) 9422 2949 fax, or www.bandt.com.au.

New Zealand Events

This monthly publication does a very good job of covering the events and sponsorship industry in New Zealand. Articles tend to be aimed more at sponsees, but the information is great for sponsors, as well. For details, contact NZ Events, 8 Judge St, Parnell, Auckland, New Zealand (64-9) 302 0405, or rendell@nzevents.co.nz.

Conferences

IEG Sponsorship Seminar

This huge conference is held every March in Chicago. It brings together 1500 sponsors and sponsees from around the world for three intense days of education and networking. For more information, contact IEG, Inc., 213 West Institute Place, Suite 303, Chicago IL 60610 USA, (1-312) 944 1727, (1-312) 789 6488 fax, or www.sponsorship.com.

European Sponsorship Conference

This well-respected conference attracts 500 delegates from across Europe for two big days, covering all facets of sponsorship. For more information, contact BDS Sponsorship, 19 Waterside, 44–48 Wharf Road, London N1 7UX UK, (44-207) 689 3333, (44-20) 7689 3344 fax, or cmarking.bds@sponsorship.co.uk.

International Sport Summit

All sides of sports business are covered, including marketing, production, industrial relations, management, licensing, and lobbying. It takes place every January in New York City. For details, contact EJ Krause & Associates, 6550 Rock Spring Drive, Suite 500, Bethesda MD 20817 USA, (1-301) 493 5500, (1-301) 493 5705 fax, or www.sportsummit.com.

Sport Business (UK)

In addition to publishing a magazine and Web site, Sport Business also hosts a large, sports-oriented conference every year in the UK. For details, contact Sport Business, 205 Blackfriars Foundry, 156 Blackfriars Road, London SE1 8EN UK, (44-171) 721 7161, (44-171) 721 7162 fax, or www.sportbusiness.com.

International Festivals & Events Association Conferences

IFEA holds conferences and seminars around the world and on a number of different themes, usually very well attended by a great cross-section of festival and event organisers. For details, contact IFEA, 2601 Eastover Terrace, Boise ID 83706 USA, (1-208) 433 0950, or www.ifea.com.

Smart Marketing Streetwise Workshops

SMSW is a partnership between the two authors of this book, Anne-Marie Grey and Kim Skildum-Reid. We provide a range of top quality, practical, and interactive sponsorship workshops around the world. Public and private workshops are available. We also work with select associations to present to their membership. For details, contact SMSW, 25 Samuel Street, Tempe NSW 2044 Australia, (61-2) 9559 6444, (61-2) 9565 4777 fax, admin@smsw.com, or www.smsw.com.

| Research

ABI/Inform Full Text Online

ABI/Inform provides the full text of articles from hundreds of publications worldwide. You can print them out or download articles onto your own disk. This service is typically found at universities and business reference libraries.

Business Periodicals On-Disk (BPO)

This is not widely available, but it is well worth finding. It is a CD-ROM-based listing of all of the articles for hundreds of publications worldwide, similar to *ABI/Inform*. The beauty is that you get the actual article, as printed, including photos and graphics. We have found the best access to this service at universities.

| Web sites

Although many of these sites are specific to one country or another, don't limit yourself geographically. Many of them feature good advice and links that will be useful to a wide range of sponsors and related organisations.

Sponsorship

IEG Network

www.sponsorship.com

This site is all about sponsorship. It is stylish, the information is complete, and it does provide free links. It also includes lots of information about seminars, publications, and other activities.

International Festivals & Events Association (IFEA)

www.ifea.com

This is a comprehensive site, listing all of the activities and publications for this international organisation.

Sport Business

www.sportbusiness.com

This is an excellent, sports-oriented site. It features articles from its eponymous magazine, as well as a directory of conferences related to sports business.

B4B Sport

www.b4bsport.com

This Australia-based site features some good articles and resources for sponsors.

Marketing and advertising

Advertising Age

www.AdAge.com

This site features lots of good information, including up to a dozen articles from each weekly publication available free. The list of articles goes back about two months and features a lot of useful stuff.

Advertising Media Internet Centre

www.amic.com

Some great general marketing and advertising features.

Advertising World

advertising.utexas.edu.world

This site has serious links, probably one of the most complete list on the Web. It is very focused on the US, but international sites are welcome and listings are free to appropriate companies.

Adworld

www.adworld.ie

This site bills itself as 'The No. 1 online information resource for the Irish marketing, advertising, and media business'. It delivers.

Brandweek

www.brandweek.com

This is the electronic version of the excellent publication, *Brandweek*. It includes lots of articles, as well as links to sister publications, *Adweek* and *Mediaweek*.

Marketing (UK)

www.marketing.haynet.com

This site has a lot of strong features, including a searchable database of articles from its hardcopy publication.

The Strategist (India)

www.bsstrategist.com

This is an excellent resource from the publishers of the *Business Standard*. Outstanding search engine, book reviews, and excerpts.

Sponsorship law

North America
Sports Lawyers Association Inc.

11250 Roger Bacon Drive, Suite 8, Reston VA 20190 USA, (1-703) 437 4377, (1-703) 435 4390 fax, or www.sportslaw.org.

Europe
British Association for Sport and Law

School of Law, The Manchester Metropolitan University, Hathersage Road, Manchester M13 0JA, UK, (44-161) 247 6445, (44-161) 247 6309 fax.

Australasia
Australian & New Zealand Sports Law Association Inc. (ANZSLA)

PO Box 689, Niddrie Delivery Centre VIC 3042 Australia, (61-3) 9378 3471, or www.anzsla.com.au.

Allens Arthur Robinson

Solicitors and Notaries, GPO Box 50, Sydney NSW 2001 Australia, (61-2) 9230 4000, (61-2) 9230 5333 fax, or www.aar.com.au.

Lionel Hogg, consultant to Allens Arthur Robinson, created the Sponsorship Agreement Pro Forma included in Appendix 3. This firm has offices throughout Australia and Asia and is happy to provide expert assistance or referrals to appropriate sponsorship lawyers. You are also welcome to contact Lionel Hogg directly on (61-7) 3334 3170 or (61-7) 3334 3444, or e-mail him on lionel.hogg@aar.com.au.

Recommended reading

The Experience Economy—Work Is Theatre and Every Business Is a Stage
By B. Joseph Pine II and James H. Gilmore, published by HBS Press
This is a great book on the role of innovation, relationships, and emotional connections in business today. It is invaluable as a sponsorship resource.

Experiential Marketing
By Bernd H. Schmitt, published by Free Press
This is another book that treads a similar path to *The Experience Economy*. Slightly more marketing-based, these two books work very well together.

Brand Spirit
By Hamish Pringle and Marjorie Thompson, published by John Wiley & Sons
Brand Spirit is a fantastic book for any company investing in cause sponsorship or cause-related marketing to foster connections with consumers and trade.

Next—Trends for the Future
By Ira Matathia and Marian Salzman, published by MacMillan
This is an excellent book that tracks the social trends that impact on how people spend their leisure time and money, their expectations of organisations and experiences, and shifting priorities.

Clicking—17 Trends that Drive Your Business and Your Life
By Faith Popcorn and Lys Marigold, published by Harperbusiness
From 'egonomics' to 'clanning' to 'femalethink', this book will make you think differently about your marketplace and how to connect with it. This is an easy read and useful to any sponsor.

EVEolution: The Eight Truths of Marketing to Women

By Faith Popcorn and Lys Marigold, published by Hyperion

This is *Clicking* on oestrogen! With women accounting for a huge percentage of sales and influencing many more, this is a must read for any sponsor targeting the consumer marketplace.

The Clustered World: How We Live, What We Buy, and What It All Means About Who We Are

by Michael J. Weiss, published by Little Brown & Company

If you are doing sponsorship marketing in the US, this is a must read. It will help you to understand that the marketplace is segmented not by age or gender, but by personal motivations and belief systems. Although most of the book is US-centric, there is a section on international segmentation, most notably Canada.

Thick Face, Black Heart

By Chin-Ning Chu, published by Warner Books

If you have trouble saying 'no' to all of those worthy organisations looking for sponsorship, this is a great book for you. Not nearly as ominous as its title, it focuses on doing the right thing while removing sentimentality from the equation.

Sponsorship agreement pro forma

 *Legal1.doc*

| Warning

This document is provided as a sample only and is not a substitute for legal advice. You should seek the advice of a suitably qualified and experienced lawyer before using this document. In particular, you or your lawyer should:

➤ Check the law in your jurisdiction—make sure this agreement works there.

➤ Check for changes to the law—law and practice might have altered since this document was drafted or you last checked the situation.

➤ Modify wherever necessary—review this document critically and never use it without first amending it to suit your needs. Remember that every sponsorship is different.

➤ Beware of limits of expertise. If you are not legally qualified or are not familiar with this area of the law, do not use this document without first obtaining legal advice about it.

Date:

[Owner]

[Sponsor]

Sponsorship Agreement

This Sponsorship Agreement comprises the attached Schedules, Special Conditions and Standard Conditions.

Schedules

Schedule 1
"Sponsor"

Title: ....

Address: ....

Representative: ....

Telephone: ....

Facsimile: ....

E-mail: ....

Schedule 2
"Owner"

(Identify the sponsee – the legal entity receiving the sponsorship. This must be the proper name of the company or association receiving the funds and controlling the team, event or venue being sponsored, not the name of the team, event or venue etc.)

Title: ....

Address: ....

Representative: ....

Telephone: ....

Facsimile: ....

E-mail: ....

Schedule 3
"Commencement Date"

(Insert when the sponsorship starts.)

....

Schedule 4
"Term"

(Insert when the sponsorship will end or for how long it will last, e.g. 5 years.)

....

....

....

....

Schedule 5

Option to renew

(See clause 1.5)
Does Sponsor have an option to renew?
Yes/No
If yes:
- *for what 'Period' (specify an extended finishing date or further Term, e.g. 3 years)?*
- *will the sponsorship fee and other Owner Benefits be the same after renewal? If not, list the new benefits.*

....
....
....
....
....
....
....
....

Schedule 6

First right of refusal

(See clause 1.6)
Does Sponsor have a first right of refusal?
Yes/No

....
....
....
....

Schedule 7

"Property"

(Identify the event, team, venue or other Property the subject of this sponsorship)

....
....
....
....

Schedule 8

"Sponsorship Category"

Identify the nature of the sponsorship, (e.g. title/category/official supplier etc.)

....
....
....
....

Schedule 9

"Territory"

(Specify the area in which the sponsorship operates, e.g. state, region, country, continent, worldwide, etc.)

....
....
....
....

Schedule 10

Sponsor objectives

(See clause 2.1)
(Be specific—list bottom-line sales objectives, measurable promotional activities, business development targets, etc.)

• ....
• ....
• ....

Schedule 11

Owner objectives

(See clause 2.2)
(Be specific—list expected leverage from Sponsor in developing event/sport, target participation or attendance numbers, entry fee and merchandise income, measurable business development targets, etc.)

- ....
- ....
- ....

Schedule 12

"Sponsor Benefits"

(See clause 1.4)
(List, in detail, the signage/tickets/ hospitality/advertising credits/ merchandising rights and other benefits that Owner must provide to Sponsor—be precise about amounts, timing etc.)

- ....
- ....
- ....
- ....
- ....
- ....
- ....
- ....
- ....
- ....

Schedule 13

"Owner Benefits"

(See clause 1.4)
(List, in detail, the sponsorship fee, contra/in-kind benefits that Sponsor must provide to Owner—be precise about amounts, timing, etc. and be careful to specify whether any fees include or exclude taxes such as goods and services or value added tax)

- ....
- ....
- ....
- ....
- ....
- ....
- ....
- ....
- ....

Schedule 14

Evaluation criteria

(See clause 8.3)
- *Is media analysis required and, if so, by whom, at whose expense, how regularly and what details must be provided?*
- *Is Owner obliged to provide reports on mutual marketing activities, demographic information, samples of printed and promotional materials and, if so, what and when?*
- *Specify, in detail, the level of performance (and how it will be assessed) which is regarded by Sponsor as unacceptable.*
- *Specify the consequences of failing to achieve this level (e.g. right of termination, reduced fees or benefits).*
- *Specify the level of performance (and how it will be assessed) above which Sponsor's reasonable expectations are exceeded.*
- *Specify the consequences of this level of performance (e.g. increased sponsorship fee or benefits).*
- *Specify any other relevant evaluation criteria, information or consequences.*

Schedule 15

"Applicable Law"

(Identify the country or state the laws of which will apply to this Agreement)

Schedule 16

Owner Marks

(Insert here all trade marks, names, logos, etc. which Sponsor is entitled to use under this Agreement. Include artwork. If nothing is listed, Sponsor may use all Owner Marks)

Schedule 17

Sponsor Marks

(Insert here all trade marks, names, logos, etc. which Owner is entitled to use under this Agreement. Include artwork.)

Schedule 18

Use of Owner Marks

(See clause 5.1)
(List here the specific purposes for which Owner Marks can be used by Sponsor)

- • ....
- • ....
- • ....

Schedule 19

Use of Sponsor Marks

(See clause 5.1)
(List here the specific purposes for which Sponsor Marks can be used by Owner)

- • ....
- • ....
- • ....

Schedule 20

Promotional and media objectives

(See clause 6.3)
(Be specific, e.g. list target media outlets, promotional events, nature of coverage, etc.).

- • ....
- • ....
- • ....
- • ....
- • ....

Schedule 21

Competitors of Sponsor

(See clauses 7.2 and 21.3)

- • ....
- • ....
- • ....

Schedule 22

Competitors of Property

(See clauses 7.3 and 21.3)

- • ....
- • ....
- • ....

Schedule 23

Sponsor's termination events

(See clause 9.2)
(Insert here the circumstances in which Sponsor can terminate this Agreement)

- • ....
- • ....
- • ....
- • ....
- • ....

Schedule 24

Owner's termination events

(See clause 9.3)
(Insert here the circumstances in which Owner can terminate this Agreement)

- ....
- ....
- ....
- ....
- ....

Schedule 25

Insurance

(See clause 16)
(Insert here the amount of public liability insurance required to be maintained by Owner and full details of any other insurance, such as product liability or event cancellation insurance, required for the purposes of this Agreement)

- Public liability—amount:

....
....

- Other:

....
....
....

Schedule 26

Ambush strategies

(See clause 8.1)
(Include here specific strategies designed to minimise the likelihood of ambush occurring, such as obligations on Owner to:
- *prevent or minimise Competitor involvement;*
- *exercise control of venue access and signage;*
- *impose contractual obligations on bidders for commercial rights not to engage in ambushing should the bids be unsuccessful;*
- *negotiate broadcasting agreements to provide Sponsor with a first right of refusal to take category exclusive advertising time during broadcasts of the event;*
- *impose ticketing restrictions;*
- *prevent the re-use of tickets or licensed products as prize give-aways;*
- *provide sponsorship fee rebates (be very specific) if serious ambush occurs, etc.)*

- ....
- ....
- ....
- ....
- ....

Special conditions

(Insert here any changes to the Standard Conditions and any special conditions not referred to in the Standard Conditions or the Schedules.)

....

....

....

Standard conditions

1 Sponsorship

1.1 EXCLUSIVITY

Sponsor shall be the exclusive Sponsor of the Property, in the Sponsorship Category, in the Territory.

1.2 TERM

Subject to this Agreement, the sponsorship starts on the Commencement Date and is effective for the Term.

1.3 CONSIDERATION

The consideration for this Agreement is the mutual conferring of benefits referred to in clause 1.4.

1.4 BENEFITS

Sponsor must confer Owner Benefits on Owner, and Owner must confer Sponsor Benefits on Sponsor, at the times outlined in, and in accordance with, Schedules 12 and 13.

1.5 OPTION TO RENEW

This clause applies if the parties specify 'Yes' in Schedule 5.

Sponsor has an option to renew this Agreement for the further Period specified in Schedule 5 if:

- Sponsor is not in breach under this Agreement; and
- Sponsor gives notice in writing to Owner no fewer than 3 months before the end of the Term stating it intends to exercise the option.

If Sponsor exercises the option, the provisions of this Agreement (except for this clause 1.5) shall continue in full force and effect for the further Period, subject to any differences in fees or Owner benefits specified in Schedule 5 for the further Period.

1.6 FIRST RIGHT OF REFUSAL

This clause applies if the parties specify 'Yes' in Schedule 6.

Owner must not enter into an agreement with any other person to Sponsor the Property in the Sponsorship Category at or immediately after the end of the Term without first offering the sponsorship to Sponsor on the same terms as it proposes to offer to (or as have been offered by) other parties. If Sponsor declines within 30 days to accept the new sponsorship terms, Owner may enter into an agreement with a third party, but only on the terms offered to, and rejected by, Sponsor.

Sponsor's first right of refusal extends to any revised terms offered to or by third parties after Sponsor declines to accept the initial terms.

1.7 NO ASSIGNMENT

Sponsor must not assign, charge or otherwise deal with Sponsor Benefits without the prior written consent of Owner.

Owner must not assign, charge or otherwise deal with Owner Benefits without the prior written consent of Sponsor.

This clause does not apply to Owner Benefits or Sponsor Benefits that the parties, on signing this Agreement, agree will be conferred on third parties.

2 Objectives

2.1 OBJECTIVES OF SPONSOR

The primary objectives of the Sponsor in entering into this Agreement are:

- to associate Sponsor's brand with the Property;
- to promote the products and services of Sponsor;
- to encourage brand loyalty to Sponsor;
- to assist in raising and maintaining Sponsor's corporate profile and image;
- to provide to Sponsor marketing leverage opportunities related to the Property;
- to promote community awareness of, affinity for and (if relevant) participation in the Property;
- to continually review and evaluate the ongoing success and performance of the sponsorship for maximum commercial advantage to all parties; and
- the objectives outlined in Schedule 10.

2.2 OBJECTIVES OF OWNER

The primary objectives of the Owner in entering into this Agreement are:

- to secure sponsorship funds and other benefits;
- to increase the profile, standing, brand value and (if relevant) participation in the Property;
- to promote the profile and corporate image of Sponsor and the use of Sponsor's products and services;
- to continually review and evaluate the ongoing success and performance of the sponsorship for the maximum commercial advantage to all parties; and
- the objectives outlined in Schedule 11.

2.3 FULFILMENT OF OBJECTIVES

The parties must act at all times in good faith towards each other with a view to fulfilling the objectives outlined in clauses 2.1 and 2.2. This Agreement is to be interpreted in a manner that best promotes the fulfilment of those objectives.

3 Warranties

3.1 OWNER WARRANTIES

Owner warrants that:

- it has full right and legal authority to enter into and perform its obligations under this Agreement;
- it owns the Property (or, if the Property is not legally capable of being owned, it holds rights which effectively confer unfettered control of the Property);
- Owner Marks do not infringe the trade marks, trade names or other rights of any person;
- it has, or will at the relevant time have, all government licences, permits and other authorities relevant to the Property;
- it will comply with all applicable laws relating to the promotion and conduct of the Property; and
- throughout this Agreement, it will conduct itself so as not to cause detriment, damage, injury or embarrassment to Sponsor.

3.2 SPONSOR WARRANTIES

Sponsor warrants that:

- it has full right and legal authority to enter into and perform its obligations under this Agreement;
- Sponsor's Marks do not infringe the trade marks, trade names or other rights of any other person;
- it will comply with all applicable laws in marketing and promoting its sponsorship of the Property; and
- throughout this Agreement, it will conduct itself so as not to cause detriment, damage, injury or embarrassment to the Owner.

4 Disclosure

4.1 INITIAL DISCLOSURE

Owner warrants that it has disclosed to Sponsor:

- the substance (other than financial details) of all agreements entered into or currently under negotiation with Owner for sponsorship, exclusive or preferred supplier status or other like arrangements relating to the Property; and
- all other circumstances which might have a material impact upon Sponsor's decision to enter into this Agreement.

4.2 CONTINUING DISCLOSURE

Owner must from time to time keep Sponsor informed of:

- new sponsorship, exclusive or preferred service or supplier status or other like arrangements conferred by Owner in respect of the Property;
- significant marketing programs and other promotional activities which might provide leverage opportunities for Sponsor; and
- research and demographic information held or commissioned by Owner about the Property and its participants.

5 Marks and title

5.1 AUTHORISED USE

Sponsor may use Owner Marks:

- for all purposes reasonably incidental to obtaining the Sponsor Benefits; and
- as permitted in Schedule 18.

Owner may use Sponsor Marks:

- for all purposes reasonably incidental to obtaining the Owner Benefits; and
- as permitted in Schedule 19.

5.2 NO UNAUTHORISED USE

Sponsor must not use or permit the use of Owner Marks (or any other trade or service marks, logos, designs, devices or intellectual property rights of Owner) and Owner must not use or permit the use of Sponsor Marks (or any other trade or service marks, logos, designs, devices or intellectual property rights of Sponsor) unless authorised by this Agreement or with the written consent of the other party.

5.3 MERCHANDISE

Unless permitted in Schedule 18, Sponsor must not manufacture, sell or licence the manufacture or sale of any promotional or other merchandise bearing Owner Marks without Owner's prior written consent.

Unless permitted in Schedule 19, Owner must not manufacture, sell or licence the manufacture or sale of any promotional or other merchandise bearing Sponsor Marks without Sponsor's prior written consent.

All authorised merchandise bearing Owner Marks or Sponsor Marks permitted under this Agreement must be:

- of a high standard;
- of such style, appearance and quality as to suit the best exploitation of the Sponsor, Owner and Property (as the case may be); and
- free from product defects, of merchantable quality and suited for its intended purpose.

5.4 IMAGE

The parties must ensure that any authorised use by them of the other's marks or intellectual property rights:

- is lawful;
- properly and accurately represents those rights;
- (in the case of Owner using Sponsor Marks) strictly complies with any trade mark and logo usage policies of Sponsor applicable at the relevant time;
- is consistent with the other's corporate image; and
- (if used in connection with the provision of goods or services) is associated only with goods or services of the highest quality.

5.5 ENFORCEMENT PROTECTION

The parties must provide all reasonable assistance to each other to protect against infringers of Owner Marks or Sponsor Marks in connection with the Property.

5.6 TITLE

Despite any rights to use another's marks conferred under this Agreement:

- Owner holds all legal and equitable right, title and interest in and to the Property and all Owner Marks;
- Sponsor holds all legal and equitable right, title and interest in and to the Sponsor Marks;

- naming, title and other rights conferred by this Agreement merely constitute licences to use the relevant Owner Marks or Sponsor Marks (as the case may be) for the purposes of, and in accordance with, this Agreement and do not confer any property right or interest in those marks; and
- the right to use another's marks is non-exclusive and non-assignable.

5.7 INFRINGEMENTS INCIDENTAL TO TELEVISION BROADCASTS, ETC.

This clause 5 does not prevent any person holding rights to televise or reproduce images associated with the Property from incidentally broadcasting or reproducing Sponsor Marks appearing as or in signage on premises controlled by Owner and relevant to the Property.

5.8 NO ALTERATION TO BROADCAST SIGNAL ETC

Owner must not authorise or permit any media rights holder contracted in respect of the Property (for example, the official broadcaster of an event or an authorised Internet site manager or multimedia provider or rights holder) in the exercise of its rights to alter any images associated with the Property (for example, by the artificial electronic insertion, removal or alteration of signage or other images) without the prior written consent of Sponsor.

6 Media, branding, leverage, etc.

6.1 MEDIA EXPOSURE

At all reasonable opportunities:
- Owner will use its best endeavours to obtain public and media exposure of the sponsorship; and
- Sponsor will use its best endeavours to obtain public and media exposure of the Property.

6.2 APPROVAL

Media releases relating to the sponsorship must:
- be issued jointly by the parties; or
- not be issued by one party without the consent of the other.

6.3 PROMOTIONAL AND MEDIA OBJECTIVES

Owner and Sponsor must use their best endeavours to achieve their promotional and Media objectives outlined in Schedule 20. Sponsor licences Owner to use Sponsor Marks, and Owner licences Sponsor to use Owner Marks, for these purposes.

6.4 LEVERAGE

Sponsor has the right at its cost to:
- promote itself, its brands and its products and services in association with the Property; and
- engage in advertising and promotional activities to maximise the benefits to it of its association with the Property,

provided that it will not knowingly or recklessly engage in any advertising or promotional activities which reflect unfavourably on the Property, the parties or any other Sponsors of the Property.

7 Exclusivity

7.1 EXCLUSIVITY WITHIN TERRITORY

If the Sponsorship Category is designed for only 1 sponsor (for example, naming rights or principal sponsorship):
- Sponsor's rights under this Agreement are exclusive within the Territory; and

- Owner must not enter into any sponsorship or supply arrangements for the Property in the Sponsorship Category within the Territory with any other person.

If the Sponsorship Category is designed for multiple sponsors (for example, official suppliers or sponsors of a particular class) Owner must not, without the prior written consent of Sponsor (which must not be unreasonably withheld), enter into any sponsorship or supply arrangements for the Property in the Sponsorship Category within the Territory with any other person.

The sponsorship categories for the Property must not be redesigned without Sponsor's prior written consent if to do so might affect adversely Sponsor's rights under this clause.

7.2 COMPETITORS

Owner must not within the Territory authorise or permit to subsist:
- the provision of any products or services to the Property, in any sponsorship category; or
- any association with the Property,

by any Competitor of Sponsor.

7.3 SPONSOR RESTRAINT

Sponsor must not enter into any sponsorship or supply arrangements with any Competitor of the Property during the Term or within a reasonable time after the end of the Term.

7.4 INJUNCTIONS

The parties acknowledge that the restraints referred to in this clause 7 cannot adequately be compensated for in damages and consent to injunctive relief for the enforcement of these restraints.

8 Marketing and service delivery

8.1 MARKETING COMMITTEE

Owner and Sponsor will establish a marketing committee to meet quarterly (or otherwise, as agreed) for the purposes of:
- reviewing the progress of the sponsorship and the mutual rights conferred under this Agreement;
- evaluating the success of the sponsorship against its objectives;
- discussing further opportunities for leverage and cross-promotional activities;
- maximising the ongoing benefits to the parties, implementing promotional strategies for the parties and identifying new, mutual opportunities; and
- maximising the Sponsor Benefits by:
  - identifying actual or potential Ambush activities;
  - using their best endeavours to prevent Ambush or minimise its potential impact on the sponsorship; and
  - directing implementation of the strategies outlined in Schedule 26.

8.2 SERVICE DELIVERY

Both Sponsor and Owner must designate a representative to be primarily responsible for the provision of the day-to-day service and support required by the other party under this Agreement. Until otherwise nominated, the representatives will be the representatives named in Schedules 1 and 2.

8.3 EVALUATION

The parties must evaluate the success of the sponsorship in accordance with the criteria outlined in Schedule 14 and with the consequences (if any) outlined in that Schedule.

9 Termination

9.1 EXPIRY

This Agreement, unless terminated earlier under this clause or extended under clause 1, will continue until the end of the Term.

9.2 EARLY TERMINATION BY SPONSOR

Sponsor may terminate this Agreement if any of the following occurs:

- Owner fails to provide a Sponsor Benefit, and failure continues for 7 days after Owner receives written notice from Sponsor to provide the benefit.
- Owner is Insolvent.
- any event outlined in Schedule 23 occurs.
- application of the evaluation criteria in Schedule 14 permits termination.
- any laws come into operation which in any way restrict, prohibit or otherwise regulate the sponsorship of, or association by Sponsor with, the Property so that:
  - the benefits available to Sponsor are materially reduced or altered; or
  - Sponsor's obligations under this Agreement are materially increased.
- for reasons beyond the reasonable control of Sponsor, Sponsor is unable to continue to exploit and enjoy fully the Sponsor Benefits.
- any major, public controversy arises in connection with the Owner, the Property or this Agreement which, in the reasonable opinion of Sponsor, reflects adversely and substantially on Sponsor's corporate image.
- any statement, representation or warranty made by Owner in connection with this Agreement proves to have been incorrect or misleading in any material respect.
- the rights conferred on Sponsor under this Agreement are directly or indirectly diminished, prejudiced or compromised in any way by the reckless acts or omissions of Owner.
- Owner has not used its best endeavours to ensure that the exclusive rights conferred on Sponsor under this Agreement are not directly or indirectly diminished, prejudiced or compromised in any way by the acts or omissions of third parties (for example, by Ambush).

9.3 EARLY TERMINATION BY OWNER

Owner may Terminate this Agreement if any of the following occurs:

- Sponsor fails to provide a material Sponsor Benefit, and failure continues for 7 days after Sponsor receives written notice from Owner to provide the benefit.
- Sponsor is Insolvent.
- any event outlined in Schedule 24 occurs.
- any major, public controversy arises in connection with the Sponsor or this Agreement which, in the reasonable opinion of Owner, reflects adversely and substantially on Owner's corporate image or upon the Property.
- any statement, representation or warranty made by Sponsor in connection with this Agreement proves to have been incorrect or misleading in any material respect when made.
- the rights conferred on Owner under this Agreement are directly or indirectly diminished, prejudiced or compromised in any way by the reckless acts or omissions of Sponsor.

9.4 IMMATERIAL BREACHES

Nothing in this clause entitles a party to terminate this Agreement for trivial or immaterial breaches which cannot be remedied, however, this does not prevent termination for regular, consistent or repeated breaches (even if they would, alone, be trivial or immaterial).

9.5 METHOD OF TERMINATION

A party entitled to terminate this Agreement may do so by notice in writing to the other at the address specified in Schedule 1 or Schedule 2, as the case may be.

9.6 EFFECT OF EARLY TERMINATION

Termination in this Agreement for any reason shall be without prejudice to the rights and obligations of each party accrued up to and including the date of termination.

10 Re-branding

10.1 CHANGE OF NAME, LOGO, PRODUCT, ETC.

If at any time Sponsor changes its name or logo, or wishes to change any Sponsor's product associated with Property, Sponsor may re-brand the sponsorship of the Property provided that, in the reasonable opinion of Owner, to do so will not affect the good name and image of the Property or Owner.

10.2 COSTS

Re-branding must be at Sponsor's cost. This includes:

- direct costs to Sponsor; and
- any costs incurred by Owner directly or indirectly resulting from the re-branding.

11 Governing law

This Agreement is governed by and must be construed in accordance with the Applicable Law.

12 Relationship of parties

The parties are independent contractors. Nothing in this Agreement or in the description of the Sponsorship Category shall be construed to place the parties in, and the parties must not act in a manner which expresses or implies, a legal relationship of partnership, joint venture, franchise, employment or agency.

13 Ongoing assistance

Each party must promptly:
- do all things;
- sign all documents; and
- provide all relevant assistance and information,

reasonably required by the other party to enable the performance by the parties of their obligations under this Agreement.

14 Costs

14.1 AGREEMENT COSTS

Each party must pay its own costs of and incidental to the negotiation, preparation and execution of this Agreement.

14.2 IMPLEMENTATION COSTS

Unless otherwise specified as a Sponsor Benefit or Owner Benefit, each party must pay its own signage, advertising, leverage, general overhead and incidental costs related to the performance of its obligations under this Agreement. Despite this, all signage, artwork, photography, film, video tape and similar expenses directly or indirectly incurred under this Agreement must be met by Sponsor unless otherwise provided for in the Schedule or Special Conditions.

14.3 TAXES

All amounts payable by Sponsor to Owner under this Agreement (for example, the sponsorship fee) include all government taxes (such as goods and services or value added taxes) unless specified to the contrary in Schedule 13.

However, if Australian taxation laws apply to any such amounts, the following provisions apply:

- the amounts payable include all applicable GST, unless specified to the contrary in Schedule 13;
- if Owner is registered for GST, the amounts are not payable (despite any other provision in this Agreement) unless and until Owner delivers a Tax Invoice for the relevant amount to Sponsor; and
- if Owner is not registered for GST, the amounts must be reduced (despite any other provision in this Agreement) by one-eleventh of the amount otherwise payable.

15 Notices

Notices under this Agreement may be delivered or sent by post, facsimile or e-mail to the relevant addresses outlined in Schedules 1 and 2 (as the case may be) and will be deemed to have been received in the ordinary course of delivery of notices in that form.

16 Insurance

16.1 LIABILITY INSURANCE

Owner must effect and keep current:

- a public liability insurance policy for an amount not less than the amount specified in Schedule 25 for any single claim for liability of Owner or Sponsor or both for death, personal injury or property damage occasioned to any person in respect of the Property (including a contractual liability endorsement to cover the obligations of Owner under clause 17);
- such other insurance as is specified in Schedule 25; and
- if Property is a one-off event (or if the parties specify in Schedule 25), event cancellation insurance in an amount equalling or exceeding the value of Sponsor Benefits.

16.2 PRODUCT LIABILITY INSURANCE

If:

- Owner is authorised under this Agreement to manufacture, sell or licence the sale or manufacture of any merchandise bearing Sponsor Marks; or
- Sponsor is authorised under this Agreement to manufacture, sell or licence the sale or manufacture of any merchandise bearing Owner Marks,

the party so authorised must effect and keep current a product liability insurance policy for an amount not less than the amount specified in Schedule 25 for any single claim for liability of Owner or Sponsor or both for death, personal injury or property damage occasioned to any person in respect of the manufacture or sale of the merchandise (for example, for claims relating to a defective product).

16.3 TERMS OF POLICIES

All insurance policies effected under this Agreement must:

- be wholly satisfactory to Beneficiary;
- identify Beneficiary as a named insured;
- remain enforceable for the benefit of Beneficiary even if invalid or unenforceable by Payer; and
- include full, automatic reinstatement cover at all times during the Term.

16.4 OTHER OBLIGATIONS

Payer must:

- not violate, or permit the violation of, any conditions of these policies; and
- provide insurance certificates and copies of the policies to Beneficiary on its reasonable request.

17 Indemnities and liability limitation

17.1 OWNER INDEMNITIES

Owner must indemnify Sponsor and Sponsor's officers, employees and agents from and against all claims, damages, liabilities, losses and expenses related to:

- any breach by Owner of this Agreement;
- the inaccuracy of any warranty or representations made by Owner;
- any wrongful act or omission by Owner (including negligence, unlawful conduct and wilful misconduct) in its performance of this Agreement;
- Sponsor's involvement with the Property (other than losses and expenses incurred solely as a result of Sponsor's decision to invest in the Property); and
- liabilities for which insurance is required under clause 16.

17.2 SPONSOR INDEMNITIES

Sponsor must indemnify Owner and Owner's officers, employees and agents from and against all claims, damages, liabilities, losses and expenses related to:

- any breach by Sponsor of this Agreement;
- the inaccuracy of any warranty or representations made by Sponsor;
- any wrongful act or omission by Sponsor (including negligence, unlawful conduct and wilful misconduct) in its performance of this Agreement; and
- all liabilities for which insurance is required under clause 16.

17.3 LIMITATION OF LIABILITY

Sponsor's liability to Owner under this Agreement (whether for breach of warranty or otherwise) is limited to the payment of sponsorship fees as and when due.

18 Dispute resolution

18.1 MEDIATION

Any dispute or difference about this Agreement must be resolved as follows:

- the parties must first refer the dispute to mediation by an agreed accredited mediator or, failing agreement, by a person appointed by the President or other senior officer of the Law Society or Bar Association in the jurisdiction of the Applicable Law;

- the mediator must determine the rules of the mediation if the parties do not agree;
- mediation commences when a party gives written notice to the other specifying the dispute and requiring its resolution under this clause;
- the parties must use their best endeavours to complete the mediation within 14 days; and
- any information or documents obtained through or as part of the mediation must not be used for any purpose other than the settlement of the dispute.

18.2 FINAL RESOLUTION

If the dispute is not resolved within 14 days of the notice of its commencement, either party may then, but not earlier, commence legal proceedings in an appropriate court.

18.3 CONTRACT PERFORMANCE

Each party must continue to perform this Agreement despite the existence of a dispute or any proceedings under this clause.

18.4 EXCEPTIONS TO MEDIATION

Nothing in this clause prevents:

- a party from seeking urgent injunctive relief in respect of an actual or apprehended breach of this Agreement;
- Sponsor from exercising its rights under the first 3 bullet points in clause 9.2; or
- Owner from exercising its rights under the first 3 bullet points in clause 9.3.

19 Confidentiality

The commercial terms of this Agreement are confidential to the parties unless they otherwise agree. However, this does not prevent:

- Sponsor or Owner disclosing the existence or the sponsorship to the general public; or
- any promotional, marketing or sponsorship activities authorised or required under this Agreement.

20 Entire agreement

This Agreement represents the entire agreement between the parties and supersedes all other agreements and conduct , express or implied, written or oral.

21 Interpretation

21.1 COMPOSITION

This Agreement comprises these Standard Conditions and the attached Schedules and Special Conditions.

21.2 PRECEDENCE

The Special Conditions and the attached Schedules have precedence over these Standard Conditions to the extent of any inconsistency.

21.3 INTERPRETATION

In this Agreement, unless the context otherwise requires:

- *Agreement* means this Agreement as amended from time to time.
- *Ambush* means the association by any person, not authorised in writing by Owner, of the person's name, brands, products or services with the Property or with a party, through marketing or promotional activities or otherwise, whether or not lawful, accurate or misleading.

- *Beneficiary* means the party for whose benefit an insurance policy must be effected under clause 16.
- *Competitor* (in connection with Sponsor) means:
  - any person who conducts any business which competes (other than incidentally), directly or indirectly, with any business conducted or services provided by Sponsor or any company related to Sponsor or whose products or services are antithetical to or incompatible with the business, products or services of Sponsor; or
  - any person listed in Schedule 21 or who conducts a business in the industry, or of the nature, described in that Schedule.
- *Competitor* (in connection with Owner) means:
  - any person who conducts any event or offers any product substantially similar to the Property anywhere in the Territory or whose operations are antithetical to or incompatible with the Property; or
  - any person or Property listed in Schedule 22 or any Property or event of the nature described in that Schedule.
- *GST* means the goods and services tax as imposed by the GST Law.
- *GST Law* has the meaning given to that term in *A New Tax System (Goods and Services Tax) Act 1999* of the Commonwealth of Australia, or, if that Act does not exist for any reason, means any Act imposing or relating to the imposition or administration of a goods and services tax in Australia and any regulation made under that Act.
- *Insolvency* in respect of a party means:
  - the filing of an application for the winding up, whether voluntary or otherwise, or the issuing of a notice summoning a meeting at which it is to be moved a resolution proposing the winding up, of the party;
  - the appointment of a receiver, receiver and manager, administrator, liquidator or provisional liquidator with respect to that party or any of its assets;
  - the assignment by that party in favour of, or composition or arrangement or entering into of a scheme of arrangement (otherwise than for the purposes solely of corporate reconstruction) with, its creditors or any class of its creditors; or
  - a party taking advantage of any insolvency laws to obtain temporary or permanent relief from the payment of its debts or from creditors generally.
- *Media* means any of communication to the public at large, whether by radio, television, newspaper, electronic media (such as the Internet) or otherwise.
- *Owner Benefits* include additional fees or benefits that accrue to Owner by application of the evaluation criteria in Schedule 14.
- *Owner Marks* means Owner's name and trade or service marks, labels, designs, logos, trade names, product identifications, artwork and other symbols, devices, copyright and intellectual property rights directly associated with the Property. If Schedule 16 is completed, the term is limited to the Owner Marks depicted or listed in that schedule.
- *Payer* means the party obliged to effect an insurance policy under clause 16.
- *Sponsor Benefits* may be reduced by application of the evaluation criteria in Schedule 14, and if reduced must be construed accordingly.
- *Sponsor Marks* means Sponsor's name and the marks and other symbols outlined in Schedule 17.
- *Tax Invoice* has the meaning given to that term by the GST Law.
- *Term* includes the period of any option to renew this Agreement if clause 1.5 applies and the option is exercised.

21.4 CURRENCY

References to currency are to the lawful currency of the country or region of the Applicable Law, unless otherwise stated.

21.5 EXAMPLES

Examples given in this Agreement do not limit or qualify the general words to which they relate.

SIGNATURES

By signing, you indicate acceptance of this Agreement (including the Standard Conditions and the Special Conditions) on behalf of the entity you represent and you declare your ability to sign this Agreement on behalf of the Sponsor/Owner (as the case may be).

Signed for and on behalf of Sponsor by:)
)
)
(signature)

Full name
Title
Witness
Date

SIGNED for and on behalf of Owner by:)
)
)
(signature)

Full name
Title
Witness
Date

Index

For more information

Smart Marketing Streetwise Workshops provides a full range of sponsorship workshops.

For sponsorship seekers

➤ Building Brilliant Partnerships: selling and retaining more sponsorship

➤ Partnerships Plus: giving yourself the edge

➤ Confident Sponsorship for Sponsees: a novice's guide to sponsorship

For sponsors

➤ Getting Remarkable Results: managing and maximising your sponsorships

➤ Advanced Skills for Sponsors: making the most of your investments

➤ Creative Power: unleashing the true potential of sponsorship

➤ Confident Sponsorship for Sponsors: a novice's guide to sponsorship

We also offer fully customised workshops and presentations, and keynote speaking, as well as a comprehensive consulting service.

For more information on these services, contact us on:

Asia-Pacific office

Smart Marketing Streetwise Workshops
25 Samuel Street
Tempe NSW 2044
Australia
(61-2) 9559 6444 phone
(61-2) 9565 4777 fax

North American office

Smart Marketing Streetwise Workshops
142 Greens Farm Road
Westport, CT 06880-6215
USA
(1-203) 222-1303 (phone/fax)

You can also e-mail us on admin@smsw.com or visit our Web site at www.smsw.com.